Object Thinking

David West

PUBLISHED BY
Microsoft Press
A Division of Microsoft Corporation
One Microsoft Way
Redmond, Washington 98052-6399

Library of Congress Cataloging-in-Publication Data pending.

Printed and bound in the United States of America.

1 2 3 4 5 6 7 8 9   QWE   8 7 6 5 4 3

Distributed in Canada by H.B. Fenn and Company Ltd.

A CIP catalogue record for this book is available from the British Library.

Microsoft Press books are available through booksellers and distributors worldwide. For further information about international editions, contact your local Microsoft Corporation office or contact Microsoft Press International directly at fax (425) 936-7329. Visit our Web site at www.microsoft.com/mspress. Send comments to *mspinput@microsoft.com*.

Acquisitions Editor: Robin Van Steenburgh and Linda Engelman
Project Editor: Denise Bankaitis and Devon Musgrave
Indexer: Shawn Peck

Body Part No. X10-25675

Table of Contents

Acknowledgments

One name appears on the cover as author of this book, hiding the fact that every book is a collaborative effort involving scores of contributors. Although it is impossible to acknowledge and thank everyone who played a role, I can and must name some individuals. Each is owed my personal thanks, and each stands as a proxy for many others whom I acknowledge in my mind and heart.

Mary—without whom this would never have been done. My muse, my friend, my spouse of twenty-one years.

Maurine, Bob, Sara, Ryan, and Kathleen—my family, whose support was required and freely given.

Kevin—the best programmer with whom I have ever worked. You proved, sometimes after a lot of discussion as to why it was impossible, that my crazy ideas could be implemented.

Tom, Pam, Don, Dion, Julie, Kyle, Dave, Steve, and J.P.—our initial contact was as student and professor, but you became colleagues and friends and represent the hundreds of St. Thomas alumni who helped shape object thinking and then applied it in the real world with notable success.

Tom and Ken—your technical review, insightful comments, correction of errors, and honest advice were invaluable. This would not have been as useful a book without your assistance.

Linda, Devon, Denise, Robin, Shawn, Joel, Sandi, and Elizabeth—the editors and staff at Microsoft Press who smoothly dealt with all the technical aspects of getting a book out the door (including an author with deadline issues). An author could not have found a friendlier, more helpful, or more professional group of editors and craftspeople with whom to work.

Preface

A Different (and Possibly Controversial) Kind of Software Book

This book will be deliberately different from almost any other object analysis/design, component-based development, software development methodology, or extreme programming (XP) book you may have encountered. It's also likely to be controversial, which is not intended but is, perhaps, inevitable. Several factors contribute to this book's differences:

- The reader will be asked to read and digest a lot of history and philosophy before embarking on the more pragmatic aspects of object thinking.

- The author will unabashedly, adamantly, and consistently advocate behavior as the key concept for discovering, describing, and designing objects and components.

- The centrality of CRC (Class-Responsibility-Collaborator) cards as an object thinking device or tool will likely be viewed as anachronistic and irrelevant since UML (Unified Modeling Language) has achieved the status of de facto standard.

- The apparent indifference, or even antagonism, toward formalism and the formal approaches to software specification that are intrinsic to the behavioral approach will concern some readers, especially those trained in computer science departments at research universities.

- The emphasis on analysis and conceptualization—that is, on thinking—instead of on implementation detail might strike some readers as academic.

It will take the rest of the book to explain why these differences are important and necessary, but the motivation behind them is found in this 1991 quote from Grady Booch:

*Let there be no doubt that object-oriented design is
fundamentally different than traditional structured design
approaches: it requires different ways of thinking about
decomposition, and it produces software architectures that are
largely outside the realm of the structured design culture.*

"Different ways of thinking" is the key phrase here, and the word *culture*
is equally important. The history of objects in software development is characterized by the mistaken notion that the object difference was to be found in a
computer language or a software module specification. But objects are fundamentally different because they reflect different ideas—particularly about
decomposition—and because they reflect a different set of values and a different worldview (that is, culture) from that of traditional software development.
Understanding objects requires understanding the philosophical roots and historical milestones from which objects emerged.

Readers will be expected to review and reflect on two competing philosophical traditions—formalism and hermeneutics-postmodernism—that are
responsible for the value systems and ideas leading to the competition and
heated disagreements between advocates of software engineering (who value
formalism) and advocates of XP/agile methodologies/behavioral objects (who
value hermeneutics). A quick look at the history of programming in general will
show that XP and agile methodologies are but the latest manifestations in this
long-standing philosophical feud, which has also influenced our (mis)under-
standing of objects and patterns.

Distractions to object thinking, such as which programming language is
"best," will be shown to be mostly irrelevant with a brief recap of classical
languages claiming to be object-oriented. This historical excursion will also
show you how ideas become manifest in tools—in this case programming
languages—and how philosophical principles and cultural values shape software development methods and processes.

Metaphor and vocabulary play a major role in shaping object thinking.
Metaphors are essential for bridging the familiar and the unfamiliar, and selection of the "right" metaphors is critical for further development of fundamental
ideas. Likewise, vocabulary provides us with one of the essential tools for thinking and communicating. It's important to understand why object advocates
elected to use a different vocabulary for object thinking and why it's inappropriate to project old vocabulary onto new concepts.

As you might expect by now, the prominent role of formally defined models, methods, and processes will be discounted in this book; their claim to be
repositories of objective truth will be challenged. This book will suggest that
methods are little more than helpful reminders of "things to think about" and
that models are only a form of external short-term memory useful in the context

of a particular group of people at a particular point in time. These biases will be linked to XP/agile approaches.

Note that I'll also provide applications of the ideas this book offers. I'll provide several examples as illustrations of how the ideas exhibit themselves in practice.

However focused on a particular topic each section of this book might be, an overarching bias or perspective colors every discussion: behaviorism. If a single word could be used to capture the "different ways of thinking about decomposition" noted by Booch, it would be *behavior*. The centrality of behavior will be most evident when we consider and compare traditional definitions and models of objects.

A majority of the published books on objects mention using behavior as the criterion for conceptualizing and defining objects. Many claim to present behavioral approaches to object development. However, with one or two exceptions,[1] they provide object definitions and specification models that owe more to traditional concepts of data and function than to behavior. Even when behavior is used to discover candidate objects, that criterion is rapidly set aside in favor of detailed discussions of *data* attributes, member *functions*, and *class/entity* relationships. This book's focus on behavior, on its aspects and implications, is consistent, I believe, with both the origins of object ideas and the design tradition assumed by XP/agile.

Material in this book is presented in a matter-of-fact style, as if everything stated were unequivocally correct. I'll cite alternative ideas and approaches, but I'll make little effort to incorporate those alternatives or to discuss them in detail. This is not because I am unaware of other viewpoints or because I am dismissive of those viewpoints. Alternative ideas are best expressed by their advocates. To the extent that this book is used as a classroom text, discussion of alternative viewpoints and alternative texts is the purview of the instructor.

Paths and Destinations

The destination is easy—to become a better software developer. Or maybe not so easy since "better" requires more than the addition of yet another skill or technique to one's repertoire. Techniques, tools, skills, and facts are part of becoming better but are insufficient in themselves. Integration with existing skills, the transformation of facts into knowledge (even wisdom), and the ability to base one's future actions on principles and ideas instead of rote procedures are all essential to becoming better.

---

1. Wirfs-Brock, Weiner, and Wilkerson's *Objected Oriented Design* offers a behavior-based method, as does Wilkinson's *Using CRC Cards*.

This book is intended to offer one path to becoming a better developer. Specifically, a better agile developer; and more specifically yet, a better extreme programmer. By better, I mean more like the acknowledged masters of agile development and extreme programming: Ward Cunningham, Kent Beck, Ron Jeffries, Alistair Cockburn, Bob Martin, Ken Auer … (Please fill in the rest of the top 20 to reflect your own heroes.)

These people are not masters merely because they practice certain techniques or exhibit certain skills. They embody, they live, they exude shared values and principles. They share similar experiences and have learned common lessons from those experiences. They share a worldview. Given a common anthropological definition of culture—"shared, socially learned knowledge and patterns of behavior"[2]—it is reasonable to assert that the agile and extreme programming masters constitute a culture—a subculture, actually—of software developers. If one aspires to be like them, one must become a member of that culture.

The process of learning a culture—enculturation—is partly explicit but mostly implicit. The explicit part can be put into books and taught in seminars or classrooms. Most of culture is acquired by a process of absorption—by living and practicing the culture with those who already share it. No book, including this one, can replace the need to live a culture. But it is possible to use a book as a means of "sensitizing," of preparing, a person for enculturation—shortening the time required to understand and begin integrating lived experiences. That is the modest goal of this author for this book.

Who Should Read This Book

A conscious effort has been made to make this book useful to a wide audience that includes professional developers and postsecondary students as well as anyone with an interest in understanding object-oriented thinking. It's assumed that the average reader will have some degree of familiarity with software development, either coursework or experience. It's further assumed that the reader will have been taught or will have experience using the vocabulary, models, and methods prevalent in mainstream software development. This book focuses on presenting objects and XP and not on providing background and details of mainstream development.

---

2. Peoples, James, and Garrick Bailey. *Humanity: an Introduction to Cultural Anthropology*. Belmont, CA: Wadsworth/Thompson Learning, 2000.

The organization of the book, front-loading the philosophical and historical material, might present some problems for the most pragmatically oriented reader, the one looking for technique and heuristics to apply immediately. The introduction attempts to make a case for reading the book in the order presented, but it's OK to skip ahead and come back to the early chapters to understand the ideas behind the technique.

Three caveats help to further define the audience for this book:

■ This is not a programming text. Some limited examples of pseudocode (usually having the flavor of Smalltalk, the language most familiar to the author) are presented when they can illuminate a concept or principle of development.

■ The book, however, is expressly intended for programmers, especially those using Java and C++. It's hoped that this book will facilitate their work, not by providing tricks and compiler insights but by providing conceptual foundations. Languages such as C++ and Java require significant programmer discipline if they are to be used to create *true* objects and object applications. That discipline must, in turn, be grounded in the kind of thinking presented in this book.

■ Although this book stresses the philosophy and history of objects/components, the author's overarching goal is assisting people in the development of pragmatic skills.

> **Note**   If this text is used in an academic course (undergraduate or graduate), roughly 40 percent of the available class time should be devoted to workshop activities. Software development of any kind is learned through experience, but objects, because they are new and different, require even greater amounts of reflection and practice. Another characteristic of an ideal course is interaction and discussion of multiple viewpoints. This book is best used in conjunction with other method books (particularly any of the excellent books on UML or RUP) that present alternative viewpoints and, of course, with at least one of the XP or agile texts, which will add depth to what is presented here.

Portions of the historical and philosophical material in this book will be familiar to those readers with their own extensive personal experience as practitioners. To them, the material might appear to be rehashed old arguments. But most readers will not share either that experience or that awareness, and they need to know, explicitly, how those ideas have shaped the profession as we see it today. I hope that even the most experienced practitioners will see some new insights or have old insights brought to the forefront of their minds when reading this material.

One final note. Readers of this book will tend to be professional software developers or those aspiring to become professionals. Both groups share a character trait—an eagerness to build, to practice. They are ready to "just do it."

To them is directed the final message of this introductory chapter: please be patient.

As a profession, we also tend to be abysmally ignorant of our own history. In the words of the oft quoted, misquoted, and paraphrased philosopher, George Santayana, "Those who cannot remember the past are condemned to repeat it." In computing, thanks to Moore's Law, our repetition is disguised a bit by scale—mainframe mistakes replicated on desktops, then notebooks, then PDAs and phones, and then molecular computers.

As a profession, we tend to ignore the various influences—such as culture, philosophy, psychology, economics, and sheer chance—that have shaped the practice of software development.

It is my belief that we cannot improve our intrinsic abilities as object and agile software developers without an examination, however brief, of the historical and philosophical presuppositions behind our profession. We should not, and cannot if we want them to truly understand, bring new members into our profession without providing them with more than tools, methods, and processes that they use by rote.

How This Book Is Organized

Readers are encouraged to proceed through the book in sequence, to accept that each chapter lays a foundation for the one that follows. Overlaying the order are several implicit logical divisions, including the following:

- The introduction and Chapter 1, "Object Thinking," advance arguments for why understanding the background and history of ideas is a necessary step in the successful application of those ideas. They also argue that both objects and extreme programming (agile methods) share common foundations.

- Chapter 2, "Philosophical Context," and Chapter 3, "From Philosophy to Culture," provide a foundational context, partly based in philosophy and partly in history.

■   Chapter 4, "Metaphor: Bridge to the Unfamiliar," introduces key ideas and meta-ideas (metaphors as ideas about how to explain ideas, simply put).

■   Chapter 5, "Vocabulary: Words to Think With," introduces vocabulary and explains why object thinking requires a different vocabulary for things that appear to be familiar but that use old labels.

■   Chapter 6, "Method, Process, and Models," revisits commonalities between object and agile ideas and the relationship of those ideas to the notion of method and process.

■   Chapter 7, "Discovery," Chapter 8, "Thinking Toward Design," and Chapter 9, "All the World's a Stage," apply the ideas of previous chapters and provide examples of object thinking in action.

■   Chapter 10, "Wrapping Up," adds a coda with short explorations of how object thinking can be extended and coordinated with unavoidable nonobject worlds, and what the ultimate outcome of object thinking might be.

I encourage you to engage the book in the order presented, but feel free to skip Chapter 1 if you're prepared to take on faith the assertions made about objects and object thinking in subsequent chapters.

Many readers will be a bit anxious to "get to the good stuff," to see how the book's ideas are applied or how they manifest themselves in practice (which is shown in Chapters 7 through 9). While I firmly believe that the book's initial chapters—as far afield as they might appear to be—need to be covered first, I also recognize the need to at least foreshadow application. To this end, I offer a continuing sidebar—the "Forward Thinking" sidebar—in these initial chapters. This sidebar presents a sample application in bits and pieces as a means of illustrating important ideas while satisfying the craving for pragmatic examples.

Introduction

The time: 1968. A software crisis has been declared. Part of the crisis derives from the fact that more software is needed than there are developers to produce it. The other part of the crisis is the abysmal record of development efforts. More than half of the projects initiated are canceled, and less than 20 percent of projects are successfully completed, meaning that the time and cost overruns associated with those projects were less than 100 percent and the software was actually used to support the business.

The time: 2003. We have a lot of developers—part of the software crisis has passed for the moment. Many of them are located in other countries because too many managers seem to believe that developers are developers and therefore go for greater numbers at lesser cost.

The skills, abilities, attitudes, and aptitudes of the development community are, unfortunately, suspect. The "development community" means the *entire* development community—from programmers to senior managers—in the United States and the rest of the world. It is still the case that almost half of all projects initiated are not completed. Those that are completed almost always incur significant cost overruns. Quality—the lack thereof—is still a major issue. Bloated, inefficient, bug-ridden, user-unfriendly, and marginally useful—these are still common adjectives used to describe software.

The lack of significant improvement is not for want of trying. Numerous proposals have been advanced to improve software development.

Software engineering provides an umbrella label for a spectrum of improvement efforts ranging from structured programming to formal (mathematical and logical) foundations for program specification to UML (unified modeling language) to ISO 9000 certification and CMM (capability maturity model) formalizations of the development process.

Sharing the goal of software improvement but rejecting the assumptions implicit in software engineering, several alternative development approaches have been championed. Creativity and art have been suggested as better metaphors than engineering. Software craftsmanship[1] is the current incarnation of this effort. Iterative development has as long a history as the linear-phased development at the heart of software engineering.

---

1. McBreen, Peter. *Software Craftsmanship: The New Imperative*. Addison-Wesley, 2001.

Extreme programming (XP) and agile software development represent a contemporary attempt to redefine and improve software and the practice by which that software comes into existence. XP/agile represents an alternative to software engineering. Further, XP/agile challenges the assumptions, the core values, and the worldview upon which software engineering is predicated. It is not surprising, therefore, that those with a vested interest in software engineering are trying very hard to marginalize ("it's OK for small projects by small teams that are not engaged in mission-critical projects"), co-opt ("XP is just a subset of RUP[2]—with a different vocabulary"), or dismiss ("XP is just a tantrum staged by a few petulant out-of-work Smalltalk programmers angry at the demise of their favorite programming language").

This book is motivated by a set of curious questions; it is based on the belief that "better people" are absolutely essential and that they can be nurtured; it is grounded in the conviction that object-oriented ideas and principles are poorly understood; and it is premised on the belief that XP (and other agile methods) and object thinking are inextricably entwined—each requires the other if they are to be successful.

Curiosities

Consider the following curious questions: Why is it that iterative development has been acknowledged—even by those proposing sequential (waterfall) development—as the "right" way to produce software, and yet

- XP is seen as a "novel" and even "radical" approach?

- So few, except those who have attempted to install an agile approach the past two or three years, "officially" use iterative development?

- There is so much resistance—by managers and professional developers—to doing things the "right" (iterative) way?

---

2. RUP—Rational Unified Process, an attempt to standardize and formally define the software development process. Created and advocated by the same individuals behind UML (unified modeling language), most notably Grady Booch, Ivar Jacobson, and James Rumbaugh.

■ Discussions between proponents and opponents of agile approaches are so heated and frequently emotional when both sides seem to agree, on the surface, on so many things?

■ "Better people" has been recognized as the most promising silver bullet for addressing the software crisis, and yet almost all of our energy has been spent on creating better tools, methods, and processes instead of better people?

■ Every effort to advance nonformal, iterative, artistic, and humane ways to develop software seem to be resisted and then co-opted and debased by formal software engineering?

■ So few developers seem to be able to adopt and practice innovations such as objects and agile methods in a manner consistent with the intent and example of those who first advanced the innovation? (Don't believe this is a fair statement? Then why, two to four years after XP and agile were introduced, is that community spending so much time and effort wrestling with questions of certification? Why does Alan Kay say the object revolution has yet to occur?)

The long answer to these and similar questions is this book. The short answer, and hopefully part of your motivation for reading this book, is that software developers tend to be so focused on what and how that they forget to explore questions of why.

The "People Issue"

Fact 1: The most important factor in software work is not the tools and techniques used by the programmers but rather the quality of the programmers themselves.

Fact 2: The best programmers are up to 28 times better than the worst programmers, according to "individual differences" research. Given that their pay is never commensurate, they are the biggest bargains in the software field.

—Robert L. Glass[3]

---

3. Glass, Robert L., *Facts and Fallacies of Software Engineering*. Boston: Addison-Wesley, 2003.

In his discussion of the foregoing facts, Glass notes that we have been aware of these human differences since 1968:[4]

Nearly everyone agrees, at a superficial level, that people trump tools, techniques, and process. And yet we keep behaving as if it were not true. Perhaps it's because people are a harder problem to address than tools, techniques, and process.

We in the software field, all of us technologists at heart, would prefer to invent new technologies to make our jobs easier. Even if we know, deep down inside, that the people issue is a more important one to work.

—Glass, 2003

This book is an attempt to address the "people issue." Specifically, it is an attempt to help developers improve their intrinsic abilities.

The Need for Better Developers

For decades, the profession of software development has relied on an implicit promise: "Better tools, methods, and processes will allow you to create superior software using average human resources." Managers have been sold the idea that their jobs will be made easier and less risky by adoption of strict formal methods and processes—a kind of intellectual Taylorism. (Taylor, Gilbreth, and others advanced the concept of scientific management, time and motion studies, and the modern assembly line. Their distrust of human workers led them to the idea that imposed process and method could compensate for weaknesses they felt to be innate in workers. The same attitude and philosophy are assumed in the field of software engineering.) For the most part, these efforts have failed miserably.

Instances of success exist, of course.[5] You can find cases in which project A using method X did, in fact, achieve notable success, but industry statistics as a whole have failed to improve much since 1968, when software engineering and scientific management were introduced as means for resolving the software crisis. Abandoned projects, cost/time overruns, and bloated, buggy software still dominate the landscape.

---

4. Sackman, H., W.I. Erikson, and E.E. Grant. "Exploratory Experimental Studies Comparing Online and Offline Programming Performances." *Communications of the ACM*, January 1968.

5. Some advocates of software engineering and process improvement will make claims of major successes (SEI Report CMU/SEI-2001-SR-014).

Even the most ardent advocates of software engineering (for example, Dykstra, Boehm, and Parnas), as well as those most responsible for popularizing software engineering among the corporate masses (Yourdon and Martin), recognized the limits of formal approaches. In "A Rational Design Process: How and Why to Fake It,"[6] Parnas acknowledged the fact that highly skilled developers did not "do" development the way that so-called rational methods suggested they should. Martin suggested that the best way to obtain high-quality software—software that met real business needs on time and within budget—was the use of special "SWAT" teams comprising highly skilled and greatly rewarded developers doing their work with minimal managerial intervention.

The only consistently reliable approach to software development is, simply, good people. So why have so much attention and effort been devoted to process and method? There have been at least three contributing reasons:

- A widespread belief, partially justified, that not enough good people were available to accomplish the amount of development that needed to be done.

- An unspoken but just as widely held belief that really good developers were not to be trusted—they could not be "managed," they all seemed to be "flaky" to some degree, and they did not exhibit the loyalty to company and paycheck of "normal" employees. Really "good" developers tended to be "artists," and art was (is) not a good word in the context of software development.

- A suspicion, probably justified, that we did not (do not) know how to "upgrade" average developers to superior developers except by giving them lots of experience and hoping for the best.

It is no longer possible to believe that either method or process (or both together) is an adequate substitute for better people. There is a resurgence of interest—spurred most recently by XP and the core practices in other agile methods—in how to improve the human developer. This interest takes many forms, ranging from XP itself to redefinition of software development as a craft (McBreen[7]) and a calling (West[8], Denning[9]) instead of a career to software apprenticeship (Auer[10]). Why do we need better developers? Because increasing

---

6. Parnas, David Lorge, and Paul C. Clements. "A Rational Design Process: How and Why to Fake It." *IEEE Transactions on Software Engineering*. Vol. SE-12, No. 2, February 1986.

7. McBreen, Peter. *Software Craftsmanship: The New Imperative*. Boston: Addison-Wesley, 2001.

8. West, David. "Enculturating Extreme Programmers" and "Educating Xgilistas."

9. Denning, Peter. ACM editorial.

10. Ken Auer, *www.rolemodelsoft.com*.

the supply of highly skilled people—rather than only adhering to particular methods and processes—is the only way to resolve the software crisis.

Note Extreme programming and agile methods derive from the actual practice of software development rather than academic theory. The critical difference between XP/agile and traditional methods is their focus on attitudes, behaviors, culture, and adaptive heuristics instead of formal technique and theory. If the "method" label is to be attached to XP/agile, it should be in terms of a method for producing better developers rather than a method for producing better software. Better software comes from, and only from, better people.

Producing Better Developers

What makes a better developer? The traditional answer is experience. Most textbooks on software engineering and formal process contain a caveat to the effect that extensive real-world experience is required before the tools and techniques provided by method/process can be effectively utilized. In this context, experience is just a code word for those aspects of development—philosophy, attitude, practices, mistakes, and even emotions—that cannot be reduced to syntactic representation and cookbook formulation in a textbook.

Today's practitioners, and some theorists, are intensely interested in teasing apart and understanding the complex elements behind the label "experience." There is great desire to understand what developers actually "do" as opposed to some a priori theory of what is appropriate for them to do. Models are seen as communication devices, unique to a community of human communicators, instead of "vessels of objective truth" with a value that transcends the context of their immediate use. Development is seen as a human activity—hence a fallible activity—that must accommodate and ameliorate imperfection and mistakes rather than seek to eliminate them. Communalism is valued over individualism. Systems are seen as complex instead of just complicated, necessitating a different approach and different insights than were required when software developers merely produced artifacts that met specification.

All of this intense interest is producing results. Although the total picture is still emerging, some facets of "the better developer" are coming into focus.

XP provides a foundation by identifying a set of discrete practices that can actually be practiced. Any developer can actually do these practices and, simply by doing them, become a better practitioner. They offer no grand theory, nor are they derived from any theory. The justification for the XP approach is based on two simple empirical observations: "We have seen master developers do these things" and "We have seen less proficient developers do these things and become better." Although XP does make claims to improve both product and process, these are side effects—one is tempted to say mere side effects—of the improvement in the human developers.

XP/agile approaches provide a solid foundation, but just a foundation. What "Xgilistas"[11] *do* is but part of what makes them master developers. What they think and how they think are critically important as well. XP relies on maximized communication and storytelling as a means for enculturating new developers in appropriate ways of thinking. Thinking includes a value system, a history, a worldview, a set of ideas, and a context. And XP encompasses an oral tradition that has not, as yet, been reduced to ink and paper (and maybe cannot be so reduced). Aspiring Xgilistas must become conversant with all of this before they can attain true "master" status.

One component of the oral tradition, of the history, and of the common worldview is the use of object-oriented approaches to design and programming. Unfortunately, this is seldom made explicit in the XP literature. The terms *object* and *object-oriented* do not appear in any of the first five books in the Addison-Wesley XP series—except once, and that occasion points to an incorrect page in the text. However, object vocabulary and concepts are abundantly evident. This discrepancy merely confirms that object thinking is presupposed by those advocating XP. The primary goal of this book is to provide one small contribution to help those following the Xgilista path—specifically, a contribution in the area of *object thinking*.

Object Thinking

Thirty plus years have passed since Alan Kay coined the term *object-oriented*. Almost all contemporary software developers describe their work using object vocabulary and use languages and specification tools that lay claim to the object label. The ubiquity of object terminology does not mean, however, that everyone has mastered object thinking. Nor does the popularity of Java. Nor does the de facto standardization of object modeling embodied in UML. A prediction made by T. Rentsch (cited by Grady Booch in 1991[12]) remains an accurate description of today's development and developers:

---

11. A neologism—useful for labeling those that embody one or more of the approaches that fall under the "agile" label.

12. Booch, Grady. *Object-Oriented Analysis and Design with Applications,* Second Edition. Boston: Addison-Wesley, 1993.

*My guess is that object-oriented programming will be in the
1980s what structured programming was in the 1970s.
Everyone will be in favor of it. Every manufacturer will promote
his products as supporting it. Every manager will pay lip service
to it. Every programmer will practice it (differently). And no
one will know just what it is.*

In fact, the situation may be worse than Rentsch predicted. An argument
can be made that the contemporary mainstream understanding of objects is but
a pale shadow of the original idea. Further, it can be argued that the mainstream
understanding of objects is, in practice, antithetical to the original intent.

Clearly the behavioral approach to understanding objects has all but disappeared. (Yes, UML does allow for a "responsibility" segment in its class diagram and description, but this hardly offsets the dominant trend in UML to treat objects as if they were "animated data entities" or "miniature COBOL programs.") This fact is important because two of the leading advocates behind XP were also the leading advocates of "behavioral objects." Kent Beck and Ward Cunningham invented the CRC card approach to finding and defining objects—the most popular of the "behavioral methods." Others deeply involved in the Agile Alliance were also identified with "object behavioralism" and with Smalltalk, the programming language that came closest to embodying behavioral objects.

It isn't unreasonable to assume that the behavioral approach to understanding objects dominates the "object thinking" of many of the best XP practitioners, in part because it was almost necessarily part of the oral tradition passed on by Kent Beck as he initiated others into the XP culture.

> **Note**   Certain aspects of XP practice are simply incarnations of earlier practices. XP "stories," for example, which deal with a system function actualized by a group of objects, are identical to the scenarios talked about in conjunction with CRC cards. Stories that are factored to their simplest form are nothing more than responsibilities. The only real difference between stories and scenarios/behaviors is the insistence that stories are always, and only, told by the domain expert (the customer) and always depict interactions in the problem domain. This was also true of good scenarios, but in the object literature scenarios tended to reflect implementation more than they did problem description.

It's also reasonable to assume that behavioral object thinking is only implicit in the XP/agile culture because so few books or texts were ever written in support of this approach. Neither Beck nor Cunningham ever wrote such a book. Rebecca Wirfs-Brock didn't update her 1991 book describing behavior-based object design until this year. Other efforts in this area (for example, Nancy Wilkerson's book on CRC cards) were not widely known and have not been updated.

This is particularly unfortunate because the CRC card "method" as described in the early 1990s did not incorporate all aspects of object thinking. In fact, I believe that object thinking transcends the notion of method just as it transcended programming languages. (You can do good object programming in almost any language, even though some languages offer you more support than others.)

Object thinking requires more than an understanding of CRC cards as presented circa 1990. It also requires understanding some of the history and some of the philosophical presuppositions behind object behavioralism, CRC cards, and languages such as Smalltalk. It requires an understanding of the metaphors that assist in good object thinking and an extension of the CRC card metaphor, in particular, to include more than object identification and responsibility assignment.

It is my hope that this book will promote such an understanding by capturing at least part of the oral tradition of behavioral objects and making it explicit.

XP and Object Thinking

This book is based on the following beliefs:

- Agility, especially in the form of extreme programming, is essential if the software development profession, and industry, are to improve themselves.

- XP offers a way to create "better developers" to improve the intrinsic abilities of human beings to develop software for use by other human beings—a way to produce "master" developers.

- XP cannot be understood, and those practicing XP will not realize the full potential of the approach, until they understand object thinking and the shared historical and philosophical roots of both object thinking and XP core values and practices.

- In particular, programmers and technical developers will fail to realize the full potential of XP-based development without a thorough understanding of object orientation—the "object thinking" promised by the title of this book.

1

Object Thinking

Let there be no doubt that object-oriented design is fundamentally different than traditional structured design approaches: it requires a different way of thinking about decomposition, and it produces software architectures that are largely outside the realm of the structured design culture.[1]

——Grady Booch

I have three main goals for this initial chapter:

- To begin showing the reader why object thinking is different and important

- To introduce arguments as to why object thinking is particularly valuable to developers hoping to master extreme programming or other agile approaches[2]

- To explain the emphasis on thinking instead of tools or technique; to explain the relevance and importance of history, philosophy, and metaphor—topics that are seldom the focus of books purporting to improve your software development skills

---

1. Booch, Grady. *Object-oriented Design: with Applications.* Redwood City, CA: Benjamin/Cummings. 1991. ISBN: 0-8053-0091-0.

2. In the remainder of this book, I will generally use *XP* instead of *XP and other agile methods* as a shorthand label for aspects common to all agile methods.

The short quote from Grady Booch that opens this chapter contains three key phrases that provide a framework for the discussion in the remainder of this chapter:

- **"fundamentally different"** Which raises the question of how object-oriented design's difference manifests itself and whether, in some aspects of development, this difference is more obvious or important than in other aspects.

- **"different way of thinking"** Not only about decomposition but about all aspects of development. Of course, this is the theme of this entire book.

- **"structured design culture"** By explicitly mentioning a structured design culture, Grady implies the existence of a corresponding *object culture.* There is an object culture and an extreme programming culture, and both cultures share a common heritage. Culture is a critical factor in how and what we think as human beings and as software developers.

Observing the Object Difference

Is Figure 1-1 or Figure 1-2 a better visual depiction of an object?

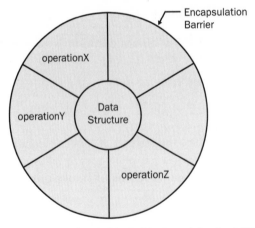

Figure 1-1   A graphical object model using UML graphical syntax.

Figure 1-2   A person as visual metaphor of an object.

A traditional developer will almost always pick the diagram in Figure 1-1. (Ken Auer calls this a "soccer ball" diagram because the segmentation resembles that of a soccer ball.) An object thinker, on the other hand, will pick the photograph. The soccer ball diagram has the advantage of familiarity to a traditional developer. It employs terms that are readily understood, and more important, it reinforces premises critical to the mindset of traditional developers and computer scientists. The diagram embodies Dykstra's definition of a program as data structures plus algorithms along with the idea of black box (enabled by the encapsulation barrier) modularization.

Anthropomorphization—a big word for the practice of projecting human characteristics onto objects—is fundamental to object thinking, which accounts for the selection of the person depicted in the photograph by object thinkers. As a thinking device—a metaphor or mental model—the soccer ball diagram impedes object thinking by perpetuating old mental habits. For example, if the diagram is an accurate depiction of an object, what is the difference between an object and a COBOL program? There is none. A COBOL program encapsulates data (data division) and operations (procedure division) and allows communication among programs (communication division). Object development—using this model—will have a tough time being anything more than the creation of lots of tiny COBOL programs.

> **Note**   A COBOL program is, of course, a very large object. Inside the program is a lot of messy stuff that's not at all object-like. Object COBOL differs from COBOL primarily in its ability to create smaller programs—closer to the scale of classes/objects in other programming languages—and enhancement of the communication division. No substantial changes have been made—object COBOL is merely COBOL rescaled. This is perhaps the best example of how the soccer ball diagram reinforces traditional program thinking.

Another illustration of where the object difference might be observed: the answer to the question of how many objects (classes actually) are required to model a complete spectrum of typical business forms. Stated another way, how many objects are required to create any possible business form? Your objects will need the ability to collect a variety of information values (dollar amounts, alphabetic strings, dates, and so forth) and make sure that each item collected on the form is valid. When this question is posed as a class exercise, students, traditional developers all, typically list 10 to 20 objects, including all kinds of "managers," "controllers," and different "widgets" for each type of data to be collected on the form (*integerDataEntryField, stringDataEntryField, dateDataEntryField*, and so on).

An object thinking solution would tend to limit the number of objects to four: a *Form*, acting as a collection; *Strings*, each label or text element being but an instance of this single class; *entryFields*, a widget object that displays itself and accepts input from a person; and *selfEvaluatingRules*, a special kind of object that embodies a business rule or, in this case, a data value validation rule. Both *entryFields* and *Form* objects would have a collection of *selfEvaluatingRules* that they could use to validate their contents.

Note   *selfEvaluatingRules* will be discussed in detail in Chapter 10. For now, think of a self-evaluating rule as an expression (for example, widget contents = integer object) in the form of an ordered sequence of operators, variables, and constants. When the rule is asked to evaluate itself, each of its variables is asked to instantiate itself (become a known value), after which the rule resolves itself (applies the operators in the expression) to a final value—a Boolean true or false, for example. A widget on a form is likely to have at least two rules, one to determine whether the entered value is of the correct class (for example, an integer or a character) and one to determine whether the value is consistent with the range of allowable values for that widget. If both of these rules resolve to true, the widget can say its contents have been validated.

Here's a final example (for now) of places to observe the object difference: three different models of a *customer*. Figure 1-3a is an entity model: customer as data. Figure 1-3b is a UML class, and Figure 1-3c is an object model. Both Figure 1-3a and Figure 1-3b reflect typical thinking about customers as a collection of facts that must be remembered by the system. Both examples name the "object" and list its attributes. An attribute is the name of some characteristic, the value of which must be remembered (stored by) the system. The UML model (Figure 1-3b) differs from the entity model (Figure 1-3a) only because it also lists operations—functions that manipulate the attributes—collocated with the attributes themselves. The similarity between entity and UML models tends to ensure that the latter are subject to the same rules of normalization as entities. This means that attributes of an object tend to get dispersed among several different objects, increasing the total number of classes created to hold facts about customers.

Figure 1-3c models a customer only in terms of what it does—what services it might provide. (The front-facing facet of the cube model contains a list of these behaviors or responsibilities.) What is known (by the system or anyone else) about the customer is not important to understanding the object itself. What the customer object needs to know to satisfy its advertised responsibilities is important and is evident (partly) in the left facet of the object cube depiction.

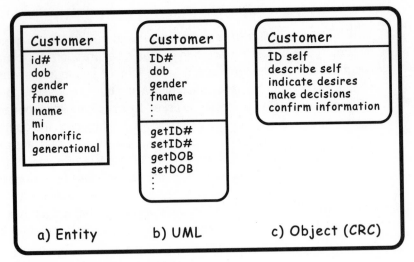

Figure 1-3   Customer depictions.

Entity modeling is most used in database applications where normalization is required to build the underlying database properly. UML models need
not be normalized, but if you intend to fully utilize an automated tool, such as
Rational's Rose, it becomes increasingly difficult to avoid normalization and the
explosion of classes that results from applying normalization rules. Object
models are seldom (if ever) concerned with normalization. The knowledge
stored in an object (leftmost facet of the model in Figure 1-3c) might be arbitrarily complex and need not be related in any formal way to whatever bit of
knowledge uniquely identifies the object.

Note   There are advantages to modeling objects differently from entities. Here are two simple examples. First, it isn't necessary to create two
different entities (classes) just because one object has an additional
attribute or needs to know an additional piece of information in compar-
ison with the other object, which reduces the total number of classes.
Second, it's possible to aggregate a number of attributes into a single
collection of values (which we will later call a *valueHolder*). The object
has an instance variable named *description*, for example, which contains a collection of discrete labeled values (dob:11/23/76, gender:F,
height:63, and so forth). The collection is itself an object with behaviors that allow it to add and delete *label:value* without the need to redefine an entity and database schema and recompile the database.

It's not necessary to fully accept the Whorf-Sapir hypothesis (see sidebar) to acknowledge that what and how we think varies with the language we employ. Every mathematician knows the difficulty of translating elegant equations into English prose. Likewise, every programmer who has used more than one programming language knows that statements easily and elegantly made in one language (Smalltalk or Lisp, perhaps) are cumbersome and verbose when translated into another (C++ or Java, perhaps). Developers are aware that different programming languages have very different idioms and styles despite being, deep under the covers, equivalent.

The Whorf-Sapir Hypothesis

Benjamin Lee Whorf and Edward Sapir advanced a theory (overstated here) to the effect that what you could and did think was determined by the language you spoke and that some languages allowed you to think "better" than others. Whorf was particularly interested in the Hopi language.

The Whorf-Sapir hypothesis is not fully accepted because most linguists and cognitive scientists believe that the hypothesis is flawed by overstatement and that the theory reflects some basic errors in the understanding of the Hopi language. However, most cognitive scientists do believe there is an element of truth in the hypothesis. In recent years, George Lakoff and others have advanced a similar theory with regard to language and thought. Lakoff's work centers on metaphor, a particular aspect of a language, and shows how metaphor influences what and how we think. Both Whorf and Lakoff are part of a school of philosophy and cognitive science focused on the role of language as a shaper of thought. The arguments for object thinking in this book reflect and are supported by this kind of cognitive science research.

These simple examples, which I'll return to and expand upon later in this book, point to some of the differences resulting from object thinking, but other more general comments can also be made about object differences. Consider the continuum depicted in Figure 1-4. At the far left, the developer is thinking about the problem and its intrinsic nature, and at the far right, the developer is thinking of the most precise details of implementing a program. As we move from left to right, we tend to think using different languages. At the far left, we employ (or, since most of you are developers, you collaborate with someone who employs) natural language and the vocabulary of domain experts. At the far right, our vocabulary and syntax are essentially equivalent to an instruction set embedded on a processor chip.

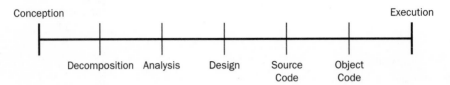

Figure 1-4   Difference continuum.

Object thinking occurs across the continuum illustrated in Figure 1-4, but it's far more critical when engaged in activities to the left of the spectrum than to the right. In fact, if you apply object thinking correctly when you are conceptualizing and decomposing your problem space, you create a context that frames and guides your thinking as you move to activities on the right half of the spectrum. Object thinking and object decomposition yield a very different set of objects (modules) than would result from using traditional decomposition thinking based on an understanding of data structures and algorithms.

Objects exist in the world. They are observed by and interact with other objects—some of them human beings—in that world. Human objects come to have expectations about the nature and the behaviors of other objects in their world and are disconcerted if an object appears different or if it behaves in a manner contrary to their expectations. The "naive" or "natural" expectations of objects represent a kind of integrity—what Alan Kay called a user illusion—that must be respected.

The set of objects produced by object thinking must eventually be designed and implemented, ideally without violating the integrity of the objects themselves and without contravening any object principles or ideals. This poses a new set of problems for developers as they design classes and code methods. As we move rightward on the continuum, thinking is constrained by the languages (remember Whorf and Sapir) that we must employ. Programming languages can lead us far from object thinking. Even if the language is relatively benign (a "pure" OO programming language), it is still quite possible to write nonobject code.

As I've said, although object thinking will yield observable differences across the thinking continuum, the differences will be far more evident, and their "correctness" will be essential, on the left. On the right of the continuum, the differences will tend to be collective rather than individual. For example, idiosyncrasies of syntax aside, it can be very difficult to differentiate a specific object-oriented method from a similarly specific procedural function. But the complete set of methods and the manner in which they are distributed among the objects (modules) will be quite different than would be the case in implementations conditioned upon traditional computer thinking.

Note I refer once again to COBOL programs to illustrate some differences. It was the case that a single COBOL program would encapsulate a bunch of functions, data structures, and some overall control logic. Object orientation is not achieved, however, merely by breaking up the monolith of a traditional COBOL program. Object COBOL implementations will use a greater number of objects (each one a separate program), but absent object thinking, each little program will be a mirror of the larger single program they collectively replaced: data structures, functions, and control logic. Without object thinking, the developer repeats old thinking habits on a smaller scale. One specific example of the perpetuation of this kind of thinking is the treating of data as something passive that must be protected, manipulated, and managed. In COBOL, data is defined separately from all the functions that operate on that data; it just sits there, and it is used (and frequently corrupted) by functions elsewhere in the program. Uniting data and procedure is far more complicated and difficult to do than is implied by the soccer ball model (discussed earlier), which simply shows the same old things stuffed in smaller containers.

In what other ways will object thinking manifest itself? What metrics will be different? Dramatic and frequently claimed measures include the oft-cited reductions in lines of code and the amount of lead time required to deliver an application. Lines of code, for example, in a well-thought-out object application will be at least an order of magnitude fewer (sometimes two orders of magnitude). This means that a 1 million–line program, written conventionally by developers thinking like a computer, can be duplicated with object thinking in 100,000 lines of code or fewer. Time to delivery is reduced by at least 50 percent and often by as much as 70 percent. Projects scheduled to take 2 years to complete can be done in 8 to 12 months.

Dramatic results were routinely reported in the early days of object enthusiasm but have died off in recent years because, I would claim, of a return to dominance of old thinking habits. This does not mean that object thinkers reverted to form—merely that as the number of people using OO programming languages and tools but not object thinking expanded dramatically, the collective ratio of object thinking to traditional thinking became smaller. When entire teams were object thinking and were almost certainly engaged in the rich iterative communication practices advocated by XP, the results were dramatic. If less than 10 percent of the team members are object thinking and the others are thinking traditionally, the overall effort will reflect the thinking style of the majority.

Mark Lorenz[3] and Jeff Kidd published a set of empirically derived metrics for successful object projects. (Although their book is somewhat dated, metrics derived from my own consulting experience—which continues to the present—are consistent with those reported by Lorenz and Kidd.) Following is a selection of metrics based on the results reported by Lorenz and Kidd but modified by my own consulting experience and observations. The debt to Lorenz and Kidd must be acknowledged, but they should not be held accountable for my interpretations and extensions.

- Application size: between 1 and 40 *stories,* with stories being roughly equivalent to the story cards talked about in XP or one-fifth of the use cases advocated in UML.

- Classes per application: fewer than 100, which are a mix of *key classes* (for example, business objects such as customer, account, inventory item) and *support classes* (for example, collections, strings, numbers, widgets). (See the sidebar "How Many Objects" in Chapter 4 for a discussion regarding the number of classes expected in a domain class hierarchy.)

- Number of classes required to model an entire domain (business enterprise): approximately 1000.

- Number of development iterations (conceive, develop, deploy, evaluate—what Grady Booch called a "roundtrip"): three, on average. Because XP iterates at the level of story and of release, this metric needs to be reinterpreted. But some variation of three cycles per defined effort seems consistent in both traditional and agile development.

- Amount of code discarded at each iteration: 25 to 30 percent. This metric is a proxy for the learning that took place and the refactoring of code done at each iteration.

- Responsibilities per class: average of seven. (We are using the term *class* in this context as an exemplar object—so these responsibilities are really *object responsibilities*, a distinction that will be made clearer in Chapter 4, "Metaphor: Bridge to the Unfamiliar." The same is true when we talk about methods.)

- Methods (the blocks of code that are invoked to fulfill a responsibility) per class: average of 12.

---

3. Lorenz, Mark, and Jeff Kidd. *Object-Oriented Software Metrics.* Englewood Cliffs, NJ: Prentice Hall. 1994. ISBN 0-13-179292-X.

- Lines of code per method: average of fewer than seven for Smalltalk (15 for languages such as C++ and Java).

- Percentage of methods requiring inline (comments) documentation: about 60. Practitioners of XP would think this a very high percentage. Refactoring, naming conventions, other idioms, and coding standards should move this figure much closer to 0 percent.

- Average method complexity using the following weights for each occurrence of the noted item—API calls 5.0, assignments 0.5, arithmetic operators or binary expressions 2.0, messages with parameters 3.0, nested expressions 0.5, parameters 0.3, primitive calls 7.0, temporary variables 0.5, messages without parameters 1.0: average fewer than 20 total points per method.

- Number of case statements, nested conditionals, and nested branching statements in methods: zero (0). Lorenz and Kidd are quite careful to cite a range for all of their metrics—a range that I have omitted for dramatic purposes. The nature of the domain being modeled, the application problem within the domain, and the relative skill of the developers will affect the metrics cited. Treat the numbers as if they were channel buoys—markers placed in the middle of the channel. You do not have to hit the number, but sail too far to the side, and you risk running aground.

Failing to achieve the metrics reported by Lorenz is a clear sign of the absence of object thinking. In cases in which traditional thinking prevails, the lines of code, the number of methods, and the complexity of methods will increase dramatically. In cases in which thinking derived from database design and data modeling prevails, the number of classes required to model any domain and to build any application in that domain explodes.[4] Another sign of the ascendancy of traditional thinking over object thinking will be a plethora of classes with the word *controller* or *manager* embedded in the class name.

---

4. One of the largest object projects of which I am aware through my consulting practice was tainted by datacentrism. At the inception of the project, management mandated the translation of a recently completed enterprise data model into the domain class hierarchy—each entity in the data model became a class in the object model. Despite using the right language, having some of the best object developers available in the country at that time, and having significant corporate support, the project took two to three times as long to complete as necessary, cost far more than it should have, and encountered numerous problems and complications that could have been avoided if the development team had been allowed to rethink what they were doing using object thinking principles. Management deemed the project "successful" because it was completed with no major overruns and saved the company a lot of money. Compared to what might have been, however, it was a dismal failure.

As the discussion of objects and object thinking proceeds, I'll note many other ways in which the object difference is observable. By the end of this book, you should be able to clearly differentiate between object thinking and traditional thinking solutions to problems. You should also be able to distinguish between "good" and "better" object solutions to a problem—recognizing that design always yields a spectrum of potential solutions to any problem and that evaluation of those solutions is partially subjective. Given that observable and real differences exist between designs that result from object thinking and from traditional thinking, what accounts for those differences? A full answer will require the rest of this book, but I'll introduce one essential difference immediately.

Object Thinking = Think Like an Object

The essential thinking difference is easily stated: "Think like an object." Of course, this statement gets its real meaning by contrast with the typical approach to software development: "Think like a computer." Thinking like a computer is the prevailing mental habit of traditional developers. And, as David Parnas noted,[5] it's a bad habit:

The easiest way to describe the programming method used in most projects today was given to me by a teacher who was explaining how he teaches programming. "Think like a computer," he said. He instructed his students to begin by thinking about what the computer had to do first and to write that down. They would then think about what the computer had to do next and continue in that way until they had described the last thing the computer would do…. Most of today's textbooks demonstrate the same method, although it has been improved by allowing us to describe the computer's "thoughts" in larger steps and later to refine those large steps into a sequence of smaller steps.

This intuitively appealing method works well—on problems too small to matter. … As we continue in our attempt to "think like a computer," the amount we have to remember grows and grows. The simple rules defining how we got to certain points in

---

5. Parnas, David Lorge. "Software Aspects of Strategic Defense Systems." *American Scientist* 73 (1985). pp. 432–440.

a program become more complex as we branch there from other points. The simple rules defining what the data mean become more complex as we find other uses for existing variables and add new variables. Eventually, we make an error.

In many of our computer systems there are several sources of information and several outputs that must be controlled. This leads to a computer that might be thought of as doing several things at once. If the sequence of external events cannot be predicted in advance, the sequence of actions taken by the computer also is not predictable. ... Any attempt to design these programs by thinking things through in the order that the computer will execute them leads to confusion and results in systems that nobody can understand completely.

When there is more than one computer in a system, the software not only appears to be doing more than one thing at a time, it really is doing many things at once. There is no sequential program that one can study. Any attempt to "think like a computer system" is obviously hopeless....

Programmers have tried to improve their working methods using a variety of software design approaches. However, when they get down to writing executable programs, they revert to the conventional way of thinking.

It should be clear that writing and understanding very large real-time programs by "thinking like a computer" will be beyond our intellectual capabilities. How can it be that we have so much software that is reliable enough for us to use it? The answer is simple; programming is a trial and error craft. People write programs without any expectation that they will be right the first time. They spend at least as much time testing and correcting errors as they spent writing the initial program. ... Software is released for use, not when it is known to be correct, but when the rate of discovering errors slows down to one that management considers acceptable.

The kind of thinking described by Parnas in 1985 persists, even though much new development is based on a data paradigm and even though most people claim to be doing object-oriented programming. Developers' thinking patterns, their mental habits, have not changed. Programmers, and software developers in general, still attempt to think like a computer.

> **Note**   Many readers will be familiar with most of the eminent scholars and practitioners cited in this book but not necessarily all of them. From time to time, it will be useful to introduce these authorities and provide some background regarding their accomplishments, confirming that their insights do indeed contribute to the issues at hand. "Behind the Quotes" will be a continuing sidebar used for this purpose.

Behind the Quotes
Dr. David Lorge Parnas

Dr. David Lorge Parnas, P. Eng., Ph.D., Dr. h.c., FRSC, FACM, Dr. h.c., Director of the Software Engineering Programme, Department of Computing and Software, McMaster University, is the Director of the Software Engineering Programme in the Faculty of Engineering's Computing and Software Department. He has also held nonacademic positions advising Philips Computer Industry (Apeldoorn), the United States Naval Research Laboratory in Washington, D.C., and the IBM Federal Systems Division. The author of more than 200 papers and reports, Dr. Parnas is interested in most aspects of computer system design. Dr. Parnas won an Association for Computing Machinery (ACM) Best Paper Award in 1979 and two Most Influential Paper awards from the International Conference on Software Engineering. He is the 1998 winner of ACM SIGSOFT's Outstanding Research Award. Dr. Parnas is a Fellow of the Royal Society of Canada and a Fellow of the Association for Computing Machinery. He is licensed as a professional engineer in the province of Ontario, Canada.

Dr. Parnas was selected to head the software portion of the Strategic Defense Initiative (President Ronald Reagan's program to develop a missile defense system, commonly known as "Star Wars")—a project from which he resigned when he and the other assembled experts concluded

(continued)

Behind the Quotes   *(continued)*

the software could not be written and tested. The quote used here is from a paper he wrote analyzing the problem and the abilities of software developers to address that problem. That paper was part of the public explanation of his resignation.

Few individuals can match the stature earned by Dr. Parnas in the realm of software development. Fewer still can match his moral conviction and willingness to uphold principle over mercenary considerations.

Now, it might be argued that the computer itself has changed substantially since 1985 such that the thing we are trying to think like is substantially different. We can investigate this claim by looking at programming languages. A programming language represents a virtual machine. Therefore, wouldn't an object-oriented language such as Java represent a very different kind of computer? If we "think in Java," don't we "think like objects" instead of engaging in the kind of "computerthink" discussed by Parnas? Unfortunately, no. As we will see in Chapter 2, programming languages are shaped by their own set of presuppositions. Although you can implement object thinking in any programming language, knowing an "OO" language is not sufficient to engender object thinking. In Chapter 3, an example is presented that shows just how easy it is to replicate traditional thinking in a "pure" object language such as Smalltalk. Languages such as Java and object-modeling tools such as UML effectively define an object as the encapsulation of data structures and algorithms. According to this kind of definition, an object (as discussed previously in this chapter) is nothing more than a very tiny COBOL program. A COBOL program is the encapsulation of data structures (data division) and algorithms that operate on those data structures (procedure division). (In fact, creating object-oriented COBOL was a relatively simple task involving making the program smaller in scope and increasing the power of the interface division to make it easier for one COBOL program to interact with others.) This example shows that developers tend to perpetuate old thinking habits, albeit sometimes to a lesser degree.

It's useful to generalize Parnas's observation to accommodate datacentric development and development in nonprocedural languages such as Prolog and Lisp. The essence of thinking like a computer is thinking in terms of the *means* of problem solution. You view every development problem through the lens of the means you intend to use to solve that problem. In datacentric development, the means of solution consists of relations and relationships; for Prolog and LISP, a set of propositions or state declarations.

The generalization being made here is a variant of the adage, "If your only tool is a hammer, every problem looks like a nail." Following Parnas, I'm suggesting that software development has been distorted and that all the problems noted by Parnas persist because "our only tool is a computer, so every problem looks like a virtual machine."

So, what is the object difference? How is thinking like an object different from thinking like a computer? Throughout this book, I'll be working to provide a complete answer to this question, but I'll preview a couple of differences here:

■ Object thinking involves a very different means of solution—a cooperating community of *virtual persons*. A virtual person is an entity capable of performing certain tasks. It has access to all the knowledge and resources required to complete its assigned tasks. Both virtual persons and virtual machines (computers) are really metaphors for how we think about problem solution—but they are very different metaphors.

■ Object thinking focuses our attention on the problem space rather than the solution space. Object thinkers take the advice of Plato, Parnas, Fred Brooks, Christopher Alexander, and many others by letting the problem define its own solution.

Problem = Solution

In *Notes on the Synthesis of Form* (Harvard University Press, 1964), Christopher Alexander argues that "every design problem begins with an effort to achieve fitness between two entities: the form in question and its context. The form is the solution to the problem; the context defines the problem." As an example of "fitness," Alexander points to the task of making a metal face smooth and level. A standard block, smooth and level to a precision greater than required by the target metal face, is inked and rubbed against the target. The presence or absence of ink on the target indicates high and low spots that need to be reground. The standard block is the context, the target face is the solution, and it is clear how the standard defines the target.

I'll develop the second point more fully in the next chapter, but again, here's a small preview. In their discussion of the principle of modular software design, Witt, Baker, and Merritt[6] quote Plato and Christopher Alexander (emphasis added):

*[First,] perceiving and bringing together under one Idea the
scattered particulars, so that one makes clear ... the particular
thing which he wishes [to do] ... [Second,] the separation of the
Idea into classes, by dividing it where the natural joints are,
and not trying to break any part, after the manner of a bad
carver ... I love these processes of division and bringing together
... and if I think any other man is able to see things that can
naturally be collected into one and divided into many, him will
I follow as if he were a god.*
                                              ——Plato, circa 400 B.C.

*In practice problems are not homogenous. They are full of knots
and crevices which exhibit a well-defined structure. An
analytic process fails only if it does not take this structure into
account.*
                                       ——Christopher Alexander, 1964

In these quotes, Plato and Alexander—and Parnas,[7] Brooks,[8] and Alexander[9] again, in other contexts—are talking about the notions of coupling and cohesion, familiar terms to any software developer. However, they're not talking about the structure of a computer program; they're talking about finding the naturally occurring divisions and classifications ("natural joints") in the problem space. This is an essential difference because the naturally occurring modules in a problem space are not isomorphic (exhibiting fitness between context and solution) with the modules discovered and defined when you are thinking about the design of a computer program.

---

6. Witt, Bernard I., F. Terry Baker, and Everett W. Merritt. *Software Architecture and Design: Principles, Models, and Methods*. New York: Van Nostrand Reinhold. 1994. ISBN 0-442-01556-9.

7. Parnas, D.L. "On the Criteria to Be Used in Decomposing Systems into Modules," *Communications of the ACM*, Vol. 15, No. 12, pp. 1053–1058, December 1972.

8. Brooks, Fred. "No silver bullet, essence and accidents of software engineering," *Computer Magazine*, April 1987.

9. Alexander, Christopher, Sara Ishikawa, and Murray Silverstein. *A Pattern Language*. Oxford University Press. 1977.

But they can be. Thinking like an object will lead to a greater degree of isomorphism between objects found in the problem space (the enterprise domain) and those employed in a solution space (the computer program) than thinking like a computer. Isomorphism of the modules (objects) in problem and solution space is a desirable, in fact essential, quality for software. I'll demonstrate the validity of these assertions in the coming pages.

Behind the Quotes

Christopher Alexander

Christopher Alexander is an architect. Not a software architect; rather, the kind who designs buildings and cities. For an "outsider," he has significantly affected the practice of software development. I'll cite the work and ideas of Alexander frequently in this book as well as add biographical and background information in later sidebars.

Alexander first came to the attention of the software community in 1968. He was frequently cited in papers at the NATO-sponsored first conference on software engineering; that conference marked the widespread adoption of software engineering as an appropriate metaphor for development. The ideas on design and formal process that he articulated in *Notes on the Synthesis of Form* were cited as appropriate for emulation by budding software engineers. Many years later, his work on architectural design patterns in *A Pattern Language: Towns, Buildings, Construction* (Oxford University Press, 1977) inspired the software patterns movement of the past decade.

Although most followers of Alexander's ideas, and Alexander himself, believe the software community missed the real essence of his ideas and settled for simply copying a syntactic form, his influence is undeniable.

Object Thinking and Agile Development Practices

The second major objective of this chapter was to provide some initial arguments for the special utility of object thinking to agile developers. To answer this question, let's look at the four XP values and a selection of the 12 XP practices introduced by Kent Beck.[10]

Values

"We will be successful when we have a style that celebrates a consistent set of values that serve both human and commercial needs: communication, simplicity, feedback, and courage." This statement introduces Kent Beck's discussion of values in *eXtreme Programming eXplained* and is a suitable introduction for our own examination.

Communication

The communication value has two aspects: advocating greater communication among all team members (developers, users, and managers) and promoting an increase in the quality of communication. Object thinking directly contributes to the latter aspect.

Imagine how much better your communication would be if all team members spoke a common vocabulary and that vocabulary reflected a common understanding of the problem domain and the essence of the problem being addressed by the team. Imagine further that the concepts behind this vocabulary reflected common understanding and did not require the customer side of the team or the developer side of the team to memorize arcane terminology employed by the other side.

Objects and object thinking promise the benefit of a common language. Users, managers, domain experts, and developers will all use the same vocabulary, grounded in a common understanding of that vocabulary, whether they are discussing workflow or programming, requirements (stories) or refactoring. It would be difficult to overstate the importance of a common language, especially in an environment shaped by XP practices, almost all of which require deep levels of communication among all participants in the development activity.

> **Note**   A domain expert is, by definition, someone with a deep understanding of the problem space and who has an ongoing involvement with that problem space—a real live customer, in other words. A software professional who has merely developed systems for "that kind of problem area" before is not a domain expert. This is one reason why XP demands an on-site customer.

10. Beck, Kent. *eXtreme Programming eXplained: Embrace Change.* New York: Addison-Wesley. 2000. ISBN 201-61641-6.

Simplicity

Every aspect of object thinking shares a common goal with this XP value, which equates to finding the simplest thing that could possibly work. Some examples:

- Object identification and responsibility assignment are based on the structure of the problem domain rather than on the structure of some potential computer program–based problem solution. However complex or complicated the natural world appears, human beings do very well in coping with that world. This suggests that a kind of natural simplicity is implicit in that world and is waiting to be discovered and employed.[11]

- Object thinking will lead to the smallest number of distinct things (represented as classes) possible—a kind of numerical simplicity.

- Objects designed and constructed following the application of object thinking will do the least amount of work possible and do it in the most direct and simplest way possible.

- Focusing on coordination of autonomous objects instead of the control and management of unruly modules and passive data structures will also contribute to simplicity.

Feedback

Object thinking's contribution regarding feedback is somewhat indirect. Object thinking evolved, in part, from the rapid prototyping school of software development and shares the values of immediate feedback that arose there. Object tools, such as the Smalltalk programming language, were optimized to provide immediate feedback to developers. Both the use of an interpreted language and the provision of multiwindowed development environments with browsers and workspaces are manifestations of this desire for rapid feedback. Consider the importance of the kind of immediate feedback described by Michael Hiltzik when talking about Apple's famous visit to Xerox PARC:

Given this rare psychic encouragement, the Learning Research Group warmed to their subject. They even indulged in some of their favorite legerdemain. At one point Jobs, watching some text scroll up the screen line by line in its normal fashion, remarked, "It would be nice if it moved smoothly, pixel by pixel, like paper."

---

11. Christopher Alexander's current works on the nature of order (*http://www.patternlanguage.com*) are a quest to find this natural—but exceedingly powerful—simplicity.

*With Ingalls at the keyboard, that was like asking a New
Orleans jazz band to play "Limehouse Blues." He clicked the
mouse on a window displaying several lines of Smalltalk code,
made a minor edit, and returned to the text. Presto! The
scrolling was now continuous.
The Apple engineer's eyes bulged in astonishment.*

Courage

Object thinking embodies precisely the kind of courage advocated by Kent
Beck:

*Every once in a while someone on the team will have a crazy
idea that just might slash the complexity of the whole system. If
they have courage, they'll try it out. It will work (sometimes).*

Object thinking is a "crazy idea" capable of increasing simplicity in software
design—crazy in the sense that it does not conform to traditional thinking about
software development, crazy in the sense that it revolts against the computer
thinking employed by most software developers, and crazy in many of the
same ways that XP is crazy. It takes courage to take a stand in opposition to
conventional wisdom as to how software should be developed. It takes courage
to suggest that formal practices, scientific practices, and engineering practices
are not necessarily the best way to develop software and that we might learn
something from philosophy, anthropology, and art.

Courage is not just "crazy ideas" and the ability to take advantage of them.
Courage is the ability to confront and overcome fear:

■   Fear that changes will break your software. Properly constructed
    objects, enforced encapsulation, and diligent refactoring based on
    solid object thinking reduce the risks associated with change to a
    negligible level.

■   Fear of mistakes. Mistakes are simply one iteration in the learning
    cycle. Object thinking is grounded in the idea that exploration and
    experimentation are intrinsically valuable and that learning what
    doesn't work is just as important as learning what does work. There
    are no mistakes: every result tells you something of value about what
    you are trying to accomplish.

- Fear that change will be costly. Change is costly only if the effects of a small incremental change in one part of a system are propagated throughout the system and somehow precipitate widespread failures in other parts of the system. Objects and object thinking assure that change is a local, not a systemic, phenomenon.

Selected Practices

Although it would be possible to link object thinking with all of the practices advocated by XP, a few merit explicit mention.

Metaphor

Metaphor is one of the most important but least understood practices of XP. Some[12] would claim that all thinking is metaphor-based. Kent Beck spent his OOPSLA 2002 keynote talking about the importance of metaphor. Object thinking introduces a very different set of metaphors to use in talking and thinking about software development. Object thinking metaphors are compatible with XP and are an important complement to XP metaphoric thinking. The common language provided by objects and object thinking provides a system of metaphors: every story, every test, every code module employs labels and terms that metaphorically connect things in the domain with their simulated coded counterparts.

Simple Design

Object thinking leads to simple design (usually the simplest design possible); the least number of classes necessary; the fewest number of methods per class possible; the simplest coding of methods; the avoidance of control, centralization, and management classes; and simple scripts to simulate simple stories.

Refactoring

Refactoring is a way for "lazy" objects to give all the hard work to other objects. Of course, when refactored and distributed to the proper objects, the work turns out not to be hard at all. Whenever a task looks too hard for a good object to perform by itself, it looks for others to share in the workload. Successive passing of hard work to others results in no object doing anything really difficult—and usually in a collective solution that is intrinsically simpler than would have been possible if the work had remained where originally assigned.

For example, suppose an airplane object has a responsibility to report its location. This is a hard task because the location is constantly changing; a

---

12. George Lakoff, for one. His work on cognition represents a fairly dramatic shift in this area of study, and his findings are very important for software developers.

location is a composite structure (latitude, longitude, altitude, direction, speed, and vector); the values of each part of that structure come from a different source; and someone has to remember who asked for the location and make sure it gets back to them in a timely fashion. If the task is broken up so that

- The airplane actually returns a location object to whoever asked for it after appending its ID to the location so that there is no confusion about who is where. (We cannot assume that our airplane is the only one reporting its location at any one time.)

- An instrument cluster keeps track of the instruments that must be asked for their current values and knows how to ask each one in turn for its value (a collection iterating across its contents).

- An instrument merely reports its current value.

- A location object collects and returns a set of label:value pairs (altitude:15,000 ft.).

None of the objects do anything particularly difficult, and yet collectively they solve a complicated problem that would be very hard for any one of them to accomplish individually.

On-Site Customer

The value of the on-site customer increases when she can fully participate in the development work by virtue of the common vocabulary described earlier in the "Communication" section. Object thinking not only creates a common vocabulary but also allows the on-site customer to actually make design suggestions and validate emerging designs as powerful representations of business context and goals because the behavior of objects is simple, transparent, and as familiar to the user as it is to the developer.

Coding Standards

Let me quote Kent Beck again: "Programmers write all code in accordance with rules emphasizing communication through the code." Object thinking promotes this kind of coding. In fact, much of what will be presented on coding later in this book is strongly influenced by Beck's *Best Smalltalk Practice Patterns* (Prentice Hall PTR, 1996), a style book for good coding. The coding metrics noted earlier—lines of code per method and number of methods requiring inline comments—are consistent with this XP practice.

As in the rest of this introductory chapter, I'm making assertions and claims about object thinking—here specifically about object thinking's compatibility with XP—that will be proved (or not) in the chapters that follow.

Thinking Is Key

There was a time when software development was considered an art. Art implies individual talent based on innate skills: "Artists are born, not made." As computers became increasingly prevalent and essential to modern industrial life, the dependence on artists to create the software that made them useful was deemed undesirable. Some were even offended that a computer—the embodiment of rationality, mathematics, and hard science—could be corrupted by "mere" art. Increasing demand for programming and development services suggested that the pool of true artists was too small; some other way would have to be found to create the mass of individuals needed to fill all the jobs available.

In the early sixties, a movement to eliminate art from development came to dominate the way we thought about the manufacture (the terms *educate* and *train* were used, but only as euphemisms for *manufacture*) of software developers. Tools would automate most of the development tasks, defined method would replace idiosyncratic problem solving, and documented process would allow every step to be monitored, measured, and controlled. Even the most mediocre human raw material could generate superior results if all the tools, methods, and processes were deployed properly.

The preface to this book begins with quotes from Robert L. Glass that suggest that the attempt to eliminate humans—or at least humanity—from software development failed. Humans and human abilities are still the key to software development success. This, in turn, suggests that we need to reconsider how we go about enhancing human abilities instead of attempting to replace them with machine capabilities.

One small step in this effort is to reconsider the "artists are born, not made" dictum. Thousands of art schools (ranging from small commercial academies to graduate academic programs) claim to make artists. While it may be true that no school "creates" artists on the order of Michelangelo or Georgia O'Keefe quality, they do enhance the innate talents of individuals and make them the best artist they can be. The education of artists is not focused on technique, process, or tools. The majority of an art education combines ideas, history, appreciation, experience, and constructive criticism.

An artist who is aware of the philosophy and history behind the practice, an artist who is attuned to the community in which art is created and appreciated, an artist who is capable of deep communication, is a better artist.

This book believes the same thing to be true of software developers—software artists, software professionals. Mastery comes first from a thorough understanding of ideas. Understanding of ideas requires an understanding of context, including historical context. Mastery is shared—it is a property less of the individual than of the group—and is shared by those participating in a common culture.

Software Development Is a Cultural Activity

To succeed, a software developer must be able to comprehend enterprise domains and perceived problems within those domains, conceptualize alternative configurations of artifacts and processes, and articulate ideas in a number of languages—at a minimum, a natural language, a modeling language, and a programming language. Because all of these activities involve thinking, improving a developer's cognitive abilities will result in improvement in the software he or she produces. This would seem obvious, but little has been done in the world of computing and software development to directly address this issue. Instead, the majority of software improvement efforts have focused on languages, tools, methods, and processes rather than on how to think about software.

In fact, efforts to reform software development by introducing a new way of thinking about software or about development are usually met with significant resistance. More often than not, new ways of thinking are dismissed out of hand or are co-opted and corrupted until they are acceptable to mainstream developers. At that point, they are but pale imitations of the original ideas.

An observer of these conflicts over the past 50 years cannot help but be struck by the similarity between the language wars, formalism wars, and method wars occurring within the software development community and ethnic and religious conflicts in the world at large. In fact, our conflicts over how to think about software development reflect real, but usually tacit, cultural differences—the most obvious example being tacit assumptions about the value of rationalism.

We live in a culture in which the value of, and the esteem given to, science and rationality are so deeply embedded that we seldom consciously consider why we have this pervasive bias. We do not question how and why this bias became entangled in other aspects of our culture—gender, for example, where a traditional association of rationality with the male gender and irrationality with the female was used as a justification for perpetuating unequal treatment based on gender. This same bias in favor of rationality is reflected in debates over method—the implicit assumption is that a method is weak unless built on a formal (rational, logical, mathematical) foundation. And it shows up in debates about programming languages, which not only must be formal but must resolve every hint of potential ambiguity, even to the point of adding features capable of resolving conflicts that are unlikely to be encountered by any programmer anytime in the next thousand years.

> **Note**   I'll say much more about cultural, and usually tacit, assumptions in the next two chapters.

Five significant software development innovations and trends have gained prominence in the past 50 years: datacentrism, software engineering, object orientation, patterns, and extreme programming. (Although computer-aided software engineering [CASE], total quality management [TQM], and capability maturity model [CMM] have been prominent innovations in software development, they were not, and are not, primarily new ideas about how to think about software.) Datacentrism—that is, focusing on data entities, relations, and databases instead of algorithms, flow charts, and data-flow diagrams—has been the most successful of the five thinking innovations, although most developers still think procedurally when writing code. Both software engineering and object orientation have achieved a strange status—everyone claims to be doing them without really doing so. The patterns movement exists mainly as a buzzword, and the jury is still out on extreme programming.

Antipathy toward new ideas, especially ideas that represent radical challenges to the perceived wisdom of formal methods and formal processes, contributes to the demise of radical new ideas. But so too does the failure to articulate radical ideas as *ideas*. Too often, proponents present their ideas in a guise supposedly more acceptable or easier to communicate—for example, objects in terms of a programming language (Smalltalk) or interface design as a set of standards, or extreme programming in terms of being a method. This kind of presentation almost always weakens the force of the new idea, making it even more difficult to overcome opposition and avoid co-option and dilution.

Extreme programming—and to a great extent all of the agile methods—represents a new and creative idea about software development (that is, an idea based on old and proven practices, reformulated, and taken far more seriously). The essence of this new idea might be distilled to a single sentence: "Software development is a social activity." Of course, it will take an entire series of books to explicate this simple idea and all of its implications. But the ultimate success of XP is dependent on people understanding and accepting the *idea*, and the body of thought presupposed by and supporting that idea, rather than on simply adopting the "twelve practices."

Behind the Quotes

Ward Cunningham and Kent Beck

Ward Cunningham is an almost mythical figure in the world of objects and extreme programming. Excepting a few papers, usually coauthored by Kent Beck, he has published little. His influence, however, has been monumental. He is considered to be the inspiration for most of the extreme programming practices, is a legendary coder and designer, and is a great mentor. Mathematicians use an "Erdos Number" as an indicator of their association with Paul Erdos, one of the most prolific and brilliant mathematicians of the past century. Erdos himself had the number 0, those who coauthored a paper with him had the number 1, coauthoring with a coauthor yielded 2, and so on. Extreme programmers are given a "Ward Number" based on pair programming with him (1), pair programming with someone who paired with him (2), and so forth.

Kent Beck is to Cunningham as Plato was to Socrates—the extender of ideas, contributor in his own right, and, in an interesting parallel, the one who published. The preeminent figure in the world of extreme programming today, Beck was equally active in object programming. Although he did not publish a book on behavioral object modeling, he did publish works on programming style and idiom (for Smalltalk).

Kent Beck and Ward Cunningham were a team when objects first became a hot technology, collaborating both as developers and as creative thinkers about object technology. Both will become quite familiar to the reader, as their ideas are central to many of the themes in this book.

Implicit in the idea of XP are other supporting ideas. Notable among these is the idea of *objects*. This is not surprising given that XP gurus Ward Cunningham and Kent Beck played a central role in the object revolution. They are the inventors of the CRC (Class-Responsibility-Collaborator) card approach to object analysis. The kind of object thinking introduced by Cunningham and Beck was, and is, far more consistent with the original *object idea* than any of the other popular approaches. The majority of developers claiming to be following object-oriented principles use the approach popularized by Rational Software under the umbrella of UML with nuances introduced by the Java programming language. Although Grady Booch, one of the principal contributors to UML thinking, clearly understood and advocated the *object idea* in his early work, little of that understanding was codified into UML.

The CRC Card Approach

The project that brought object programming into the mainstream was the development of Smalltalk at Xerox PARC in the 1970s. The first ideas about discovery and specification of objects arose in that context—Object Behavior Analysis (OBA) was the method developed by Adele Goldberg and Ken Rubin. This method was never published—except for one brief paper—but despite the flaw of overzealous formalism, it created part of the foundation for behavioral object thinking.

Ward Cunningham developed the foundation for what was to become a simple and powerful mechanism for capturing and understanding object behavior—a simple 3 × 5 index card. The index card provided a means for exploring and documenting a development team's understanding of objects. The format of the card was simple: a class name appeared at the upper left corner, and two column headers, Responsibility and Collaborator, appeared on the next line of the card. Class, Responsibility, Collaborator (CRC) headings yielded the popular name for the cards and the approach to analysis and design based on those cards.

Figure 1-5 shows part of a completed CRC card for an airplane object.

Airplane

Responsibility	Collaborator
ID self	a location
provide current location	an InstrumentCluster
maintain instruments	a Navigator
move to new location	
describe self	

Figure 1-5   A partial completed CRC card for an airplane.

Chapter 6, "Method, Process, and Models," will introduce more detail about CRC cards and how they became the foundation for the "Object Cube" at the center of applied object thinking and modeling introduced in this book.

Object thinking is central to extreme thinking. This is true even though there is little explicit mention of objects in the XP books. Object thinking is so basic to XP that it is simply assumed. As with cultural practices, it seldom occurs to members of a given culture that there is any need to explicitly talk about those practices—you simply do them the way everyone does. Many of the XP values and practices—for example, simplicity, stories, and refactoring—are dependent in important ways on object thinking.

XP values and practices aren't based on just any flavor of object thinking. Object thinking in XP is based on the behavior-centric ideas about objects exemplified in the CRC card approach. This approach to object thinking was always a minority view and almost disappeared as UML attained dominance and C++ challenged Smalltalk. (Visual Basic and Java superseded C++ in popularity and offered an improvement for object thinking, but still not an optimal environment.) Minority status was almost assured because of the close association of the Smalltalk programming language with behavioralism, an "informal, human-centric method" in a culture dominated by a bias in favor of formalism and engineering.

Oft-cited reasons for the demise of Smalltalk and the behavioral ideas behind informal methods (such as CRC cards) include performance issues, scaling issues, and hyperbolic promises by expensive consulting companies leading to dramatic failures. These reasons appear to be little more than rationalizations since every innovation in software has been subject to the same criticisms. If an innovation can claim a formal foundation (relational databases), it's given time to overcome its limitations (or those limitations are ignored, and the innovation is used in spite of them).

> **Note**   The same forces that are bringing XP to the forefront of software development have generated a resurgent interest in the behavioral approach to object thinking. In addition to this work, Rebecca Wirfs-Brock and Alan McKean have published *Object Design* (Addison-Wesley, 2003), and Richard Pawson and Robert Mathews have published *Naked Objects* (John Wiley & Sons, 2002), both of which strongly advocate and update behavior-based object thinking.

The purpose of this book is to help you become a better software developer and a better agile developer by improving the way you think. Thought, however, is not simply a matter of rote memorization and repetition of a few facts; it requires an understanding of ideas, of metaphors, and of history, topics that many readers will find unusual in a computer book. Changing your mind requires that you change your worldview, your culture, to include not only new ideas but new values and new perspectives. This, in turn, requires a temporary suspension of your current mindset. You must be prepared to take objects and object thinking seriously. An important aspect of taking the object idea seriously is a willingness to change your mind, to give up (at least temporarily) old and sometimes cherished ideas that are in conflict with new ones. Many of the original proponents of object ideas overdramatized the need for a mental change. ("Step one in the transformation of a successful procedural developer into a successful object developer is a lobotomy.") Predictably, this alienated potential converts to the new ideas more often than it convinced them. I'll try to avoid this error in this book, while at the same time emphasizing those occasions when you really must think differently in order to think in an object-oriented fashion.

Of course, the object idea is not a single idea. It's a complex of interrelated ideas that provide a kind of philosophy or, perhaps more accurately, a mental perspective. This perspective shapes the software developer's thoughts constantly and pervasively whenever a decision needs to be made, a problem needs evaluation, or a design requires formulation. It matters little whether the actual development act involves coding, testing, analysis, or design—the object perspective influences that mental activity.

Object thinking will be most effective only after the developer internalizes the object perspective. The same thing can be said about extreme programming. In both cases, the novice is confronted with an array of terms, of practices, of examples that constitute a "gate" (to use Christopher Alexander's and many a Zen mystic's terminology) that must be "passed through" to attain full mastery. As I introduce vocabulary, models, and examples, remember that these are but expressions of the idea (the gate), not the idea itself.

My excursion into history and philosophy in this book is intended to expose the cultural foundations of our thinking about software development. It will accomplish, hopefully, two things: expose the origins of divergent schools of thought (XP and objects on one side; traditionalist computer scientists and software engineers on the other) and provide the cultural context necessary to fully assimilate the material in later chapters.

Onward

In this chapter, I tried to make a case for reading the rest of this book. Some promises have been made, including that object thinking will make you a much better software developer and that object thinking will make you a much better XP practitioner.

The journey toward mastery of object thinking is not direct. I will ask you to take a short detour into history and philosophy in order to develop the context from which object thinking emerges. This context should make it easier to understand the advocacy of behaviorism as well as why terms and concepts are developed as they are in later chapters.

A secondary, and in many ways more important, reason for looking at philosophy and history is to establish in the reader's mind the themes and principles that can help you expand and shape the details of object thinking to accommodate new situations. It's my hope that you learn object thinking not by rote but by actively and creatively applying ideas, concepts, and philosophical principles.

Object thinking predates agile thinking, and both share deep common roots. Object thinking and agile development, especially extreme programming, are natural partners, sharing values and following common practices. Understanding these commonalities at the level of ideas and values is essential to the mastery of both. Exploration of these similarities will allow you to develop synergies of thinking and to become more agile.

Welcome to the journey.

Forward Thinking

Introduction

The first five chapters of this book introduce a lot of ideas and background information that are fundamental to object thinking. As critical as these ideas are, many readers will find themselves anxious to get to the material that illustrates application of the ideas. This continuing sidebar—an example application problem—will partially satisfy the urge to get to the "good stuff" while providing illustration of the ideas presented in early chapters.

Be forewarned: the example may involve concepts and models that have not been introduced in the main text. You may have to take a few things on faith until they are discussed properly.

(continued)

Forward Thinking   *(continued)*

Problem Statement:
The Universal Vending Machine Project

It's your first big XP project—you are to head a team building the software for a "better vending machine." Vending machine sales are flat, but your CEO notes that in Japan almost anything can be purchased from vending machines, and in Scandinavia people can buy products from machines using their cell phones. The hardware side of the company is busy designing and building customized vending machines of all types, and your team is to develop a common software base to run every type of vending machine they might come up with.

The Universal Vending Machine (UVM) will be capable of dispensing liquids as well as packages (cans or products in wrappers of various kinds). Payment can be made using any or all of three kinds of currency and coins (U.S. dollars, euros, and yen), debit cards (including a line of prepaid debit cards sold by your company), and credit cards. Customers can purchase goods from the machine via a Web-based transaction—also using debit and credit cards. Each vending machine will initiate product reordering via the Web. Restocking will be adjusted based on demand—which products sell the most in the least amount of time.

To save money, your team will create a single program, one capable of supporting the entire line of planned UVMs.

Given that this is an XP project, your customer will provide you with stories, and you will write tests and code programs. Getting from stories to code requires a fair amount of thinking, some open discussion, definition of tests, occasional writing of notes, and drawing of diagram fragments. Fortunately, you and your team are conversant in object thinking, so this will not present an insurmountable challenge.

2

Philosophical Context

More often than not, the first question programmers ask when embarking upon a new development project is, "What language will be used for implementation?" There is usually no need to ask about method because some variation of a formal structured approach is assumed. This is a very unfortunate situation.

The rising popularity of extreme programming (XP) and agile development makes the method question an open one—again. I say again because in terms of observable actions, XP and agile approaches are just the latest incarnation of iterative development. Some form of iterative development has been practiced in software since the 1960s and has usually been held to be superior to the structured "waterfall" approach that is officially practiced. And yet, when XP was proposed about four years ago, management and most practitioners reacted as if it were a radical departure from accepted and acceptable practice. Later in this chapter, we'll look at the philosophical context behind this reaction. But first it's useful to explore how philosophy shapes the development and utility of programming languages.

Whatever the answer to the programming language question, it is almost always given for the wrong reasons. Even worse, it is given for reasons that are never articulated and therefore never subject to reasoned judgment. Common reasons (not necessarily expressed out loud) for adopting a programming language include, in no particular order, the following:

- **Loyalty**   "We are a Microsoft shop; we use Visual Basic (or, today, Visual C#)."

- **Bandwagon**   "Everyone is doing Java."

- **Economics**   "Java programmers are a dime a dozen and completely interchangeable—if we lose one, we can find a replacement easily."

■ **Culture**   "You can't do telecom/real-time/embedded applications in anything except C++."

■ **Resumé**   "All the job ads ask for C# experience, so I had better get some exposure."

■ **Inertia**   "I wrote my first program in COBOL and am most familiar with COBOL, so COBOL is the right language for this project. Using COBOL makes it easier for me to manage the project."

Given that all programming languages are ultimately equivalent—"anything you can do, I can do also"—are there any legitimate reasons for selecting one language over another? I would suggest three:

■ **Pragmatics**   Mature libraries, compatibility with external systems (if you want to be a supplier to Wal-Mart, you make your systems compatible with theirs), availability of labor force, or other economic reasons. However, my professional experience suggests that 70 to 80 percent of the pragmatic cases made for a particular language have been rationalizations, not rationales. The pragmatic case has usually been a surrogate for loyalty, bandwagon, and similar reasons.

■ **Performance**   If, and only if, performance mandates cannot be satisfied with effective design, it might be appropriate to select a language that provides more direct access to and control of hardware. Here again, performance is more often than not an excuse and not a reason. It's possible to build hard real-time embedded systems using "slow and cumbersome" languages such as Smalltalk without paying any performance penalty compared with C or C++ implementations. It takes excellent design and the occasional programming trick (precompiling methods, for example), but performance is rarely a true reason for selecting a particular implementation language.

■ **Philosophy**   Programming languages are created for a reason. Language designers have specific intentions for their language, and those intentions are grounded in and shaped by particular philosophical values and ideas. Developers and development teams should select an implementation language that has been shaped by philosophical ideas and ideals similar to their own and to their problem space.

The philosophy implicit in the implementation language should be the reason for selection. There are some problems with putting this dictum into practice. Most developers, especially programmers, might be quite surprised that philosophy plays any role, let alone a critical role, in language design because few have had the occasion or opportunity to explore the ideas behind languages. Most object developers are not conversant with the philosophy of objects—the subject of this book—and are therefore in a poor position to select an implementation language reflective of object philosophy.

Developers who specialize in software for large-scale switching networks (such as the phone system) should choose a language such as C because the ideas and ideals that shaped that language are the same ones that shape the thinking of developers working in that problem domain. (Even C++ will be seen as an intrusion by those developers.) Scientific or engineering number crunching? No reason not to use FORTRAN. Business applications? COBOL or Visual Basic is perfectly fine.

Philosophical compatibility will allow you to be more expressive than if you are trying to translate your thoughts into a "foreign" language because your thoughts will naturally flow into the syntax of the implementation language.

Note   Every programmer has a first language—the one she learned first and used most. Most programmers have occasion to learn additional languages during their careers. Languages can be classified into families like procedural (C, COBOL, PASCAL) and declarative (Lisp, Prolog). Learning a new language within a family is relatively easy (Java in 40 hours, if you learned Pascal first; however, learning a language across families is quite difficult (C programmers learning Lisp). Object languages like Smalltalk proved most difficult for expert C programmers and expert database developers precisely because it required them to cross language family lines. Unless the programmer also learns a great deal of idiom and convention (not included in the formal syntax of the language or even in its libraries), she will continue to write (for example) COBOL using Java syntax.

Developers might, initially, be surprised at the significant and often hidden role played by philosophy. Many, if not most, have experienced moments of frustration when a language provided no direct and obvious way to express the ideas they had in their heads. Such moments are frustrating precisely because the true source of friction is hidden—it's based on unstated philosophic incompatibilities. On the other hand, many programmers have experienced the exhilaration that comes when design thinking and implementation language are compatible and productivity soars. (Users of script languages for Web development are likely to enjoy this type of experience.)

On a macroscopic level, it's impossible to truly understand the acrimony and the bitterness of the debates about object programming languages without looking beyond the languages themselves to the philosophy implicit in those languages. In the case of object language debates, the philosophic problem is twofold: first, very few people have explored the philosophy behind the languages claiming to be object-oriented (even though that history is well documented); second, few have understood object philosophy, making it difficult to match that philosophy with the one behind a given programming language. A short foray into the history of three languages of particular interest to object thinkers—SIMULA, C++, and Smalltalk—will illustrate the problem.

Philosophy Made Manifest—Dueling Languages

Computers—actually the engineering behind the construction of various hardware devices—and mathematics are the binary stars around which the world of computer science has revolved for more than fifty years. Programming once was a matter of rewiring. It was a decade before machine-level problems were solved to the extent that we could turn our attention to larger issues of program design. Another decade elapsed before we worked on analysis of applications and systems employing computers and programs. Significant attention is now being paid to the "soft" issues of usability, human/machine interaction, and even culture.

Despite these advances, whenever a new idea is introduced in computer science, it receives little attention until it has been made concrete and explicit—frequently as a new programming language[1]. Debates about ideas are then transformed into debates of the relative merits of the artifact languages. Arguments about design, analysis, method, and process inevitably follow, but those discussions are more often grounded in the programming language artifacts than in the original ideas. In this process, the original ideas become secondary if they are not lost entirely.

This has certainly been true in the case of the "object idea" and the programming languages that lay claim to that idea. The most vituperative debates in the object community have tended to center on questions of programming language. The overt focus of those debates has been on programming language features and technical benchmarks. But it is the emotions induced by covert (not consciously hidden, merely assumed and unspoken) philosophical positions that have accounted for the intensity and the hostility evident in those debates.

---

1. All of the quotations regarding SIMULA, Smalltalk, and C++ languages are taken from the respective chapters in *ACM History of Programming Languages*, ACM Press, 1978, Richard Wexelblat (ed.), or *History of Programming Languages II*, Addison-Wesley, 1996, Thomas J. Bergin Jr. (ed.).

Until the appearance of Java and C#, Smalltalk and C++ were the prime contenders for the hearts and minds of object developers. The intensity of argument between advocates of each language is legendary. Both sides tended to see Java as an interloper and tended to criticize those aspects of Java that reflected their more traditional nemesis. Disagreement between Smalltalkers and C++ers gains added interest from the fact that both claim to be the direct heirs of another, older, language, SIMULA.

Behind the Quotes

Alan Kay, Kristen Nygaard, and Bjarne Stroustrup

Each of these individuals is known for designing and promoting a particular programming language (which we will be discussing shortly). Each individual is also known for many other contributions to the world of software development and computer science.

Alan Kay designed, and Dan Ingalls implemented, the Smalltalk programming language while working at Xerox PARC. After leaving Xerox PARC, they both worked at Apple Computer, where they reinvented Smalltalk and called it Squeak. Squeak underwent further development when both men moved to The Walt Disney Corporation. Today they are independent developers focused on educational applications of the Squeak language and its multimedia capabilities.

Dr. Kay, who received his Ph.D. in computer science from the University of Utah, developed the idea of a *Dynabook*—a network-enabled laptop computer with the Smalltalk environment—also while at Xerox PARC. Arguably, the Pad Computer version of the Microsoft Windows operating system would be—if coupled with Smalltalk/Squeak—a pretty close approximation of his ideas.

Kay's biggest contribution was changing the way industry and users think of computers. Before Kay, computers were impersonal tyrants that required you to speak their language and limited their interaction to text-based communications. Kay personalized the machine: he expanded the means of interaction to include graphics, point-and-click, and multimedia using a language designed for humans rather than machines. The PC on your desktop reflects more of Kay's ideas than most people realize.

Kristen Nygaard developed, with Ole Johan-Dahl, the SIMULA programming language, introducing the concepts upon which all later object-oriented programming languages are built: objects, classes, inheritance,

(continued)

Behind the Quotes   *(continued)*

---

virtual quantities, and multithreaded program execution. He was also a social activist greatly concerned with the use of information technology and spent a good part of his career concerned with the social impact of computer technology. His work became the foundation of what today is called the Scandinavian school of system development, closely linked to the field of participatory design.

Nygaard has received the Norbert Weiner prize from Computer Professionals for Social Responsibility (CPSR) for responsibility in social and professional work; the Rosing Prize, awarded by the Norwegian Data Association for exceptional professional achievements; the John von Neumann Medal, awarded by the Institute of Electrical and Electronics Engineers (IEEE); and the A. M. Turing Award, issued by the Association of Computing Machinery (ACM) for 2001. In August 2000, he was made Commander of the Order of Saint Olav by the King of Norway.

Bjarne Stroustrup designed and implemented C++. He pioneered the use of object-oriented and generic programming techniques in application areas where efficiency is at a premium—for example, switching systems, simulation, graphics, embedded systems, and scientific computation. *The C++ Programming Language* (Addison-Wesley, 1985, 1991, 1997, and "special" edition in 2000) has been translated into 14 languages. In addition to his five books, Stroustrup has published more than 60 academic and more popular papers.

Dr. Stroustrup (Ph.D. in computer science from Cambridge University) is an ACM Fellow and has received that society's Grace Murray Hopper award for his work in C++. He is an ATT Bell Labs Research Fellow and an ATT Fellow and currently holds the position of professor at Texas A&M University.

SIMULA

SIMULA did not start as a programming language, and during all of its development stages, reasoning outside traditional programming played an important part in its design.

From the very outset SIMULA was regarded as a system description language.... *[emphasis Nygaard's]*

SIMULA 67, however, was a general-purpose programming language. Was the original purpose abandoned, or did SIMULA have a "dual personality"? The latter option is correct. This will be important when we examine what Smalltalk and C++ chose to borrow from SIMULA.

The concept of SIMULA began with an analysis of operations research and the kind of complex systems being modeled and analyzed in that domain. The first goal was to develop a "useful and consistent set of concepts" for modeling the "structure and interaction" of elements in complex systems. The initial objectives for the language were as follows:

1. The language should be built around a general mathematical structure with few basic concepts. This structure should furnish the operations research worker with a standardized approach in his description so that he can easily define and describe the various components of the system in terms of these concepts.

2. It should be unifying, pointing out similarities and differences among various kinds of network systems.

3. It should be directing, and it should force the operations research worker to consider all aspects of the network.

4. It should be general and allow the description of very wide classes of network systems and other systems that can be analyzed by simulation, and it should for this purpose contain a general algebraic dynamic language, such as ALGOL or FORTRAN.

5. It should be easy to read and to print, and it should be suitable for communication among scientists studying networks.

6. It should be problem oriented and not computer oriented, even if this implies an appreciable increase in the amount of work that has to be done by the computer.

Perhaps the most dramatic of these objectives was number 6, which is at odds with typical objectives for programming languages: efficiency, speed of execution, smallest possible executable footprint, and more intuitive and useful representations for computer primitives (memory addresses, operation codes, and so forth). Subsequent statements of objectives for SIMULA significantly modified this original goal.

One reason for the change was market driven: "The success of SIMULA would, regardless of our insistence on the importance of problem orientation, to a large extent depend on its compile and run-time efficiency as a programming language" (Wexelblat, p. 447). The other reason for the change was a perceived lack of conflict between problem orientation and computer orientation. SIMULA's developers discovered that "good system description capabilities seem to result in a more simple and logical implementation," thereby reducing the load on the computer's capabilities.

The focus on problem description—and the resulting simplification of the implementation—promoted by SIMULA's developers is paralleled in a paper called "On Decomposition," by David Parnas. Parnas's paper examined two conceptual abstractions for decomposing complex systems for the purposes of developing software. One was top-down functional decomposition, the approach that was gaining widespread acceptance under the label "structured design." Functional decomposition is based on an attempt to model the performance of the computer and software and to translate the requirements of the domain problem into those computer-based constructs.

Parnas offered an alternative approach called "design decision hiding," in which the problem or problem domain is modeled and decomposed without consideration of how the component parts of that domain or problem would be implemented. He was able to show that his alternative led to simpler, easier to read, easier to maintain, and more composable software modules than functional decomposition. Unfortunately, his advice was essentially ignored as the juggernaut of structured development came to dominate, at least officially, the manner in which software was conceived and implemented.

Both Parnas and the SIMULA team point to an important principle. Decomposition into subunits is necessary before we can understand, model, and build software components. If that decomposition is based on a "natural" partitioning of the domain, the resultant models and software components will be significantly simpler to implement and will, almost as a side effect, promote other objectives such as operational efficiency and communication elegance. If, instead, decomposition is based on "artificial," or computer-derived, abstractions such as memory structures, operations, or functions (as a package of operations), the opposite results will accrue.

Remember the minor reason for selecting a programming language noted earlier: only if performance mandates cannot be satisfied with effective design is it appropriate to consider selecting a language based on whether it provides more direct access to and control of hardware. Nygaard's and Parnas's observations are consistent with that assertion. Object thinking leads to better designs that reduce the demand placed on the machine, so raw efficiency and speed are far less critical than presumed by most developers.

As the SIMULA team expanded their understanding of the simulation problem domain and of the kinds of systems to be simulated, they identified needs for more generalized and interrelated components. These components had to be implemented, and implementation required adding sophistication to the language, resulting in the ideas of objects, classes of objects, data and implementation hiding, virtual procedures, and inheritance.

The legacy of SIMULA is twofold. First and most important from the perspective of object thinking, it provided an orientation (a philosophy) of giving primary importance to understanding and modeling the problem domain. This philosophy suggested the need for an elegant and powerful language that would allow direct mapping of components in a domain to the modules employed in the computer. Second, a number of original concepts, with appropriate vocabulary (object, class, inheritance), and some important implementation tricks (such as abstract data types and compiler-generated structures) were invented or advanced as the language developed. What use did the inheritors of SIMULA make of this legacy?

C++

Bjarne Stroustrup was motivated by the desire to create "a better C." The C programming language is noted for its power and conformity to machine architecture, which ensures that C programs are maximally efficient in terms of machine resources. This same power, however, made its misuse almost inevitable. Bugs were easy to create and difficult to track down. Too many C programmers lacked the discipline necessary to properly use the language. In SIMULA, Stroustrup saw a model for introducing discipline into the C language:

C++ was designed to provide SIMULA's facilities for program organization together with C's efficiency and flexibility for systems programming.... While a modest amount of innovation did emerge over the years, efficiency and flexibility have been maintained without compromise.

Stroustrup was concerned with creating a "suitable tool" for projects such as the writing of "a significant simulator, an operating system, and similar systems programming tasks." His focus was on the machine—system-level programming—and on the program. Even though he found SIMULA to be an excellent tool for describing systems and directly mapping application concepts into language constructs, he seemed to be more concerned with performance features of SIMULA than its descriptive capabilities.

SIMULA's class-based type system was a huge plus, but its run-time performance was hopeless:

The poor runtime characteristics were a function of the language and its implementation.... The overhead problems

were fundamental to SIMULA and could not be remedied.
The cost arose from several language features and their
interactions: run-time type checking, guaranteed initialization
of variables, concurrency support, and garbage collection....

SIMULA was conceived to make it easier to describe natural systems and simulate them in software, even if that meant the computer had to do more work. The inefficiencies noted by Stroustrup were indeed intrinsic to the language and the paradigm created by SIMULA. Stroustrup essentially rejected the SIMULA philosophy because his problem domain was the computer itself and performance was the primary goal:

C with Classes [precursor to C++] was explicitly designed to
allow better organization of programs; "computation" was
considered a problem solved by C. I was very concerned that
improved program structure was not achieved at the expense
of run-time overhead compared to C. The explicit aim was to
match C in terms of run time, code compactness, and data
compactness. To wit: someone once demonstrated a three
percent systematic decrease in overall run-time efficiency
compared with C. This was considered unacceptable and the
overhead was promptly removed.

C++ maintained the goal of adding program structure without a loss of performance. The constant measure of the language was the machine, either the physical computer platform or the virtual machine—the program. This constant focus on performance limited what could be borrowed from SIMULA—most important, SIMULA's goal of being a general systems description language.

Although the claim is made that C++ is a general-purpose programming language, that assertion should be modified. C++ is a general-purpose language for describing and efficiently implementing programs that model software implementation constructs (for example, control structures, data structures, and algorithms), virtual machines, or hardware elements.

The focus on the machine is C++'s greatest strength and its greatest weakness. Stroustrup explicitly rejected the philosophy and values behind SIMULA and merely borrowed some of its implementation tricks, thereby creating a language that inhibits the direct expression of application designs in any domain except that of the computer itself. The "simple and logical implementations" observed by Nygaard and advocated by Parnas of noncomputer problem domain designs cannot be expressed in C++ without some degree of compromise with those principles upon which the language is predicated.

Smalltalk

Philosophically, Smalltalk's objects have much in common with the monads of Leibniz and the notions of 20th century physics and biology. Its way of making objects is quite Platonic in that some of them act as idealizations of concepts—Ideas—from which manifestations can be created. That the Ideas are themselves manifestations (of the Idea-Idea) and that the Idea-Idea is a-kind-of Manifestation-Idea—which is a kind-of-itself, so that the system is completely self-describing—would have been appreciated by Plato as an extremely practical joke.

Alan Kay describes Smalltalk as a "crystallization of style" language, one that is an expression of "the insight that everything we can describe can be represented by a single kind of behavioral building block"—in essence, an object. From the outset, Kay is characterizing Smalltalk as deriving from the same goals that motivated SIMULA—a desire to have a simple and expressive language for describing and representing (simulating) naturally occurring complex systems.

Object-oriented design is a successful attempt to qualitatively improve the efficiency of modeling the ever more complex dynamic systems and user relationships made possible by the silicon explosion.

Note the absence of any reference to computer or program efficiency or organization. When Kay first encountered SIMULA and its objects and object manipulation constructs, he experienced a kind of epiphany, as ideas from mathematics, philosophy, and biology came together.

Bob Barton had said... "The basic principle of recursive design is to make the parts have the same power as the whole." For the first time I thought of the whole as the entire computer and wondered why anyone would want to divide it up into weaker things called data structures and procedures. Why not divide it up into little computers. ... I recalled the monads of Leibniz, the "dividing nature at its joints" discourse of Plato, and other attempts to parse complexity. ... It is not too much of an exaggeration to say that most of my ideas from then on took their roots from SIMULA—but not as an attempt to improve it. It was the promise of an entirely new way to structure computations that struck my fancy.

Another major stream of influences that shaped the development of Small-talk was education and cognitive theories—ideas about how people (often children) think or can be encouraged to develop thinking skills. The computer, for Kay, promised a potential vehicle for supporting and promoting thinking, the foundation for an alternative advocated by Marvin Minsky.

*It was clear that education and learning had to be rethought
in the light of 20th century cognitive psychology and how good
thinkers really think. Computing enters as a new representation
system with new and useful metaphors for dealing with
complexity, especially of systems.*

Although Kay's account of the origins of Smalltalk addresses issues of machine efficiency (almost always in the context of making performance conform to human user expectations for dialog) and compactness (an overriding goal was to create a Dynabook or at least a notebook computer), the goals of machine efficiency and compactness are overwhelmed by other goals. Expressiveness in describing complex systems, support for education and dialogic interaction between children and machines, and even a search for beauty in programming languages are important examples.

*One part of the perceived beauty of mathematics has to do
with a wondrous synergy between parsimony, generality,
enlightenment, and finesse. ... When we turn to the various
languages for specifying computations, we find many to be
general and few to be parsimonious. For example, we can
define universal machine languages in just a few instructions
that can specify anything that can be computed. But most of
those we would not call beautiful, in part because the amount
and kind of code that has to be written to do anything
interesting is so contrived and turgid. ...*

*A fertilized egg that can transform itself into the myriad of
specializations needed to make sure a complex organism
has parsimony, generality, enlightenment, and finesse—in
short, beauty. ... Nature is wonderful at both elegance and
practicality—the cell membrane is partly there to allow
evolutionary kludges to do their necessary work and still be
able to act as components by presenting a uniform interface
to the world.*

Alan Kay clearly was not interested so much in what went on inside the machine as in how the existence of the machine redefined the act of communication between person and machine. He saw the personal computer as a potentially liberating and creative device, but its potential impact was inhibited by the mode of communication. He saw that a better *language*, not *programming* language, was required.

We should derive two lessons and one assertion from this brief historical retrospective:

- **Lesson** The true differences among programming languages are those that reflect philosophical ideals and values. Those values and ideals, in turn, determine the degree to which a language naturally and simply expresses design concepts without resorting to "contrived and turgid" code.

- **Lesson** If you *think* about design using an implementation language—as programmers and especially extreme programmers are wont to do—your *designing* will be enhanced or severely restricted by that language.

- **Assertion** If your development project involves modeling, designing, and solving problems in the domain defined by the boundaries of the computer itself (for example, operating systems, device drivers, network infrastructure), you will best be served by languages such as C++, C#, and Java. If, like the vast majority of software developers, you are interested in modeling, designing, and solving problems in an application space, you will be far better served by languages such as Smalltalk, Lisp, FORTRAN, COBOL, and Visual Basic (with Smalltalk and Visual Basic being generally applicable to a wider variety of application domains).

Of course, choice of language is not the only implementation decision that affects design in a particular way. The decision to employ a relational database is an implementation decision with the same kind of implications as selecting a language. Consider the following example. A customer in the real world might use many different addresses for different reasons. A domain-reflective object model might have the partial diagrammatic representation in Figure 2-1. *Address* is a collection—a recurring field—and therefore, according to the dictates of relational database design, cannot be an attribute of *Customer*. In fact, we have to create two entities with a relationship between them, as shown in Figure 2-2.

Object modeling allows
'attributes' with
multiple values, e.g.,
description or address.

Figure 2-1   Domain-reflective customer model (partial).

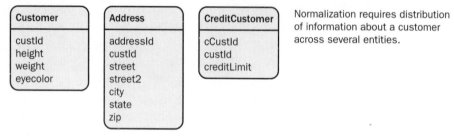

Figure 2-2   Relational customer model (partial).

In a store I might ask a customer, "Where would you like your purchase delivered?" The customer would think a bit and give me back an address. But in the relational example, I cannot ask the customer this question because the customer does not know the answer. Instead, I have to ask the customer for his customer number and then ask the collection of addresses in the Address relation, "Which of you belongs to customer *custNo* and also has the type value *delivery*?" The implementation code gets even more "contrived and turgid" when I attempt to account for the fact that the customer might want to use different delivery addresses at different times or for different situations. Analogous design problems occur when you use strongly typed languages—the real world is pretty fuzzy when it comes to classification—or other constructs that effectively represent the computer but not the application domain.

Programming languages are concrete manifestations of a set of values, ideals, and goals, which in turn reflect a more inclusive worldview or philosophical context. Sometimes the language designer makes explicit philosophic decisions, as did the three language developers just discussed. At other times, the philosophy that shapes the programming language is invisible even to the designer. Designers are humans and participate in a human culture. Most humans are oblivious to their own culture: as the saying goes, "as blind to their own culture as a fish is to the water in which it swims." It would be expected, therefore, that the general culture in which language designers live and work also plays a role in shaping the design of the language. And programming languages are not the only artifact shaped by a prevailing culture. So too are methods, processes, and even models.

Note   The philosophy behind Smalltalk (and object thinking) does not make the problem of selecting a correct address trivial, nor does it solve problems with classification, but it does lead you in the direction of simpler-to-implement and easier-to-modify solutions. For example, we ask a human customer, "Where would you like this shipped?" Object thinking suggests we create a customer object that can respond to essentially the same message: *shipTo*. We assume that the customer has a collection of possible addresses in mind and a rule that they employ to decide which address to use. We probably assume that the rule is context sensitive in some way, evaluating to different addresses at different times. If we simulate all three of these objects—*Customer*, *addressCollection*, and *selectionRule*—and distribute the problem of "which address?" across the three, the solution is far simpler than what would be necessary using a relational schema and an SQL query. The classification problem is finessed, in a way, rather than solved by object thinking and Smalltalk philosophy, which suggests that the real world is fuzzy and any kind of hard-and-fast classification should be avoided unless absolutely necessary. (Protecting programmers from making errors is not an absolute necessity.) And when making classifications, use set criteria that are intrinsic (such as DNA) instead of extrinsic (such as presence of hair, warm blood, and lays eggs).

We now return to an issue raised at the very beginning of this chapter: why is XP perceived as a radical departure from accepted practice, and why does it evoke such strong reactions—both positive and negative—from software development practitioners and theorists? The answer to this question lies in the philosophical context within which software development emerged.

Given that most of computing and software development emerged in the Western world,[2] a common worldview or philosophical context might be assumed.

---

2. This is a historical observation, not an expression of ethnocentrism or an attempt to claim computing for Europe and the United States. As will be seen in the rest of the discussion, this is more of an indictment of the history of computing than a boast. Clearly the roots of computing and many of the most important contributions to our understanding of computing come from many different places and cultures. The argument will be made in the next few pages that most of computing, however, is firmly grounded in a philosophical tradition that arose in Europe and formed the foundation of the Age of Reason.

If this were true, all programming languages, methods, approaches, tools, and processes would share a common, albeit deeply hidden, philosophical foundation.

This is clearly not the case. Every culture contains variations, or subcultures, which exist at various levels of scale. In the next section, we'll explore two competing philosophical themes that have long been present in Western culture.

Formalism and Hermeneutics

For philosophers, the eighteenth century is considered the Age of Enlightenment, or the Age of Reason. Other descriptive labels for the era include the Age of Science and the beginning of the Age of the Machine. The universe was considered a kind of complicated mechanism that operated according to discoverable laws. Once understood, those laws could be manipulated to bend the world to human will. Physicists, chemists, and engineers daily demonstrated the validity of this worldview with consistently more clever and powerful devices.

Forward Thinking
Metaphor and Initial Stories

In this particular case, our system metaphor is easy: it's the vending machine itself since our task is to provide software simulations of the behaviors expected of a Universal Vending Machine. Even more helpful, we have an entire row of vending machines in the hallway just outside our office that we can use as references as we talk about what we are building.

The team sits down with the on-site customer to discuss the project. We have all heard the CEO's excited description of the UVM, so we have a common starting point. The first cards that the customer writes include the following. (The story title precedes the colon; the story narrative follows the colon.)

- Payment: The UVM accepts payment.

- Selection: The UVM allows the customer to make a selection.

- Change: The UVM dispenses change.

- Inventory: The UVM updates its inventory.

- Dispense: The UVM dispenses the selected product.

Rather obvious stories, but a starting point. The team discusses whether it can estimate the stories provided, decides that it cannot, and works with the on-site customer to refactor the story list. This effort yields a modified list:

Chapter 2 Philosophical Context 49

Forward Thinking *(continued)*

1. VerifyCC: The UVM verifies the credit card.
2. VerifyDBT: The UVM verifies the debit card.
3. ChargeCC: The UVM charges the credit card.
4. DeductFunds: The UVM deducts funds from the debit card.
5. Cash: The UVM accepts cash.
6. CurrencyConversion: The UVM converts currencies.
7. WebConnect: The UVM accepts a Web connection.
8. Menu: The UVM informs the customer of what is available to purchase, making sure only in-stock items are presented.
9. Selection: The customer is allowed to make a selection. Do we allow her to change her mind?
10. ValidateSelection: Make sure that the amount of money available is equal to or greater than the cost of the selected item.
11. ChargeIt: Charge the credit card.
12. DeductIt: Deduct funds from the debit card.
13. DispenseItem: Give the customer what she asked for.
14. Change?: Calculate whether change is due.
15. DispenseChange: Return change to customer.
16. NoChange: Ask the customer to enter correct change only, or offer to post the change amount to a credit card or debit card instead of dispensing money.

The next step is to turn the stories into objects. Yes, yes—the next explicit XP step is to write tests, but what tests, and what should be the focus of the tests be? You know that the code you produce will consist of class definitions and methods. You know that the refactoring you will eventually do involves breaking up methods and redistributing methods among your classes. So even though your next activity may be to write tests, your next thinking will involve finding objects.

Because you have internalized object thinking, you can look at the list of stories and foreshadow some likely outcomes. Stories 1 and 2 are likely to involve the same set of objects and might be a single story. The same thing is true of stories 13 and 15—dispensing is dispensing.

(continued)

Forward Thinking *(continued)*

Developers separate into pairs, select a story, and begin development. Everyone is confident that we can begin development with such sparse definition of requirements and in the absence of any kind of formal modeling. Everyone fully expects a final solution to emerge from ongoing discussions, elaborations, and implementations of this initial set of stories. No one feels the need to create syntactically precise models, but it is surprising how much gets jotted down and drawn in the process of discussing and writing code. Interestingly enough, those that have been doing objects longer tend to make fewer notes as they proceed, while those that are relatively new to objects have many more bits of paper on and near their workspace. Object thinking is a mental exercise: all the ideas, definitions, heuristics, and models presented in this book are internalized as developers put them into practice.

Writers such as Descartes, Hobbes, and Leibniz provided the philosophical ground that explained the success of science and extended the mechanical metaphor to include human thought. For these thinkers, the universe comprised a set of basic elements: literally, the periodic table of elements in the case of chemistry, properties such as mass for the physicists, and mental tokens in the case of human thought. These basic elements could be combined and transformed according to some finite set of unambiguous rules: the laws of nature in the case of the physical sciences, or classical logic in the case of human thought.

Note Descartes, Hobbes, and Leibniz are likely to be familiar to most readers as rationalist philosophers. Perhaps less well known is the fact that all three were convinced that human thought could be simulated by a machine, a foundation idea behind classical artificial intelligence (AI) research in the 1970s. All three built or attempted to build mechanical thinking/calculating devices. Leibniz was so entranced with binary arithmetic (he invented aspects of binary logic) that it influenced his theology—"The void is zero and God is one and from the One all things are derived"—and prompted an intense interest in the Chinese *I Ching* (Book of Changes), which has a binary foundation.

This tradition of thought, this worldview or paradigm, has been labeled *formalism*. Other names with various nuances of meaning include *rationalism*, *determinism*, and *mechanism*. Central to this paradigm are notions of centralized control, hierarchy, predictability, and provability (as in math or logic). If someone could discover the tokens and the manipulation rules that governed the universe, you could specify a syntax that would capture all possible semantics. You could even build a machine capable of human thought by embodying that syntax in its construction.

As science continued to advance, other philosophers and theoreticians refined the formalist tradition. Russell and Whitehead are stellar examples. In the world of computing, Babbage, Turing, and von Neumann ensured that computer science evolved in conformance with formalist worldviews. In some ways, the ultimate example of formalism in computer science is classical artificial intelligence, as seen in the work of Newell, Simon, and Minsky.

Formalist philosophy has shaped Western industrial culture so extensively that even cultural values reflect that philosophy. For example, *scientific* is good, *rational* is good, and being *objective* is good. In both metaphor ("Our team is functioning like a well-oiled machine") and ideals (*scientific* management, computer *science*, software *engineering*), Western culture-at-large ubiquitously expresses the value system derived from formalist philosophy.

Computer science is clearly a formalist endeavor. Its roots are mathematics and electrical engineering. Its foundation concepts include data (the tokens), data structures (combination rules), and algorithms (transformation and manipulation rules). Behind everything else is the foundation of discrete math and predicate calculus. Structured programming, structured analysis and design, information modeling, and relational database theory are all prime examples of formalist thinking. These are the things that we teach in every computer science curriculum.

As a formalist, the computer scientist expects order and logic. The "goodness" of a program is directly proportional to the degree to which it can be formally described and formally manipulated. Proof—as in mathematical or logical proof—of correctness for a piece of software is an ultimate objective. All that is bad in software arises from deviations from formal descriptions that use precisely defined tokens and syntactic rules. Art has no place in a program. In fact, many formalists would take the extreme position: there is no such thing as art; art is nothing more than a formalism that has yet to be discovered and explicated.

Countering the juggernaut of formalism is a minority worldview of equal historical standing, even though it does not share equal awareness or popularity. Variously known as *hermeneutics, constructivism, interpretationalism,* and most recently *postmodernism*, this tradition has consistently challenged almost everything advanced by the formalists. Iterative development practices, including XP, and object thinking are consistent with the hermeneutic worldview.

Unfortunately, most object, XP, and agile practitioners are unaware of this tradition and its potential for providing philosophical support and justification for their approach to software development.

Hermeneutics, strictly speaking, is the study of interpretation, originally the interpretation of texts. The term is used in religious studies in which the meaning of sacred texts, written in archaic languages and linguistic forms, must be interpreted to a contemporary audience. Husserl, Heidegger, Gadamer, Dilthey, and Vygotsky are among the best-known advocates of hermeneutic philosophy.

> **Note**   Hermeneutics (*her-me-NOO-tiks* or *her-me-NYOO-tiks*) is derived from the name of the Greek god Hermes, the messenger or god of communication. It is a difficult name and does not flow easily off the tongue like "formalism." Unfortunately, there is no comfortable alternative term to use. Most of the philosophers most closely associated with this school of thought—excepting Heidegger—are probably unknown to most readers. Unfortunately, there isn't space to fully explicate the ideas of these individuals in this book. It's strongly suggested, however, that your education—and your education as a software developer in particular—will not be complete without a reasonably thorough understanding of their ideas. The bibliography contains a section of references that can help the reader begin exploring hermeneutics.

The ideas of the hermeneutic philosophers are frequently illustrated with examples from linguistics, but hermeneutic principles are not limited to that domain. For example, words (the tokens of thought, according to formalists) do not have clear and unambiguous meaning. The meaning (semantics) of a word is negotiated, determined by those using it at the time of its use. Semantics are ephemeral, emerge from the process of communication, and are partially embodied in the minds of those involved in creating them.

According to the hermeneutic position, the meaning of a document—say a Unified Modeling Language (UML) class diagram—has semantic meaning only to those involved in its creation. However precise and correct the syntax of such a diagram may be, a significant portion of its meaning (its semantics) is not in the diagram but exists only in the minds of the developers that created the diagram. If a team of analysts and designers create a UML diagram and pass it to a team of programmers to implement, the programmers will not be able to discern the "meaning" of the diagram. The programmers will, of necessity, have to interpret the document and find their own meaning (semantics) in its syntax. And of course, it will be the programmer's semantics, not the analyst's/designer's syntax, that actually get implemented.

The hermeneutic conception of the natural world claims a fundamental nondeterminism. Hermeneuticists assert that the world is more usefully thought of as self-organizing, adaptive, and evolutionary with emergent properties. Our understanding of the world, and hence the nature of systems we build to interact with that world, is characterized by multiple perspectives and constantly changing interpretation. Contemporary exemplars of this paradigm are Gell-Mann, Kauffman, Langton, Holland, Prigogine, Wolfram, Maturana, and Varela.

> **Note**   Murray Gell-Mann, Stuart Kauffman, Christopher Langton, and John Holland are closely associated with the Santa Fe Institute and the study of complexity and artificial life. This new discipline challenges many of the formalist assumptions behind classical science, suggesting that significant portions of the real world must be understood by using an alternative paradigm based on self-organization, emergent properties, and nondeterminism. Ilya Prigogine is a Nobel prize–winning physicist (as is Gell-Mann) whose work laid many of the foundations for the study of emergent and chaotic physical systems. Steven Wolfram, developer of Mathematica and an expert in cellular automata, has recently published *A New Kind of Science* (Wolfram Media, Inc., 2002), which suggests that all we know can be best explained in terms of cellular automata and emergent systems. Humberto Maturana and Francisco Varela are proponents of a "new biology" consistent with complex systems theory and are collaborators with Terry Winograd on a hermeneutic theory of design strongly influenced by the philosophy of Heidegger.

As exotic and peripheral as these ideas may seem, they have been at the heart of several debates in the field of computer science. One of the best examples is found in the area of artificial intelligence—the formalists, represented by Newell and Simon, arguing with the Dreyfus brothers and others representing hermeneutic positions.

> **Note** Allen Newell (before his death) and Herbert Simon were among the leading advocates of traditional artificial intelligence—the theory that both humans and machines are instances of "physical symbol systems." According to them, both humans and machines "think" by manipulating tokens in a formal way (Descartes *redux*), and therefore it is perfectly possible for a digital computer to "think" as well as (actually better than) a human being. Hubert L. Dreyfus, working with his brother, Stuart, has been one of the most vocal and visible critics of traditional AI. *What Computers Can't Do* (HarperCollins, 1979) and *What Computers Still Can't Do* (MIT Press, 1992), written by Dreyfus, present arguments based on the work of Husserl and Heidegger against the formalist understanding of cognition.

Another example centers on the claim for emergent properties in neural networks. *Emergence* is a hermeneutic concept inconsistent with the formalist idea of a rule-governed world. Arguments about emergence have been heated. The stronger the claim for emergence by neural network advocates, the greater the opposition from formalists. Current work in cellular automata, genetic algorithms, neural networks, and complexity theory clearly reflect hermeneutic ideas.[3]

> **Note** Marvin Minsky is another leading advocate of traditional AI. Originally, he was vehemently against the idea of emergent properties in systems—a view that has seemed to soften in later years. His book *Society of Mind* (Touchstone Books, 1988) attempted to use object-oriented programming ideas to develop a theory of cognition that could rely on interactions of highly modularized components without the need for emergent phenomena.

The hermeneutic philosopher sees a world that is unpredictable, biological, and emergent rather than mechanical and deterministic. Mathematics and logic do not capture some human-independent truth about the world. Instead, they reflect the particularistic worldview of a specific group of human proponents.

---

3. Do not confuse *formalism* with the use of formal tools, such as mathematics, that are employed in the cited fields of study.

Software development is neither a scientific nor an engineering task. It is an act of *reality construction* that is political and artistic.

As you can see, formalism and hermeneutics contest each other's basic premises and assumptions about the nature of the universe and the place of humanity within that universe. Challenges to basic assumptions are frequently challenges to core values as well. And often, fundamental assumptions and core values are seldom examined. Like articles of faith, they are blindly defended.

As noted previously, Western culture in general is largely formalist (using the labels *rationalist* and *scientific* rather than *formalist*) in its orientation. Anything challenging this position is viewed with suspicion and antagonism. It is for this reason that the conflict between hermeneutic and formalist worldviews frames the debate about an object paradigm.

Forward Thinking

An Observation

A quick glance around the development room reveals some interesting graphical models drawn on paper or on the whiteboard. We also see people pointing to and modifying these models as they engage in developing tests or writing code. Figure 2-3 and Figure 2-4 are examples of two such artifacts. Figure 2-3 is just a rectangle with some text, but it seems to be a model of an object that one team is working on. Figure 2-4 consists of some labeled boxes, lines, and arrows; judging from the conversation of the development pair, it's a model of object interactions that they are trying to understand as a basis for writing a test.

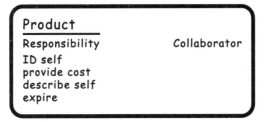

Figure 2-3   A graphical representation of one aspect of an object: its behaviors or responsibilities.

Both of these models are sketches—nothing formal about them. Both are tools to facilitate communication among the developers. Neither tool is likely to be useful to those outside the team. Neither contains any "truth." Both are ways for the developers to explore and share the thinking

(continued)

Forward Thinking   *(continued)*

in their individual heads with each other. Both provide a kind of external memory for those involved in the development activities at hand. Neither is worth keeping around once the task that prompted their creation is completed.

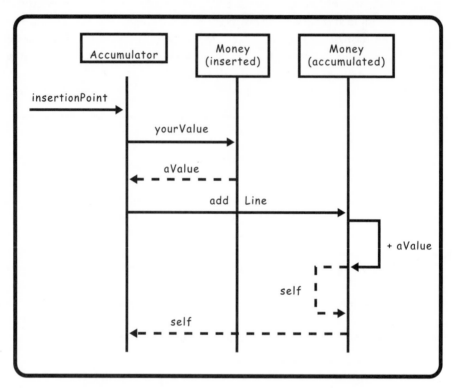

Figure 2-4   A graphical model of objects communicating (interacting) with one another.

These artifacts are quite consistent with hermeneutic philosophy and at odds with formalist philosophy. They are quite useful for extreme programmers.

XP is the most recent example of a series of attempts to apply hermeneutic, human-centric, and aformal ideas to software development. Some antecedents include the "Greek versus Roman" software development cultures identified by Robert L. Glass[4] and the associated debates over the role of creativity in software

---

4. Glass, Robert L. *Software Creativity*. Englewood Cliffs, NJ: Prentice Hall, 1995.

development, the conflicts between "fuzzies" and "neats" in AI, and the classic debates between devotees of Smalltalk and C++.

Behind the Quotes
Robert L. Glass

A prolific writer and chronicler of ideas in software development as well as a leading practitioner, Robert L. Glass appears frequently in publications ranging from *ACM Communications* to his own newsletter, *The Software Practitioner*. His extensive experience in the real world and the world of academe make his insights into the conflict between how it is done and how theorists think it is done invaluable for everyone involved in any kind of software development. One of his main themes is that practice requires a great deal more creativity and experimentalism than computer scientists, software engineers, and academicians are willing to publicly acknowledge. His latest work, *Facts and Fallacies of Software Engineering* (Addison-Wesley, 2003), presents in a concise and highly readable fashion many of the critiques of formalist software development methodology that are presented here as foundation positions for object thinking and extreme programming.

More recently, Michael McCormick notes that

What XP uncovered (again) is an ancient, sociological San Andreas Fault that runs under the software community—programming versus software engineering (a.k.a. the scruffy hackers versus the tweedy computer scientists). XP is only the latest eruption between opposing continents.[5]

XP is the latest assertion of the view that people matter. XP is the latest challenger to the dominant (and hostile) computing and software engineering culture. XP is the latest attempt to assert that developers can do the highest-quality work using purely aformal methods and tools. And XP is the latest victim of the opprobrium of the formalists and the latest approach to be described as suitable only for dealing with small, noncritical problems.

To the extent that objects (our present focus) are seen as an expression of a hermeneutic point of view, they have been characterized as antirationalist, or

---

5. McCormick, Michael. "Programming Extremism." *Communications of the ACM* 44(6), June 2001, 109–110.

at best nonrationalist, challenges to the prevailing philosophy. It is my assertion that objects are, or are perceived to be, a reflection of hermeneutic philosophy. A way to test this assertion is to compare objects with other ideas about software development that are clearly hermeneutic—for example, postmodernism.

Postmodern Critiques

There is a controversy smoldering in the computer science world at the intersection of two important topics: formal methods and heuristics. The controversy, though it may sound esoteric and theoretic, is actually at the heart of our understanding of the future practice of software engineering.

What is meant by formal methods? Techniques, based on a mathematical foundation, which provide for systematic approaches to problem solution. What is meant by heuristics? Techniques that involve trial-and-error approaches to problem solution.

It should be noted that careful reading will disclose a potential middle ground. Formal methods, perhaps, are appropriate for solving mechanistic and well-understood problems or parts of problems; heuristics are necessary for more complicated and creative ones.

—Robert L. Glass[6]

Robert L. Glass probably would not identify himself as a postmodernist, but he does provide a good transition to a consideration of postmodern philosophy and computer science. The preceding quotes are consistent with the contrast between formalist and hermeneutic philosophy discussed in the preceding section. The third quote additionally suggests the superiority of heuristics over formalism when we need to address large-scale, complicated (and possibly complex) systems that involve human beings.

Glass's arguments in favor of heuristics and creativity in software design mirror the hermeneutic arguments against formalism. Formal approaches simply will not work beyond a certain scale. Formalism works close to the computer, is highly questionable at the level of an application, and fails at the level of complete systems and architectures.

---

6. Glass, Robert L. *Software Creativity*. Englewood Cliffs, NJ: Prentice-Hall PTR. 1995. (p. 42)

The work of Terry Winograd provides a complementary parallel to Glass while making a more direct link to hermeneutic philosophy. Early in his career, Winograd was a strong advocate of classical AI and was a strong formalist. Exposure to the ideas of Humberto Maturana and Francisco Varela, along with the philosophical works of Martin Heidegger, prompted his reconsideration of AI's formalist tenets. Winograd has turned his attention from formal modeling of the world to the issue of designing software to be used in the real world. He characterizes design as a conscious act, human-centric, conversational or dialogic in nature (between artifacts such as software and hardware and human beings who are users of those artifacts), creative, communicational, with social consequences, and done as a social activity.

One of the influences on Winograd's thinking was the work of Humberto Maturana and Francisco Varela regarding the evolution of autopoietic (self-organizing) biological and cognitive systems. The structural-coupling mechanism used by cells to establish cooperative complex structures, and eventually all the familiar forms of flora and fauna, provided one bridge to the social nature of computer systems and their development. Another influence was the work of Martin Heidegger, a hermeneutic philosopher. Writing with Fernando Flores, Winograd explored the work of Heidegger and its implications for computer system design.

One of the most important implications was the denial of "intrinsic truth or meaning" in any artifact—whether it was a computer, a piece of software, or a simple statement in a natural language. This claim is also central to the school of thought that has been labeled *postmodern*. It is also one of the core claims of all the hermeneutic philosophers. Because of this implication, the design of computer systems must, for Winograd and other postmodernists, be refocused on the use of software and hardware as communication devices for a particular group of people at a particular point in time.

While Winograd and Flores concentrated on Heidegger's notion of *breakdown* and issues of communication, Christiane Floyd and her coauthors extended the discussion to include other facets of postmodern philosophy.[7] The role of politics and power relationships in both the imposition of a software artifact on a community of users and the group dynamics of those charged with the creation of the software artifact in the first place are central concerns of Floyd and her colleagues. In a similar vein, Richard Coyne[8] addresses the issue of design in a postmodern age.

The importance of all this work—beginning with Glass's concerns about creativity and including the postmodernists' concerns with computer system

---

7. Floyd, C., H. Zullighoven, R. Budde, and R. Keil-Slawik (eds.). *Software Development and Reality Construction*. Springer-Verlag, 1992. Also Dittrich, Yvonne, Christiane Floyd, and Ralf Klischewski. *Social Thinking, Software Practice*. MIT Press, 2002.

8. Coyne, Richard. *Software Development in a Postmodern Age*.

design—is its clear extension of hermeneutic arguments against formalism. It's also the context in which objects as a software development metaphor were coined. The first expression of "object thinking" by Alan Kay and the researchers at Xerox PARC was concerned, like the postmodernists, far more with people and communication issues than it was with technical computer and formalist issues.

Knowingly or not, the object community was concerned in the 1960s and 1970s with the same issues raised by the hermeneuticists in the nineteenth and twentieth centuries, as well as the issues that would be raised by the postmodernists of the 1990s. To an object advocate, objects are valuable because they facilitate user/computer interaction and communication among members of development teams. Objects enhance the art of software development but not necessarily the engineering.

Adherents to formalist ideas, including many computer scientists and software engineers, dismissed objects as irrelevant. When object technology looked as if it might make serious inroads into real-world development, the formalists attacked in the same manner that they attack other critiques of formalist approaches—for example, the creativity discussed by Robert Glass.

Simultaneous with the attack on basic philosophy, the traditionalists began to lay claim to the *form* of objects by equating them with the *black box module*. They were also quick to adopt less threatening innovations such as abstract data types as logical extensions of traditional software engineering theory. As a consequence, the object technology that became widely adopted was the formalist recasting of object ideas rather than the "pure" object paradigm itself.

A similar phenomenon is evident in the *patterns movement*, wherein many of the core philosophical ideas of Christopher Alexander, the original inspiration for the attention paid to patterns, are being dismissed or co-opted by traditional software developers who like the form of patterns but are uncomfortable with the more esoteric ideas.

Rejecting Mysticism

Although *A Pattern Language: Towns, Buildings, Construction* (Oxford University Press, 1977), by Christopher Alexander, was published before his *The Timeless Way of Building* (Oxford University Press, 1979), the latter provides the philosophical foundation for the former. *A Pattern Language* is cited by everyone in the patterns movement as an inspiration for their own efforts, but *The Timeless Way* is seldom mentioned. Of

Rejecting Mysticism *(continued)*

course, it is in the latter book that Alexander's mysticism is most evident. Consider the following:

A building or town will only be alive to the extent that it is governed by the Timeless Way. *To seek the* Timeless Way *we must first know the* Quality Without A Name. *To reach the* Quality Without A Name *we must then build a living pattern language as a* Gate. *Once we have built the* Gate, *we can pass through it to the practice of the* Timeless Way. *And yet the* Timeless Way *is not complete, and will not fully generate the* Quality Without A Name, *until we leave the* Gate *behind.*

The emphasized statements are actually chapter headers from *The Timeless Way of Building.* They read far more like the Taoist (and later Zen) story of the Boy and the Bull, which is an allegory of the process of obtaining enlightenment.

It's not surprising that computer scientists and software engineers, embedded in a formalist culture, find little of value in this aspect of Alexander's work. You have to wonder, however, how deeply they understand Alexander's ideas about patterns if they dismiss what are clearly, for Alexander, fundamental philosophical presuppositions. Is it not possible, even likely, that they are reading into Alexander's pattern ideas their own philosophical biases? And if so, how valuable was Alexander's contribution after all?

This example exposes a bias of the author. You cannot claim to understand something—in this case, object thinking and extreme programming—unless you are able to understand the form, the substance, and the presuppositions that support the form and the substance.

Deciding to be an object thinker or an extreme programmer is a decision to set oneself in opposition, in very important ways, to mainstream software development thought and practice to become a revolutionary.

Revolutions, especially in the arena of software development, seldom succeed. They are resisted, and attempts are made to marginalize the proponents of new ideas. Opponents from the mainstream have already suggested that object thinking, as presented in this book, and XP are "good," but only in a small niche, for small teams, and for noncritical software. What the critics fail to realize, however, is that object thinking and agile thinking are not a means for solving software problems; they are a means for creating better people and better teams of people. Object thinking and XP will produce a culture (see note), not a technique; they will give rise to better people capable of attacking any kind of problem and able to develop systems on any level of complication and scale.

Note A culture already exists that is friendly to object thinking and extreme programming. As Ken Auer points out, there were hundreds of people employed by Smalltalk vendors and thousands of projects written in Smalltalk (many still flourishing). Add in all the people in consulting organizations and all the members of all the project teams, and you have a sizable number of people. Include the growing number of XP/agile experts. Even if most of them have failed to grasp the fullness of object philosophy and culture, the society, with a culture of shared values and worldviews, clearly exists and is not limited to a handful of researchers in Palo Alto, consultants in the woods of Oregon, and a few strange academicians in odd corners of the globe.

3

From Philosophy to Culture

Philosophy provides roots, determines some values, and affects the design of some tools, but the fullness of the object thinking difference must be understood in terms of a broader context—as a culture. The cultural perspective suggests the need to look for the shared, socially learned knowledge (norms, values, worldviews) and patterns of behavior (individual actions and organizational relationships) that characterize a group of people. The philosophical positions discussed in the preceding chapter are part of the cultural knowledge shared by object thinkers as members of an object culture.

Robert Glass used the metaphor of culture to explain differences in how different groups of people conceive of and develop software and how the results of their work are evaluated. His contrast of Roman and Greek cultures directly parallels the contrast made in the preceding chapter between formalist and hermeneutic philosophies. The Greek culture described by Glass is a close match to the XP culture[1] and the object culture we will explore in this chapter.

---

1. West, David. "Enculturating Extreme Programmers," Proceedings XP Universe. Chapel Hill, N.C., 2001.

Greek and Roman

Robert Glass makes the argument for two cultures within the realm of software development, two cultures that frequently find themselves in conflict based on cultural values. He uses an analogy with Greek and Roman culture to illustrate the differences as follows:

In ancient Greece, an individual would act as his own agent in his own behalf, or combine with other people to act together as a team. In a Greek work environment, you bring your tools to work with you, you do your stuff, and then you pack up your tools and take them home. You are an individual—an independent contractor. You are not owned body and mind. You are merely providing a service for compensation.

In Rome, one's first duty was to the group, clan, class, or faction upon which one depended for status. Known as gravitas, this meant sacrificing oneself for the good of the organization, and giving up one's individuality and identifying closely with the group. In a Roman environment you go to work, the company hands you your tools, and then it holds you and your mind hostage until you sever your relationship with the organization. You are not an individual: you are owned by the organization body and mind, twenty-four hours a day. There are substantial rewards for this, however. The organization provides you with security, money, and power.

Glass is particularly interested in the degree to which the two cultures support creativity and asserts that the Roman culture is likely to take the creativity, passion, and magic out of the work of software development. He further notes that Roman culture will emphasize up-front planning, control, formal procedures as a means of control, and maximum documentation and will value logical, analytical thinking above empirical and inductive thinking.

Even a cursory evaluation of XP values and practices reveals their incompatibility with Roman thinking. When objects were first introduced, they too reflected a Greek and not a Roman culture. Smalltalk was motivated by a need to empower people, to make interaction with a computer fun and creative. Exploratory development, a kind of rapid prototyping, was seen as the proper way to develop new software—as opposed to the notion of up-front, detailed design and rote implementation favored by the (Roman) structured development culture.

Our exploration of the object culture begins with a rough enumeration of some groups likely to be included in this culture. The original proponents of object ideas (the original SIMULA team, the Smalltalk team), advocates of behavior-based object methods, and the first XP and agile practitioners are likely candidates, and of course, any who recognize themselves as members of the "Greek" culture described by Glass.

Absent a full ethnography, a cursory look at the object culture reveals some important traits and characteristics. Specifically:

- A commitment to *disciplined informality* rather than defined formality

- Advocacy of a local rather than global focus

- Production of minimum rather than maximum levels of design and process documentation

- Collaborative rather than imperial management style

- Commitment to design based on coordination and cooperation rather than control

- Practitioners of rapid prototyping instead of structured development

- Valuing the creative over the systematic

- Driven by internal capabilities instead of conforming to external procedures

Cultures will usually have an origin myth, various heroes and heroines, and stories about great deeds and important artifacts, as well as a set of core beliefs and values. All of these are evident in the object culture and someday will be captured in a definitive ethnography. It is not my intent to elaborate that culture here, merely to draw the reader's attention to the fact that such a culture exists.

Being aware of object culture is valuable for object thinkers in four ways. First, it provides insight into the dynamics of interaction (or lack of it) between objectivists and traditionalists. Often the only way to understand the mutual miscommunications and the emotional antipathy of the two groups comes from understanding the underlying cultural conflict.

Second, and most important, it reminds the aspiring object thinker that he or she is engaged in a process of enculturation, a much more involved endeavor than learning a few new ideas and adopting a couple of alternative practices. Most of the material in the remainder of this book cannot be fully understood without relating it to object culture in all its aspects.

Third, it suggests a way to know you have mastered object thinking. When all of your actions, in familiar and in novel circumstances, reflect "the right thing" without the intervention of conscious thought, you are an object thinker.

Fourth, it reminds the object thinker that culture is not an individual thing; it is rooted in community. To change a culture, you must change individuals and the way that individuals interact and make commitments to one another. Culture is shared.

Subsequent chapters will deal with object thinking specifics, all of which are intimately related to a set of *first principles*, or presuppositions reflective of the object culture as a whole. The four principles introduced here are frequently stated, stated in a manner that implies that the value of the principle is obvious. Just as a member of any culture makes assertions that are indeed obvious—to any other member of that culture.

Four Presuppositions

To those already part of the object culture, the following statements are obvious ("they go without saying") and obviously necessary as prerequisites to object thinking:

- Everything is an object.

- Simulation of a problem domain drives object discovery and definition.

- Objects must be composable.

- Distributed cooperation and communication must replace hierarchical centralized control as an organizational paradigm.

For those just joining the object culture, each of these key points will need to be developed and explained. For those opposed to the object culture, these same presuppositions will be major points of contention.

One: Everything is an object.

This assertion has two important aspects. One is essentially a claim to the effect that the object concept has a kind of primal status—a single criterion against which everything else is measured. Another way of looking at this claim would be to think of an object as the equivalent of the quanta from which the universe is constructed. The implication of this aspect of everything-is-an-object suggests that any decomposition, however complicated the domain, will result in the identification of a relatively few kinds of objects and only objects.

There will be nothing "left over" that is not an object. For example:

- *Relationships*, which are traditionally conceived as an association among objects that is modeled and implemented in a different way than an object—would themselves become just another kind of object, with their own responsibilities and capabilities.

■   *Data* traditionally is seen as a kind of "passive something" fundamentally different from "active and animated things" such as procedures. Something as simple as the character D is an object—not an element of data—that exhibits behavior just as does any other object. Whatever manipulations and transformations are required of an object, even a character, are realized by that object itself instead of some other kind of thing (a procedure) acting upon that object. The commonsense notion of data is preserved because some objects have as their primary, but not exclusive, responsibility the representation to human observers of some bit of information.

■   *Procedures* as a separate kind of thing are also subsumed as ordinary objects. We can think of two kinds of procedure: a script that allows a group of objects to interact in a prescribed fashion and the "vital force" that actually animates the object and enables it to exhibit its behaviors. A script is nothing more than an organized collection of messages, and both the collection and the message are nothing more than ordinary objects. The vital force is nothing more than a flow of electrons through a set of circuits—something that is arguably apart from the conceptual understanding of an object, just as the soul is deemed to be different from but essential to the animation of a human being.

Equating, even metaphorically, a procedure to a soul will strike most readers as a bit absurd, but there is a good reason for the dramatic overstatement. It sometimes takes a shock or an absurdity to provide a mental pause of sufficient length that a new idea can penetrate old thinking habits. This is especially true when it comes to thinking about programming, wherein the metaphysical reality of two distinct things—data and procedures—is so ingrained it is difficult to transcend. So difficult, in fact, that most of those attempting object development fail to recognize the degree to which they continue to apply old thinking in new contexts.

Take object programming, for example—using Smalltalk as an example merely because it claims to be a pure object language. Tutorials from Digitalk's Smalltalk manuals illustrate how programmers perpetuate the notion that some things "do" and others are "done to."

The code in **Listing One—Pascal** is a Pascal program to count unique occurrences of letters in a string entered by a user via a simple dialog box. (Pascal was designed to teach and enforce that algorithms [active procedures] plus [passive] data structures = program mode of thinking.)

Listing Two—Naive Smalltalk shows an equivalent Smalltalk program as it might be written by a novice still steeped in the algorithms plus data structures mode of programming. Both programs contain examples of explicit control and overt looping constructs. The Pascal program also has typed variables—an implicit nod to the need for control over the potential corruption of passive data.

Listing One—Pascal

```
program frequency;
    const
      size 80;
    var
      s: string[size];
      i: integer;
      c: character;
      f: array[1..26] of integer;
      k: integer;
    begin
      writeln('enter line');
      readln(s);
      for i := 1 to 26 do f[i] := 0;
      for i :=  1 to size do
          begin
          c := asLowerCase(s[i]);
          if isLetter(c) then
              begin
              k := ord(c) - ord('a') + 1;
              f[k] := f[k] + 1
              end
          end;
      for i := 1 to 26 do
          write(f[i], ' ')
    end.
```

There is some evidence of object thinking in Listing Two—mostly conventions or idioms enforced by the syntax of the Smalltalk language—the use of the *Prompter* object, the control loops initiated by integer objects receiving messages, discovery of the size of the string being manipulated by asking the string for its size, and so forth.

Listing Two—Naive Smalltalk

```
| s c f k |
f := Array new: 26.
s := Prompter prompt: 'enter line' default: ' '.
1 to: 26 do: [:i | f at: i put: 0].
1 to: s size do: [
    :I | c := (s at: i) asLowerCase.
    c isLetter ifTrue: [
      k := c asciiValue - $a asciiValue + 1.
      f at: k put: (f at: k) + 1.
                      ].
            ].
 ^ f
```

A programmer better versed in object thinking (and of course, the class library included in the Smalltalk programming environment) starts to utilize the innate abilities of objects, including *data* objects (the string entered by the user and character objects), resulting in a program significantly reduced in size and complexity, as illustrated in **Listing Three—Appropriate Smalltalk**.

Listing Three—Appropriate Smalltalk

```
| s f |
s := Prompter prompt: ' enter line ' default: ' '.
f := Bag new.
s do: [ :c | c isLetter ifTrue: [f add: c asLowerCase]].
^ f.
```

Types, as implied earlier, create a different kind of thing than an object. Types are similar to classes in one sense, but classes are also objects and types are not. This distinction is most evident when variables are created. If variables are typed, they are no longer just a place where an object resides. Typing a variable is a nonobject way to prevent all but a certain kind of object from taking up residence in a named location. Many people have advanced arguments in favor of typing, but none of those arguments directly challenges the everything-is-an-object premise. The arguments in favor of types are orthogonal to the arguments in favor of treating everything as an object. (See note.)

> **Note**   Programs are written by human beings, and human beings make mistakes. One response to this truism is to assume that the quantity of mistakes is both high and essentially constant, which mandates the existence and use of error detection and prevention mechanisms—such as typing. Mechanisms, such as typing, are always constrictive, so much so that every typed language I know of allows ways to escape the confines of strict typing—casting, for example—which reintroduce the potential for the errors that typing was intended to prevent. An alternative response, one consistent with the ideas and ideals of object thinking, is to reduce the programmer's proclivity for making errors by teaching the programmer the precepts of simplicity and testing. Most of the time, data moves about a program with little chance of error arising from the wrong kind of data being in the wrong place at the wrong time. (User input is the obvious major exception.) If your thinking about objects and object communication reveals the potential for a type error, you should create a test for such errors and include an explicit check in your code at that point. ("Element of data occupying variable *X*, what class are you an instance of?") Since everything is an object, your element of data is an object quite capable of telling you its class. You can have all the benefits of typing without the constraints and the complications arising from escape valves such as casting.

The everything-is-an-object principle applies to the world, the problem domain, just as it applies to design and programming. David Taylor[2] and Ivar Jacobson[3] use objects as an appropriate design element for engineering, or reengineering, businesses and organizations. (See the sidebar, "David A. Taylor and Convergent Engineering.")

David A. Taylor and Convergent Engineering

Traditional modeling of businesses and organizations is flawed according to Taylor because of the lack of consistency among the set of models utilized. For example, neither a financial model nor a data model captures the cost of a bit of information, and inconsistency in design philosophy prevents the two models from collectively revealing such costs—they cannot be coordinated.

In his book *Business Engineering with Object Technology* (John Wiley and Sons, 1995), Taylor suggests creating a single object model incorporating everything necessary to produce traditional financial, simulation, process, data, and workflow models as *views* of the unifying object model. His process for accomplishing this goal is *convergent engineering*, and it, in turn, is based on a behavioral, CRC (Class, Responsibility, Collaborator) card, approach to object discovery and specification.

In addition to describing how to conceptualize objects and classes, Taylor describes a process for discovery and specification leading to the creation of the organizational object model. That model identifies all the objects in an organization and how they interact—not just the ones that will eventually be implemented as software. He also provides a framework for business objects that illustrates the power of object thinking in generating simple but powerful objects. His framework defines four classes (*Business Elements*, *Organizations*, *Processes*, and *Resources*), describes the behaviors of each, how those behaviors contribute to the generation of the five standard types of business model, how they can be customized, and how their interoperation can be optimized to reengineer the organization as a whole.

---

2. Taylor, David. *Business Engineering with Object Technology*. John Wiley & Sons, 1995.

3. Jacobson, Ivar. *The Object Advantage: Business Process Reengineering with Object Technology*. ACM Press. Reading, MA: Addison-Wesley. 1994.

The programming example shown earlier illustrates one dimension of treating everything as an object. Applying the everything-is-an-object principle to the world—finding and specifying objects that are not going to be implemented in program code or software—can be illustrated by considering a *Human* object. Objects, as we will discuss in detail later, are defined in terms of their behaviors. A behavior can be thought of as a service to be provided to other objects upon request.

What services do humans provide other objects? For many, this is a surprising question because human beings are not "implemented" by developers and are therefore considered outside the scope of the system. But it is a fair question and should result in a list of responsibilities similar to the following:

- Provides information

- Indicates a decision

- Provides confirmation

- Makes a selection

The utility of having a *Human* object becomes evident in the simplification of interface designs. Acknowledging the existence of *Human* objects allows the user interface to reflect the needs of software objects for services from *Human* objects. This simple change of perspective—arising from application of the everything-is-an-object principle—can simplify the design of other objects typically used in user-interface construction.

Additional implications of the everything-is-an-object premise will be seen throughout the remainder of this book.

Two: Simulation of a problem domain drives object discovery and definition.

Decomposition—breaking a large thing up into smaller, more easily understood things—is necessary before we can solve most of the problems we encounter as software developers. There are different approaches to decomposition. For example, find the data and data structures, find the processing steps, and find the objects. In object thinking, the key to finding the objects is simulation. The advocacy of simulation for object discovery has four primary roots:

- The system description language philosophy behind SIMULA, as discussed in the preceding chapter.

- Alan Kay's ideas about user illusions and objects as reflections of expectations based on an understanding of how objects behave in a domain.

■ David Parnas's arguments in favor of a "design decision hiding" approach to decomposition—partitioning the problem space and not the solution space as did functional decomposition approaches—as discussed in the preceding chapter.

■ Christopher Alexander's[4] ideas about design as the resolution of forces in a problem space and his subsequent work on patterns that underlie the organization of a problem space and provide insights into good design. These will be elaborated later in this book in the discussion of patterns and pattern languages as an aspect of object thinking.

Proper decomposition has been seen as *the* critical factor in design from very early times. This quotation from Plato (which you might recall from Chapter 1) is illustrative.

[First,] perceiving and bringing together under one Idea the scattered particulars, so that one makes clear the thing which he wishes to do... [Second,] the separation of the Idea into classes, by dividing it where the natural joints are, and not trying to break any part, after the manner of a bad carver... I love these processes of division and bringing together, and if I think any other man is able to see things that can naturally be collected into one and divided into many, him I will follow as if he were a god.

Plato suggests three things: decomposition is hard (and anyone really good at it deserves adoration), any decomposition that does not lead to the discovery of things that can be recombined—composed—is counterproductive, and the separation of one thing into two should occur at "natural joints." By implication, if you decompose along natural joints—and only if you do so—you end up with objects that can be recombined into other structures. Also by implication, the natural joints occur in the domain, and "bad carving" results if you attempt to use the wrong "knife"—the wrong decomposition criterion.

If you have the right knife and are skilled in its use—know how to think about objects and about decomposition—you will complete your decomposition tasks in a manner analogous to that of the Taoist butcher:

The Taoist butcher used but a single knife, without the need to sharpen it, during his entire career of many years. When asked how he accomplished this feat, he paused, then answered, "I simply cut where the meat isn't."

---

4. Alexander, Christopher. *Notes on the Synthesis of Form.* Harvard University Press, 1970.

According to this traditional story, even meat has natural disjunctions that can be discerned by the trained eye. Of course, a Taoist butcher is like the Zen master who can slice a moving fly in half with a judicious and elegant flick of a long sword. Attaining great skill at decomposition will require training and good thinking habits. It will also require the correct knife.

Decomposition is accomplished by applying abstraction—the "knife" used to carve our domain into discrete objects. Abstraction requires selecting and focusing on a particular aspect of a complex thing. Variations in that aspect are then used as the criteria for differentiation of one thing from another. Traditional computer scientists and software engineers have used data (attributes) or functions (algorithms) to decompose complex domains into modules that could be combined to create software applications. This parallels Edsger Wybe Dijkstra's notion that "a computer program equals data structures plus algorithms."

Behind the Quotes

Edsger Wybe Dijkstra

Professor Edsger Wybe Dijkstra, a noted pioneer of the science and industry of computing, died in August 2002 at his home in the Netherlands.

Dijkstra was the 1972 recipient of the ACM Turing Award. (Some consider this award the Nobel Prize for computing.) He was a member of the Netherlands Royal Academy of Arts and Sciences and a Distinguished Fellow of the British Computer Society. He received the 1989 ACM SIGCSE Award for Outstanding Contributions to Computer Science Education. The C&C Foundation of Japan recognized Dijkstra "for his pioneering contributions to the establishment of the scientific basis for computer software through creative research in basic software theory, algorithm theory, structured programming, and semaphores." He is credited with the idea of building operating systems as explicitly synchronized sequential processes and for devising an amazingly efficient shortest-path algorithm. He designed and coded the first Algol 60 compiler.

Dijkstra is one of the best examples of the formalist position in computer science. He believed and argued in favor of the position that mathematical logic must be the basis for sensible computer program construction. He added the term *structured programming* to the language of our profession and led the fight against unconstrained "GO TO" statements in program code.

(continued)

Behind the Quotes   *(continued)*

Some other common computer science concepts and vocabulary credited to Dijkstra include separation of concerns (which is important to object thinking), synchronization, deadly embrace, dining philosophers, weakest precondition, and the guarded command. He introduced the concept of semaphores as a means of coordinating multiprocessing. The Oxford English Dictionary credits him for introducing the words *vector* and *stack* into the computing context.

The fact that a computer program consists of data and functions does not mean that the nonsoftware world is so composed. Using either data or function as our abstraction knife is exactly the imposition of artificial criteria on the real world—with the predictable result of "bad carving." The use of neither data nor function as your decomposition abstraction leads to the discovery of natural joints. David Parnas pointed this out in his famous paper "On Decomposition." Parnas, like Plato, suggests that you should decompose a complex thing along naturally occurring lines, what Parnas calls "design decisions."

Both data and function are poor choices for being a decomposition tool. Parnas provided several reasons for rejecting function. Among them are the following:

- Resulting program code would be complicated, far more so than necessary or desirable.

- Complex code is difficult to understand and test.

- Resulting code would be brittle and hard to modify when requirements changed.

- Resulting modules would lack composability—they would not be reusable outside the context in which they were conceived and designed.

Parnas's predictions have consistently been demonstrated as the industry blithely ignored his advice and used functional decomposition as the primary tool in program and system design for 30 years (40 if you recognize that most object development also uses functionality as an implicit decomposition criterion). Using data as the decomposition abstraction leads to a different set of problems. Primary among these is complexity arising from the explosion in total data entities required to model a given domain and the immense costs incurred when the data model requires modification.

Note   Some examples of the kind of explosion referred to in the preceding paragraph are from my own consulting practice. One organization designed a customer support system that identified 15 different customer classes because they were using a data-oriented approach and had to create new classes when one type of customer did not share attributes of the other types. In a much larger example, a company had just completed a corporate data model (costing millions of dollars) when they decided to build a very large object system. They mandated the use of the data model for identifying objects, resulting in a class library of more than 5000 classes. This became the foundation of their system, causing enormous implementation problems. A final, midrange, example was a database application for billing and invoicing wherein management demanded 1:1 replication of the existing system. This was accomplished, but it took more than a year with an offshore development team of 10 or 15 developers. My colleague and I duplicated the capabilities of the system, using object thinking, in a weekend. Management, however, was not impressed.

What criterion should be used instead of data or functions? Behavior! Coad and Yourdon[5] claimed that people have natural modes of thought. Citing the *Encyclopedia Britannica*, they talk about three pervasive human methods of organization that guide their understanding of the phenomenological world: differentiation, classification, and composition. Taking advantage of those "natural" ways of thinking should, according to them, lead to better decomposition.

Behind the Quotes
Ed Yourdon and Peter Coad

Edward Yourdon is almost ubiquitous in the world of software development—publishing, consulting, and lecturing for decades on topics ranging from structure development to various kinds of crises (for example, the demise of the American programmer and Y2K).

(continued)

5. Yourdon, Edward, and Peter Coad. *Object Oriented Analysis*. Yourdon Press. Englewood Cliffs, NJ: Prentice Hall, 1990.

Behind the Quotes   *(continued)*

The foundation for his reputation arose from his popularization of structured approaches to analysis and design. His textbook on structured analysis and design was a standard text through several editions. In 1991, he published two books, a new edition of *Structured Analysis and Design* and a small book, coauthored with Peter Coad, called *Object Oriented Analysis.*

In the object book, Yourdon made a surprising admission: the multiple model approach—data in the form of an entity relation diagram, process flow in the form of a data flow diagram, and implementation in the form of a program structure chart—advocated in his structured development writings (including the one simultaneously published) never, in his entire professional career, worked! In practice, it was impossible to reconcile the conceptual differences incorporated into each type of model.

Objects, he believed, would provide the means for integrating the multiple models of structured development into one. Unfortunately, he chose data as the "knife" to be used for object decomposition. Other ideas advanced in that book proved to be more useful for understanding objects and object thinking—especially the discussion of natural modes of thought.

Peter Coad parted ways with Yourdon after the publication of this book and developed a method and an approach to object modeling and development that was far more behavioral in its orientation. He has several books on object development that are worthy of a place in every object professional's library.

Classification is the process of finding similarities in a number of things and creating a label to represent the group. This provides a communication and thinking shortcut, avoiding the need to constantly enumerate the individual things and simply speak or think of the group. Six different tubular, yellow, and edible things become "bananas," while five globular, red, edible things become "apples." The process of classification can continue as we note that both apples and bananas have a degree of commonality that allows us to lump them into an aggregate called "fruit." In continuing the process of classification, we create a taxonomy that can eventually encompass nearly everything—the Linnaean taxonomy of living things (and its more sophisticated DNA-based successors) being one commonly known example.

Composition is simply the recognition that some complicated things consist of simpler things. Ideally, both the complicated things and the simple things they are composed of have been identified and classified. Grady Booch suggested that all systems have a canonical form. His book *Object Oriented Design* includes a diagram captioned, "Canonical Form of Complex Systems," which captures both classification and composition hierarchies and the relationship that should exist between the two.

Classification requires differentiation, some grounds for deciding that one thing is different from another. The differentiation grounds should reflect natural ways of thought, as do classification and composition. So how *do* we differentiate things in the natural world?

Consider a tabby and a tiger. What differentiates a tiger from a tabby? Why do we have separate names for them? Because one is likely to do us harm if given the chance, and the other provides companionship (albeit somewhat fickle). Each has at least one expected behavior that differentiates it from the other. It is this behavior that causes us to make the distinction.

Some (people who still believe in data, for example) would argue that tabbies and tigers are differentiated because they have different attributes. But this is not really the case. Both have eye color, number of feet, tail length, body markings, and so on. The values of those attributes are quite different—especially length of claw and body weight—but the attribute set remains relatively constant.

Behavior is the key to finding the natural joints in the real world. This means, fortunately, that most of our work has already been done for us. Software developers simply must listen to domain experts. If the domain expert has at hand a name (noun) for something, there is a good chance that that something is a viable, naturally carved, object.

> **Note**   Listening to the domain expert and jotting down nouns captures the essence of finding a natural decomposition. A full and shared domain understanding requires the negotiation of a *domain language*, a term used by Eric Evans in his forthcoming book *Domain-Driven Design: Tackling Complexity in the Heart of Software*.

Using behavior (instead of data or function) as our decomposition criterion mandates the deferral of much of what we know about writing software and almost everything we learned to become experts in traditional (structured) analysis and design. That knowledge will be useful eventually, but at the outset it is at best a distraction from what we need to accomplish. We must relearn how to look at a domain of interest from the perspective of a denizen (user) of that domain. We need to discover what objects she sees, how she perceives them, what she expects of them, and how she expects to interact with them. Only when we are confident that our understanding of the domain and of its decomposition into objects mirrors that of the user and the natural structure of that domain should we begin to worry about how we are going to employ that understanding to create software artifacts. (Our understanding may come one story at a time, à la XP.)

Note   The focus of decomposition is understanding the domain as it is. Developers and domain experts should always be aware that "what is" is not necessarily "what is best." Just because an object exists in the domain in a particular form and has specific expectations associated with it doesn't mean that the object should and must continue to exist in that form. Domains are subject to redesign, as are the objects and the relationships and communications among objects in that domain. As developers and domain experts work together, it's quite possible that they will define new objects and redesign existing objects. This is not only acceptable but highly desirable—as long as the basis for redesign activities remains the domain, not implementation environments.

Three: Objects must be composable.

As Plato noted, putting things together again is just as important as taking them apart. In fact, it is the measure of how well you took them apart. Any child with a screwdriver and a hammer can take things apart. Unless another child can look at the pieces and determine how to put them together again (or even more important, see how to take a piece from one pile and use it to replace a piece missing from another pile), the first child's decomposition was flawed.

Composability incorporates the notions of both reusability and flexibility and therefore implies that a number of requirements must be met:

- The purpose and capabilities of the object are clearly stated (from the perspective of the domain and potential users of the object), and my decision as to whether the object will suit my purposes should be based entirely on that statement.

- Language common to the domain (accounting, inventory, machine control, and so on) will be used to describe the object's capabilities.

- The capabilities of an object do not vary as a function of the context in which it is used. Objects are defined at the level of the domain. This does not eliminate the possible need for objects that are specialized to a given context; it merely restricts redefinition of that same object when it is moved to a different context. Objects that are useful in only one context will necessarily be created but should be labeled appropriately.

■ When taxonomies of objects are created, it is assumed that objects lower in the taxonomy are specialized extensions of those above them. Specialization by extension means that objects lower in the taxonomy can be substituted for those above them in the same line of descent. Specialization by constraint (overrides) might sometimes be required but almost inevitably results in a "bad" object because it is now impossible to tell whether that object is useful without looking beyond what it says it can do to an investigation of how it *does* what it says it can do.[6]

Although relatively simple to state, these requirements are difficult to satisfy. The general principle guiding the creation of composable objects is to discover and generalize the expected behavior of an object before giving any consideration to what lies behind that behavior. This is a concept that has been a truism in computer science almost from its inception. The most pragmatic consequence of this principle is the need to defer detailed design (coding) until we have a sure and complete grasp of the identification and expected behaviors of our objects (the objects relevant to the story we are currently working on) *in the domain where they live.*

Forward Thinking

A Problem of Reuse

In "Forward Thinking: Metaphor and Initial Stories," which appeared in Chapter 2, it was noted that two stories dealt with dispensing (change and product) and might involve the same objects. Further discussion of dispensing revealed three variations of a story involving some kind of dispense action: dispense a measured volume of liquid, dispense a product, and dispense change due the customer.

It would be nice if we had a single class, *Dispenser*, that could be used in all three stories. This would mean that *Dispenser* would have to be a composable object, able to be reused in different contexts without modification of its essential nature.

(continued)

---

6. The exception occurs when a method is declared high in the hierarchy with the explicit intent that *all* subclasses provide their own unique implementation of that method and when the details of *how* are idiosyncratic but irrelevant from the perspective of a user of that object.

Forward Thinking   *(continued)*

Because of the work of the team of developers on three different stories involving dispensing, three versions of the *Dispenser* object have been created. The pairs of developers involved meet to look at each other's code and see whether they can refactor and redesign the *Dispenser* object to make it more composable—more reusable.

In one case (product dispensing), the code for the dispense method looked like the following pseudocode:

```
IF dispenserType = "Gate"
Gate open.
Else
    Set timer = 10.
    Open switch.
End-if
When timer =< 0 close switch.
```

The code in question reveals an awareness of two types of vending evident in the machines in the hall: opening a gate to drop a can of soda and pushing a product out of a coil.

The dispense method for the change dispenser looked like the following:

```
While amountToBePaid >= SmallestDenominationAvailable
AND
    AmountToBePaid > LargestDenominationAvailable
    LargestDenominationDispenser ejectCoin
    AmountToBePaid = (AmountToBePaid - largestDenomination).
```

Yes, I know you would never write code this ugly and that the second example will not really work, but code is not the issue here; refactoring is. After some discussion, the teams decided that the dispenser object was really just a façade for some mechanism that did the actual work of dispensing: a valve that opened for a period of time, a motor that ran for a period of time, or a push bar that kicked an item out of the dispenser storage area. It was also decided that the quantity to be dispensed should be supplied to the dispenser rather than calculated by the dispenser. These decisions simplified the method dramatically. In all cases, the pseudocode would look something like this:

```
For 1 to quantityToBeDispensed
    DispensingMechanism dispense.
End-loop.
```

Forward Thinking   *(continued)*

The only other behaviors of *Dispenser*—to disable itself when empty or when not functioning and to identify itself—were already simple and common in all contexts. *Dispenser* was now defined in such a way as to be truly composable.

Was this accomplished only at the expense of moving some essential complexity to another object? No. Two other objects are probably involved in every dispensing operation: a collection object that contains the actual dispensers and relays dispense requests to the appropriate dispenser within the collection—a trivial behavior already built into well-designed collection objects—and a *dispensingRule* object, which is an instance of (not a subclass of) a *SelfEvaluatingRule* object. (See "Forward Thinking: Communication and Rules," for more discussion of rules in the UVM.)

Four: Distributed cooperation and communication must replace hierarchical centralized control as an organizational paradigm.

Consider one of the more widely used models in traditional software development, the program structure chart (Figure 3-1), popularized by Meillor Page-Jones.[7] At the top of the chart is the puppet master module, attended to by a court of special-purpose input, transform, and output modules. The puppet master incorporates all the knowledge about the task at hand, the capabilities of each subordinate module, and when and how to invoke their limited capabilities. The same thinking characterizes structured source code, wherein a main-line routine (frequently a *Case* statement) consolidates overall control. Each paragraph of a collection of special-purpose subroutine paragraphs is individually invoked and given limited authority to perform before control reverts to the main line.

Unlike puppet modules, objects are autonomous. They are protected from undue interference and must be communicated with, politely, before they will perform their work. It is necessary to find a different means to coordinate the work of objects, one based on intelligent cooperation among them.

It is sometimes difficult to conceive how coordination among autonomous objects can be achieved without a master controller or coordinator. One simple example is the common traffic signal. Traffic signals coordinate the movement of vehicles and people but have no awareness of what those other objects are about or even if any of them actually exist. A traffic signal knows about its own state and about the passage of time and how to alter its state as a function of elapsed time. In this model, the necessary "control" has been factored and

---

7. Page-Jones, Meillor. *The Practical Guide to Structured Systems Design.* Yourdon Press Computing Series. Englewood Cliffs, NJ: Prentice-Hall, Inc.1988.

distributed. The traffic signal controls itself and notifies (by broadcasting as a different color) others of the fact that it has changed state. Other objects, vehicles, notice this event and take whatever action they deem appropriate according to their own needs and self-knowledge.

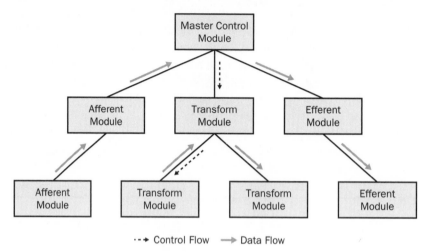

Figure 3-1 Program structure chart.

Note But what about intersections with turn arrows that appear only when needed? Who is in control then? No one. Sensors are waiting to detect the "I am here" event from vehicles. The traffic signal is waiting for the sensor to detect that event and send it a message: "Please add turn arrow state." It adds the state to its collection of states and proceeds as before. The sensor sent the message to the traffic signal only because the traffic signal had previously asked it to—registered to be notified of the "vehicle present" event. Traffic management is a purely emergent phenomenon arising from the independent and autonomous actions of a collectivity of simple objects—no controller needed. If you have a large collection of traffic signals and you want them to act in a coordinated fashion, will you need to introduce controllers? No. You might need to create additional objects capable of obtaining information that individual traffic signals can use to modify themselves (analogous to the sensor used to detect vehicles in a turn lane). You might want to use collection objects so that you can conveniently communicate with a group of signals. You might need to make a signal aware of its neighbors, expanding the individual capabilities of a traffic signal object. You will never need to introduce a "controller."

Eliminating centralized control is one of the hardest lessons to be learned by object developers.

Object Principles—Software Principles

Stating and explaining object presuppositions is important. It is also important to show the relationship between those principles and generally accepted principles of software design criteria. Exploring that relationship will further explain and illustrate the object principles and show how they recast thinking about design without rejecting traditional design goals.

Witt, Baker, and Merritt have written an excellent encapsulation of the fundamental ideas about software design and architecture.[8] Chapter 2 of their book identifies a set of generally accepted axioms and principles that define software quality:

- **Axiom of separation of concerns**   Solve complex problems by solving a series of intermediate, simpler problems.

- **Axiom of comprehension**   Accommodate human cognitive limitations.

- **Axiom of translation**   Correctness is unaffected by movement between equivalent contexts.

- **Axiom of transformation**   Correctness is unaffected by replacement with equivalent components.

- **Principle of modular design**   Elaborates the axiom of separation of concerns.

- **Principle of portable designs**   Elaborates the axiom of translation.

- **Principle of malleable designs**   Provides the means for compositional flexibility.

- **Principle of intellectual control**   Appropriate use of abstractions.

- **Principle of conceptual integrity**   Suggests a limited set of conceptual forms.

Few would argue with these axioms and principles, although they would certainly argue about the appropriate means for realizing them. Object thinkers strive to achieve the goals implied by these axioms and principles as much as

---

8. Witt, Bernard I., F. Terry Baker, and Everett W. Merrit. *Software Architecture and Design: Principles, Models, and Methods.* Van Nostrand Reinhold, 1994.

any other software developer *and* believe that objects provide the conceptual vehicle most likely to succeed.

For example, the separation-of-concerns axiom and the principle of modularity mandate the decomposition of large problems into smaller ones, each of which can be solved by a specialist. An object is a paradigmatic specialist. Large problems (requiring a number of objects, working in concert to resolve the problem) are decomposed into smaller problems that a smaller community of objects can solve, and those into problems that an individual object can deal with. At the same time, each object addresses the principles of intellectual control (individual objects are simple and easy to understand) and the principle of conceptual integrity (there should be a small number of classes). Properly conceived, an object is a natural unit of composition as well. An object should reflect natural, preexisting decomposition ("along natural joints") of a large-scale domain into units already familiar to experts in that domain. Conceived in this fashion, an object clearly satisfies the principle of intellectual control. Objects will also satisfy the principle of conceptual integrity because there will be a limited number of classes of objects from which everything in the domain (the world) will be constructed. In Chapter 4, "Metaphor: Bridge to the Unfamiliar," an argument will be presented suggesting that the total number of objects required to build anything is around 1000.

Objects are designed so that their internal structure and implementation means are hidden—encapsulated—in order to satisfy the axiom of transformation and the principle of portable designs.

The principle of malleable designs has been the hardest one for software to realize: only a small portion of existing software is flexible and adaptable enough to satisfy this principle. In the context of object thinking, malleability is a key motivating factor. Object thinkers value designs that yield flexibility, composability, and accurate reflection of the domain, not machine efficiency; not even reusability, although reusability is little more than cross-context malleability.

In fact, it might be said that for object thinkers, all the other axioms and principles provide the means for achieving malleability and that malleability is the means whereby the highest-quality software, reflective of real needs in the problem domain, can be developed and adapted as rapidly as required by changes in the domain. Agile developers and lean developers[9] value malleability as highly as object thinkers. XP software systems emerge from software that satisfies the demands of a single story, an impossibility unless it is easy to refactor, adapt, and evolve each piece of software (each object); impossible unless each bit of software is malleable.

---

9. Poppendieck, Mary, and Tom Poppendieck. *Lean Software Development: An Agile Toolkit for Software Development Managers*. Addison-Wesley. 2003.

Fred Brooks wrote one of the most famous papers in software development, "No Silver Bullet: Essence and Accidents of Software Engineering."[10] In that paper, he identified a number of things that made software development difficult and separated them into two categories, *accidental* and *essential.*

Accidental difficulties arise from inadequacies in our tools and methods and are solvable by improvements in those areas. Essential difficulties are intrinsic to the nature of software and are not amenable to any easy solution. The title of Brooks's paper refers to the "silver bullet" required to slay a werewolf—making the metaphorical assertion that software is like a werewolf, difficult to deal with. Software, unlike a werewolf, cannot be "killed" (solved) by the equivalent of a silver bullet.

Brooks suggests four essential difficulties:

- **Complexity**   Software is more complex, consisting of more unlike parts connected in myriads of ways, than any other system designed or engineered by human beings.

- **Conformity**   Software must conform to the world rather than the other way around.

- **Changeability**   A corollary of conformity: when the world changes, the software must change as well, and the world changes frequently.

- **Invisibility**   We have no visualization of software, especially executing programs, that we can use as a guide for our thinking.

He also investigates potential silver bullets (high-level languages, time sharing, AI, and so on) and finds all of them wanting. Object-oriented programming is considered a silver bullet and dismissed as addressing accidental problems only.

Although I would agree with Brooks in saying that *object technology*—languages, methods, class hierarchies, and so on—addresses only accidental problems, *object thinking* does address essential difficulties, and it does so with some promise. Objects can conform to the world because their design is predicated on that world. Objects are malleable, resolving the changeability issue. Objects provide a way to deal with the complexity issue and even allow for the emergence of solutions to complex problems not amenable to formal analysis. The metaphors presented in Chapter 4 provide the tools for visualization to guide our thinking.

Object thinking suggests we deal with software complexity in a manner analogous to the ways humans already deal with real-world complexity—using behavior-based classification and modularization. Object thinking is focused on the best means for dealing with conformity and changeability issues—the

---

10. IEEE Computer, April 1987.

malleability principle—as a kind of prime directive. And invisibility is addressed, not with an abstract geometry as suggested by Brooks, but via simulation (working software using an XP perspective)—direct, albeit metaphorical, simulation of the real world. If we can understand the complex interactions of objects in the real world (and we do so every day), we should be able to visualize our software as an analogous interaction of objects.

Forward Thinking

Communication and Rules

Because the UVM might be dispensing food items and because we want the customer experience to be always positive, we want to ensure that no spoiled products are vended. This leads to a story—*Expire: no product is sold after its expiration date has been reached.*

The development team discusses (and codes) various ways this might be accomplished. Through a combination of refactoring efforts and arguments, it is decided that the expiration problem will best be solved by a group of objects communicating with one another, with those communications being triggered by events.

Whenever a product is placed in the vending machine, it asks itself for its expiration date. It then asks the *SystemClockCalendar* to add an *eventRegistration* (consisting of the *productID* and the "die" message) for the event generated whenever a new day is recognized by the *SystemClockCalendar*. (Programmers, even extreme programmers, often have a rather grim sense of humor; hence the "die" message to effect product expiration.) At the same time, the *Dispenser* object asks the new product to accept a registration for the "I'm dead" event that the product will generate when it receives the "die" message from its own event registration that was placed with the *SystemClockCalendar*. The dispenser's *eventRegistration* with the product will cause the message "disableYourself" to be sent to the dispenser, who will, indeed, "disable" itself (with the accompanying event that other objects—such as the menu or the dispenser collection—might register for).

Breaking up a potentially complex decision-making and cascading-effects problem into pieces that can be distributed among many objects while at the same time relying on simple, reusable components such as an *eventRegistration* and a *Dispatcher* greatly reduces the complexity that worries Brooks. It also accommodates the conformity and changeability requirements imposed on software: event registrations can be added or

---

Forward Thinking   *(continued)*

deleted as needed, redirected to other objects, or transformed so that the registering object receives different messages at different times without the need to rewrite and recompile source code.

The development team found another opportunity for simplification as they worked with various types of rules that governed actions in different parts of the UVM. One kind of rule was, "Don't vend a product unless sufficient funds have been accumulated." Another rule was, "Refund money using the largest coins available, moving to lower-denomination coins only when the larger denomination is greater than the sum yet to be refunded."

Using a combination of refactoring and *appropriate* abstraction, the development team defined and designed a rule object. (XP philosophy warns against premature abstraction: abstraction that is not derived from refactoring, meaning not grounded in efforts to achieve simplification. Hence the adjective *appropriate* in the preceding sentence.) A rule is an ordered collection of constants, variables, and operations. A variable consists of an object and a message to be sent to that object. When a variable sends the message to the target, the resultant value replaces the unknown value of the variable. When asked to evaluate to a result, a rule iterates across its elements, asking each variable to instantiate itself to a real value, and then applies the operators to the instantiated variables and constants.

All four of Brooks's concerns about software's essential difficulties are addressed: simplification of complexity, ease of conformity and adaptability, and visualization. A rule is an easy thing to visualize—we see examples of them in everyday life frequently—and the process of instantiation and resolution is very straightforward—we can see it operating in our mind's eye with no difficulty. Reliance on simulation constantly provides other visualizations of the software we are creating.

Cooperating Cultures

Arguing for the existence of an object paradigm or object culture is not and should not be taken as an absolute rejection of traditional computer science and software engineering[11]. It would be foolhardy to suggest that nothing of value has resulted from the last fifty years of theory and practice.

---

11. The ideas in this section were first published in a short editorial by the author in *Communications of the ACM*, 1997.

Claiming that there are clear criteria for determining whether software is object oriented is not the same as saying all software should be object oriented. Expecting a device driver implemented with 100 lines of assembly language to reflect full object thinking is probably pointless. It's possible that Internet search engines must be implemented using "database thinking" rather than object thinking—at least for the immediate present. Different problems do require different solutions. The vast majority of problems that professional developers are paid to deliver, however, almost certainly require object solutions.

Traditional approaches to software—and the formalist philosophy behind them—are quite possibly the best approach if you are working close to the machine—that is, you are working with device drivers or embedded software. Specific modules in business applications are appropriately designed with more formalism than most. One example is the module that calculates the balance of my bank account. A neural network, on the other hand, might be more hermeneutic and objectlike, in part because precision and accuracy are not expected of that kind of system.

Traditional methods, however, do not seem to scale. Nor do they seem appropriate for many of the kinds of systems being developed 50 years after the first computer application programs were delivered. Consider the simple graph in Figure 3-2.

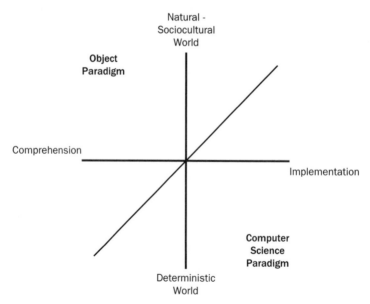

Figure 3-2   Applicability graph.

The horizontal axis represents the spectrum of activities involved in systems modeling and application development. It ranges from analysis (with the accompanying tasks of comprehending the real world, making useful abstractions, and decomposition) to implementation (compiling, testing, and executing).

The vertical axis opposes the deterministic world (the domain of hardware, discrete modules, algorithms, and small-scale formal systems) to the natural world (businesses and organizations, societies, composite systems, and cultures).

A diagonal bisects the graph to demarcate two realms. To the lower right is the realm where mainstream computer science and formalist ideas have demonstrated success. Emphasis in this realm is on defining and building hardware and using a finite set of representations (binary and operation codes) and manipulation rules (the grammar of a compiler) to implement software designs. This is the realm of formalism, where systems can be complicated and even large but not complex—that is, they do not exhibit nondeterministic behavior, they are not self-organizing, and they do not have emergent properties.

At the upper left is an area that is largely terra incognita as far as computer scientists are concerned. This is the realm of social, biological, and other complex (as that term is coming to be understood) systems. Meaning in this realm is not defined; it is negotiated. Rules are not fixed but are contextual and ephemeral. Constant flux replaces long-term consistency. This is the arena in which hermeneutic and object ideas offer an expansion of our ability to model and build systems capable of interacting with the natural systems in which they will have to exist.

This is the realm where objects and the object paradigm should dominate.

Objects provide a foundation for constructing a common vocabulary and a process of negotiated understanding of the complex world. Behavioral objects offer a decomposition technique that will yield adaptable constructs for building highly distributed, "intelligent," and flexible computer artifacts and computer-based systems.

Object thinking provides a foundation for attaining an integration of artificial systems (computer and software) with the natural systems (social and cultural contexts). Object thinking requires an awareness of the domain and the fitness of our artifacts as they operate in that domain in ways that traditional thinking ("Make the artifact meet specification") cannot. Object thinking coupled with the values of XP, especially communication, create a basis for true collaboration among users, managers, and developers.

All of this, once we learn object thinking.

4

Metaphor: Bridge to the Unfamiliar

Along the philosophical fringes of science we may find reasons to question basic conceptual structures and to grope for ways to refashion them. Old idioms are bound to fail us here, and only metaphor can begin to limn the new order.

—Willard Van Orman Quine

Explanations without metaphor would be difficult if not impossible, for in order to describe the unknown, we must resort to concepts that we know and understand, and that is the essence of metaphor.

—Earl MacCormac

Object philosophy generates a different view of the world, one that is strange to most and especially to developers trained in conventional methods and ideas. This raises the question of how best to assist developers to understand the new world of objects. In other disciplines, metaphor is frequently used to help those new to an area of study comprehend its fundamental concepts.

Consider the Bohr model of an atom, as one example. Physicists and chemists need to explain atomic structure to lay people and to new students. One common way to do so is to employ Bohr's metaphoric model that says an atom is like a tiny solar system—a nucleus (sun) surrounded by orbiting electrons (planets). This metaphor is technically inaccurate, of course, but it remains a useful tool for introducing atomic concepts.

Unsurprisingly, metaphors have also been used to convey object concepts. One of the earliest, coined by Brad Cox, is the *software integrated circuit* (IC). This metaphor juxtaposes a desirable trait for software objects with hardware components, that is, the ability to use them as standardized and interchangeable parts to "mass-produce" larger constructs. It's possible, for example, to shop at a number of electronics stores, buy standard components from a variety of manufacturers, and use those components to assemble a working personal computer. Construction of software in a similar manner is one goal of object orientation; hence the applicability of the metaphor.

Behind the Quotes

Brad Cox

Brad Cox was one of the earliest advocates of object-oriented programming and was the developer of the Objective-C programming language, which was the core of the Next Computer operating system and development environment. (Next was the first company started by Steve Jobs when he left Apple Computer.) Objective-C extended the standard C programming language with Smalltalk characteristics—an attempt to realize the expressiveness and simplicity of Smalltalk while retaining the efficiency and power of C.

Dr. Cox coined an early metaphor for object components—*software ICs*—suggesting that software components should be as modular and as composable as the ICs used to build hardware. Given an appropriate set of ICs, software could be mass-produced—cheaply and with quality—just as guns were after Colt and Remington invented standardized parts for guns.

One of Dr. Cox's most intriguing ideas was the concept of *superdistribution*. The core idea of superdistribution was to make individual software modules available via the Web and charge for their use, component by component—a concept that is evident in Microsoft's vision of Web services.

Dr. Cox recently resigned from George Mason University to concentrate on a company that will make superdistribution a reality. He has many other interests, and his Middle Of Nowhere (*http://www.virtualschool.edu/mon*) is well worth a visit.

The software IC metaphor is less helpful, however, when our concern is object discovery and specification because it tells us only of a desirable trait for the finished product. Alan Kay, Adele Goldberg, Ken Rubin, and Philippe Kahn, among many others, employ the metaphor of a person when engaged in the process of discovery and analysis. An object is like a person. This metaphor is sufficiently important to object thinking that it warrants its own special term— anthropomorphization. And of course, the more syllables a word has, the more important it must be. We will return to this metaphor later.

Metaphors are not just a tool to explore the unfamiliar. Metaphor is essential to everyday thinking as well. The full importance of metaphor in shaping our thoughts has received a lot of attention in recent years, notably in the work of George Lakoff.

Behind the Quotes

George Lakoff

Professor Lakoff teaches and researches linguistics, cognitive science, and cognitive philosophy at the University of California, Berkeley. His books most likely to be of interest to readers of this book include *Metaphors We Live By*; *Women, Fire, and Dangerous Things*; and *Philosophy in the Flesh*. Lakoff's work is frequently cited by those criticizing traditional approaches to software development—especially the kind of set-based category theory underlying traditional approaches to data and data modeling—as well as by those advocating a more human-centric approach to computing and the software development process.

Dr. Lakoff's research reveals the central role of metaphor in all human cognition and provides a foundation for Kent Beck's ideas about metaphor in extreme programming—everything from the value of a system metaphor (in lieu of architecture) to the need for metaphorical awareness when creating object and method naming conventions.

Metaphor shapes our thinking in many different ways.

- **It helps in discovery.**   "If our system is like an *X*, this component is probably like a *Y*."

- **It helps us make design decisions.**   "When a person is asked for ID, she usually hands over some sort of document (such as a driver's license), so our Person probably should store identifying information in a similar kind of object instead of as a sequence of instance variables containing single values."

- **It provides handy ways to remember principles of object thinking.** "Objects are naturally lazy, and this is starting to look hard. We had better refactor our design and split this work up among several objects."

- **It helps us avoid old ways of thinking by avoiding the metaphors that are associated with those kinds of thinking.** "Instead of 'next the machine needs to do this,' we use, 'Just ask object X to do that.'"

Metaphor plays a critical role in XP as well as in object thinking. Kent Beck used his keynote address at OOPSLA 2002 to explore all the ways that metaphor affects all aspects of XP. One of the 12 practices in XP is the system metaphor, which is deemed powerful enough to eliminate the need for detailed up-front architectural design to guide development. In Kent's book on test-driven development,[1] he talks about how different metaphors led to several different designs and implementations of multicurrency money.

Forward Thinking

A Vignette

Roger and Suroor are working on the "accumulate money" story, the user story about how the vending machine accepts coins and currency and reports back a total. They have test cases based on random selection from among all the possible denominations of coins and paper money from all three target currencies (euros, yen, and dollars) and are starting to code the *Accumulator* class.

"I guess we will need a method to determine what kind of currency we have and what its value is," suggests Roger, "and one to convert the currencies into some kind of common value—all dollars, or yen, or euros. A method to report the total amount in the accumulator and one to actually add each instance of inserted money to the current accumulation," he continued.

"Don't forget some kind of reset-to-zero method," added Suroor. "Two of these methods are really easy." Suroor is talking while typing code for two methods: *reset –total = 0*; and *total*, which just returns the amount in the instance variable named *total*.

"Determining the kind and value of the currency looks like it might be complicated," says Roger, reaching for the keyboard, "some kind of case statement probably."

---

1. Beck, Kent. *Test Driven Development by Example*. Boston Addison-Wesley, 2003. ISBN 0-321-14653-0.

Forward Thinking   *(continued)*

"No, no," interjected Suroor. "Remember, object code shouldn't need case statements—we need to rethink which object is responsible for identifying currency type and value. When I was pairing yesterday on the credit card story, we created a *Money* class that identified its value and its currency. We should use that."

"You're right; some way or another, every bit of money put in the machine identifies itself with a currency type and a value," Roger agreed, nodding. "After all, that is what happens now—somehow money uses inertia and shape to tell the machine what it is. Maybe someday there will be a chip in coins and currency that does the job easier—but whatever, it is the money's responsibility."

"That makes the *add* method real easy," said Suroor as she typed the new method: *amount in total, add amount inserted.*

"But wait, what about currency conversion?" Suroor was talking out loud to herself.

"Money should do that too," suggested Roger. "All money objects should have methods to convert themselves into other currencies—something like *asEuro* or *asDollar.*"

"The team creating the *Money* object is doing that—using a currency conversion lookup table for the actual exchange rate—a collaborator for the money object."

"How do we know what currency to convert to?"

"Ask the *VendingMachine* object—it will be a global object that can be used to store bits of information that all the other objects in the vending machine application might need to access. It can have a variable named *localCurrency* or *defaultCurrency.* Make a note."

"What does the code look like now?"

"Well, we only have three methods—*reportTotal*, *resetTotal*, and *addToAccumulation.* The first two are just one line of code each. The last one is more complicated, but not much. The method name is *addToTotal*, and it has an argument, *moneyInserted.* The actual method has three levels—see how it is nested:

```
total addToTotal (moneyInserted as (vendingMachine.localCurrency)).
```

"Looks like we kept our object appropriately lazy—making the money object do all the work of identifying itself, conversion, and addition."

"Yeah, but those methods are easy for money to do for itself—we actually simplified the system by doing this."

Metaphors are very powerful. Object thinking is absolutely dependent on selecting and employing the "right" metaphors. Each metaphor—whether general or specific to design details—must be consistent with the philosophy behind objects as discussed in previous chapters. In this chapter, we will introduce several key metaphors.

The Lego Brick Metaphor

Our first metaphor helps us think of important object characteristics, such as composability, simple interfaces, and comprehensibility (limited number of forms). It also illuminates important aspects of the object-oriented software development process, most notably the fact that two distinct but related processes are required.

Let's express the metaphor as a dictum: *software should be assembled from a finite set of composable units the way that dinosaurs and castles and spaceships are constructed from a common set of Lego bricks*. It is no accident that the first special issue of the *Communications of the ACM* devoted to objects had a cover photo of stacked red and yellow Legos.

On its face, this seems to be a restatement of Brad Cox's software IC metaphor. But there are depths and nuances to this metaphor that are missing from the simpler software IC idea. Like Cox's metaphor, this one tells us that we should be able to construct an arbitrary number of software artifacts from a finite set of standard parts. This is a characteristic of many other aspects of nature as well as of mass-produced products. For example, the world around us is constructed from a very finite set of parts—atoms of the periodic table or, below them, quarks—especially given the variety and complexity of the things manifest in the world. Houses are constructed from two-by-fours, nails, 4-by-8-foot sheets of plywood, and so forth. Even societies are built from "butchers, bakers, and candlestick makers."

By focusing on the composable nature of Lego bricks, the metaphor reminds us of how object thinking views the importance of decomposition and composition. (Remember Plato's views, quoted earlier in this book.) The metaphor also reminds us of the importance of composability across contexts, a generalization of the concept of reuse. Removing a Lego brick from a dinosaur and using it to shore up the antenna on your space station is an example of composability (reuse) across contexts.

More important, perhaps, the metaphor reminds us that simple and obvious interfaces are required if our objects are to be as composable and as useful as Lego bricks. (The standard physical dimensions of a Lego brick are but another aspect of its public interface.) Further exploration of the metaphor and its implications suggests ways to discover, design, and build truly reusable and composable objects. This alone would make the metaphor extremely valuable. Given that developers have pursued the dream of reusable code libraries from the very advent of computing—with very limited success—a way to actually accomplish that goal would be invaluable.

> **Note**   Almost all software development has focused on a very limited concept of reuse instead of the composability implicit in the axiom of Witt, et al. and Plato's philosophy of "taking apart and putting together again." Some would claim that the industry track record with reusable libraries, class libraries, components, and widget libraries suggests that reuse across contexts is impossible. At issue, however, is not the possibility of composability but the means of achieving it. Reuse efforts (as opposed to composability efforts, which have been almost nonexistent) have been characterized by a focus on the solution space—computer code, algorithms, and data structures. True composability will require an understanding of the problem space—of the natural world as advocated by object thinking. In Chapter 10, we will explore the issue of composability further in a discussion on the future of objects.

Exploration of the metaphor begins with considering what it implies about the development process: that there is a necessary separation between the process required to create objects (Lego bricks) and the process of assembling those objects into useful products (software, in our case). The metaphor suggests that

- Creators are (probably) adults working for the Lego Company.

- Users are children (at least at heart), ages 4 to adult.

- Creators have specific concerns and use specialized processes to accomplish their goals.

- Users care little about the components, as components. Their concerns focus on what can be built with the components and the ability of the artifact to satisfy their needs.

- The component "engineers" need to be very concerned with the internal structure of the bricks, what kind of plastics will yield the correct degree of malleability, colorfastness, friction to keep them together, spacing of the pips at the top of the brick, and so on. They also have to create components that transcend particular applications because their goal is to build bricks equally useful for dinosaur and spaceship construction. More important, they want bricks that can be used successfully by unknown end users to build whatever it is that they have imagined.

■   Users want to move easily from concept to construction without the need to concern themselves with technical details. They want rapid feedback, they want to be able to change their mind in mid-construction, and they want the artifact constructed to operate in their world as it is.

Applied to software, the metaphor suggests separation of domain decomposition and object definition from the tasks of assembling applications and solving specific operational problems. To some degree, with some implementation languages, this separation has started to occur. Consider the class libraries that come with a language such as Smalltalk or Visual Basic. Many of the classes (the collection and magnitude classes, for instance) in such libraries reflect the same kind of general and abstract thinking that leads to good "software Legos." Another example of this separation is the attempt to create visual programming environments for application assembly that are at least quasi-independent of the underlying implementation language. Such attempts are but a start toward an object-mature world, where the two tasks are as clearly separated as they are in the world of Legos.

> **Note**   I would like to bring to the reader's attention a nuance of this metaphor as something to think about without attempting to fully develop the idea. The metaphor suggests differentiation between users and creators that, in the case of the Lego brick, is very different from the similar distinction made in this book. A Lego user is a child— a kind of ultimate consumer. In the case of objects and software, we are treating other programmers as users.
>
> If we were to be completely consistent with the Lego metaphor, we would have to argue in favor of delivering objects to end users, those filling roles in business and organizational worlds, and not to programmers. The "objects" would have to be directly usable without the need to use programming environments and compilers. Each component would need to be a small executable program, modifiable via user messages, not modules of source code made available to programmers.

Another, critically important, aspect of the metaphor is the ability of users to successfully employ the bricks based solely on their intuitively obvious external characteristics. A child can look at a brick and instantly tell whether it is suitable for inclusion in the project at hand. It is not necessary to know anything about the chemistry of plastics or whether this particular brick was made at "Sun BuildingBlock Corporation" or "Microsoft BuildingBlock Corporation." There is no need to read a complex user manual that explains either the brick or how to use it. There are, however, patterns: diagrams suggesting proven ways that you can construct a family of similar artifacts—houses, for example.

Software objects cannot even approximate this degree of composability, but the metaphor suggests that full realization of object potential requires satisfaction of this characteristic.

The fact that two different groups of people, and two different processes, are involved in brick creation and artifact assembly, one group being adults and the other children, might lead one to believe that the metaphor de-skills the task of application assembly—after all, it can be done by children (or end users, perhaps). This would be a misleading conclusion.

The Legoland store in the Mall of America periodically sponsors two events. (Located in Bloomington, Minnesota, the MOA is the largest shopping mall in the United States.) In the first event, children are invited to use the unlimited set of bricks at hand to construct various things. Prizes are given to the best constructions. The second invites professional architects and designers to use the same bricks to create various structures, which are then sold as part of a charity auction.

As should be expected, there was a large qualitative difference between the constructions of the architects and those of the children. The building bricks remained the same. The architects, however, were able to bring to bear other skills—proportion, geometry, aesthetics, and so on—that the children did not yet possess. The architects were domain experts (end users) who were able to use the bricks to build solutions that fully exploited their domain knowledge. They were able to use the Lego bricks to simulate the way they wielded girders and bricks in the real-world domain where they worked.

Note   Following up the immediately preceding note, perhaps the users of objects would not have to be the ultimate end user but could be a new kind of professional assembler or collage artist, with a set of skills not available to the end user but quite different from those required by traditional programmers and software developers. The demand that objects be run-time modifiable executable programs would not change.

Two other items suggested by the metaphor are related. Objects should be simple, and there should be relatively few of them. There are fewer than 10 basic Lego brick types. (Kits contain additional parts, each of which is highly specialized, such as tiny human figures and motors, but these cannot be considered true Legos.) There are only 134 elements and only six quanta. The vast majority of houses in this country are built with fewer than 10 standard sizes of dimension lumber. In all of those cases as well, the base elements are simple and highly specialized.

How Many Objects?

One of the heuristics for object discovery is "Find the nouns." Each noun in a domain description is a potential object class. Estimating the minimal class set could involve a simple count of nouns employed in a domain.

Expanding on this heuristic, how many classes would be required to model the universe? Well, how many nouns are required?

The Oxford English Dictionary has about 550,000 words. An English teacher once told me that about 40 to 45 percent of the words in a dictionary will be nouns.

If we eliminate proper nouns and synonyms, that percentage will be reduced to around 25 to 30 percent of the words describing potential objects. Eliminating archaic nouns—bodkin and amanuensis, for example— will reduce the percentage still further, to 15 or 20, perhaps. This translates into about 110,000 classes. A pretty large number but clearly finite.

Instead of the OED, however, a better estimate might be obtained using the vocabulary required to read the average daily newspaper. Most things are quite adequately described in a newspaper.

Vocabulary required to read a typical newspaper: about 1400 words!

Using the 30 percent estimate (we don't have archaic terms to eliminate, hopefully) suggests a need for only 420 classes. Allowing liberal ability to add classes representing objects that do not make the paper, we still come up with fewer than a thousand classes to model all typical domains of human interest.

If your problem domain—or worse, your application—has thousands of classes (and I have seen some), you probably have yet to master object thinking.

This suggests that there are a similarly small number of objects from which we can construct any type of software needed to model any domain or organization. (See the sidebar "How Many Objects?")

It's frequently convenient to build a large construct from small, but not the smallest possible, components. It's easier to build living things with hydrocarbon molecules than directly with individual atoms. It's easier to build a roof with a truss made of standard-dimension lumber and gang nails than a board and a nail at a time. Intermediate constructs, such as trusses used to build houses, are components. The number of components will be much larger than the number of objects from which those components are constructed. Moreover, they will likely reflect stylistic differences reflective of the designers and potential users of such components.

The last item suggested by the metaphor deals with process. Watching a child work with the bricks reveals a process of discovery filled with a certain amount of trial and error and supportive of rapid change as prototypes fail to meet satisfaction criteria and so are taken apart and reassembled in another attempt to reach the envisaged goal.

XP development closely resembles playing with Lego bricks in the sense that it too allows discovery and emergent solutions, tolerates and leverages mistakes, encourages taking things apart and reassembling them into more elegant solutions (refactoring), and relies heavily on feedback as to the extent to which the current assembly meets user expectations.

Both XP and the metaphor suggest a need for a development environment that supports this kind of development process model. Smalltalk and visual programming environments, such as Visual Studio, provide examples of development environments and tools that are superior to, in this regard, compile-link-test environments such as C++ (even Visual C++ with incremental compilation). This notion would seem to be borne out in experience. It typically takes about half as long to develop an application with Smalltalk as with C++, given equivalent levels of skill in the developers, even with current incremental compilers. Even advocates of languages such as C++ will tend to concede the speed-of-development issue and focus instead on characteristics-of-product issues such as speed of execution.

The Object-as-Person Metaphor

People are objects, and objects should be conceptualized as if they were people. Projecting human characteristics onto inanimate things is called anthropomorphization. Anthropomorphizing in a philosophy class might earn you a poor grade, but it's essential to a good understanding of objects.

Philippe Kahn starred in *The World of Objects*, a video he produced to illustrate object concepts. He used musicians, a specialized type of human being, to illustrate the anthropomorphization of objects. Mr. Kahn noted that he is capable of playing numerous instruments and splicing the results together to create a finished piece of music. Better results with less work, however, would be obtained by engaging a group of talented musicians—each of whom was a specialist in some instrument or aspect of music. He could then communicate his desires to them, allowing them to respond to those desires using their innate skills, knowledge, and abilities. The musicians would be asked, at a relatively high level, for some service (asking the percussionist for some "color," for example). They in turn would interpret (make sense of) those instructions in terms of their own abilities, experience, and even awareness of the context in which the request was made and then respond in an appropriate manner.

Behind the Quotes

Philippe Kahn

Philippe Kahn is the founder of Borland International, once one of the largest software companies in the world and still a leader in the field of integrated development environments (IDEs), which combine programming language, editing, incremental compiling, debugging, and visual tools to simplify and speed software development.

Borland was an aggressive early adopter of object ideas for its own software development and enjoyed numerous early successes with object technology. Mr. Kahn left Borland, and the world of the PC, to concentrate on network applications as CEO of Starfish Software. His current work still reflects a commitment to object ideas.

The object-as-person metaphor tells us that an object needs to be an agent capable of providing a specified set of services. It has access to a body of knowledge (some of it internalized) that it uses to respond to our service requests as well as any necessary mechanisms (talents and skills) and resources (instruments, a computer, or whatever else it may need). It also tells us that the (only) appropriate way to determine whether an object will suit our needs is by a careful review of its interface (résumé).

Applying this metaphor can feel a bit strange at first. What, for example, are the talents or skills possessed by a book? What services can or does it provide? What knowledge does it require to respond to requests for those services? What resources does it need? These appear to be hard or nonsensical questions to answer. But with some practice, a book is revealed as

- A collection of page objects.
    - ❑   Working with those page objects, it maintains order (sequence).

- An object capable of identifying itself.

- An object that can describe itself.

  - ❏ The description is a separate object that can provide individual elements of the description, such as date published, author or authors, publisher, and so on.

- An object that can provide the reader with access to a specific page or a group of pages (chapters) upon request (also in collaboration with the page or chapter objects).

- An object that acts as a front for a community of objects (pages, tables of contents, indexes, chapters, and the like), allowing users of the community a convenient point of contact. Requests can be sent to the book, knowing that the book will relay those requests to the actual objects capable of responding, without interference.

- At one point in its life (in the days when it was a mere unpublished manuscript), an object that was also able to add pages to and delete pages from its collection and still maintain the proper order.

If objects are similar to persons, they are limited in some of the same ways that human persons are limited. For example, they need to know certain things to complete an assigned task. When the book was young and still being composed (playing the role of manuscript), it might have been asked to add a page to its collection of pages. To do this, it would have needed to know the page to be added.

Like people, software objects are specialists. They are also lazy. A consequence of both these facts is the distribution of work across a group of objects. Take the job of adding a sentence to a page in a book. Granted, it might be quite proper to ask the book, "Please replace the sentence on page 58 with the following." (The book object is kind of a spokesperson for all the objects that make up the book.) It would be quite improper, however, to expect the book itself to do the work assigned. If the book were to do that kind of work, it would have to know everything relevant about each page and page type that it might contain and how making a simple change might alter the appearance and the abilities of the page object. Plus the page might be offended if the book attempted to meddle with its internals.

The task is too hard (lazy object) and not the book's job (specialist object), so it delegates—merely passes to the page object named #58 the requested change. It's the page object's responsibility to carry out the task. And it too might delegate any part of it that is hard—to a string object perhaps.

Following these patterns, we let the book and the page do what each does best and what is appropriate for each. If we need a service that requires a contribution from more than one object, either we assume responsibility for asking the objects for their individual contributions and assembling those results in a way that suits our purpose or we send the request to whichever object is acting as spokesperson for the group and allow it to delegate tasks and assemble responses in order to reply to our request.

The person metaphor guides our decomposition and our assignment of responsibilities to software objects that always reflect the demands of the domain, not their eventual implementation. Our software object should simulate the services provided by our real-world object, both of which we metaphorically regard as people. Even though it's true that we must be more precise in specifying our software object, it's critically important that we continue to use the real world and not the computer (implementation) world as the foundation for our conceptualization of the software object.

Forward Thinking

Hey, Coach!

"Hey, coach," Lori waved to Ron, who was playing the role of coach for the teams today, "could you grab Hector [their on-site customer] and mediate a quick conversation about this 'make selection' story?"

"Sure thing, be right over."

Ron and Hector saunter up to Lori and Sally's work area. "What's up?"

"Sally and I have been working on this 'make selection' story, and we think it might need to be broken up—refactored. Either that or we are misthinking our objects. The story reads, 'Allow the customer to make a selection from the available products, making sure that no expired products are sold and that sufficient funds are available to pay for the product selected.'"

"We visualize this story going like this: 1) a selection object is created when a customer inserts money or a debit/credit card; 2) the selection object then monitors the console buttons for selection input; 3) when buttons are pushed, the selection object puts them together as a kind of key or index value and then asks the dispenser collection whether it has a dispenser matching that key and whether it is operational (its product has not expired and it is not empty); 4) the selection then asks the dispenser for the price of the product and the accumulator for the amount of money available; 5) if we get all yeses, we tell the dispenser to do its thing and give the customer the product. This seems to capture the story, but it will involve a lot of potential error-handling methods—in case the dispenser doesn't exist or there are other problems."

Hector looked a bit puzzled. "That seems to capture the story all right. I don't see any problem, but you are uncomfortable. Can you tell me why?"

Forward Thinking   *(continued)*

"It just seems too complicated. The way we envisage building and testing this, it isn't simple enough."

Ron said, "I think you have the story right, but you might want to consider involving some different objects, and you might want to assume that some of the things you are trying to do in this story are actually done at a different point in time. Check me on this, Hector, to make sure that we don't invalidate your story.

"Your selection object is a good idea, but let's simplify it. It will be what Rebecca Wirfs-Brock and Alan McKean would call a *structurer* stereotype object—that is, it will exist primarily to maintain a structural relationship: in this case, the parts of a selection. Some selections will have only one part, as with the soda machine: a selection is just a numbered button. For the candy machine, the parts are a letter and an integer. Your idea of having it constitute itself in response to a money-inserted event and button-pressed events is a good one.

"But we will introduce another object—a menu object. This will be a collection kind of object, and it will represent, or proxy, the dispenser collection. Visualize it like a two-dimensional table: column 1 is a key, and column 2 is a variable.

"You remember variables? An object that contains an object reference and a message to be sent to that object in order to change from an unknown to a known value?"

"Yes." Everyone agreed that they remembered what a variable object was.

"OK, now—assume that the menu is constantly updated whenever a dispenser is activated or deactivated and that, at the time when a selection is made, all you have to do is ask the menu whether it contains an entry at the *key* value that matches your selection object. If it does not, a message is sent to a *userMessage* object, which prompts the user for a different selection.

"If the selection is included in the menu, we involve another object—a *dispenseRule* object. This is probably a singleton object, and it lives in an instance variable of the *vendingMachine* object. Oh, and by the way, your selection probably lives in another instance variable of the *vendingMachine* while it is alive. The *dispenseRule* has registered with the *currentSelection* variable (that is where your selection will live) to be notified if the object-in-residence (your selection object again) generates a *selectionMade* event. This is what will happen if the menu object confirms that you are a valid selection.

(continued)

Forward Thinking   *(continued)*

"The dispense rule has two variables: one that sends a price message to the product at the front of the dispenser, or maybe to the dispenser itself, and a second one that sends the total message to the accumulator. It also has one operator, and that is less-than (or greater-than, depending on how you actually write your code to relate the two variables), and it evaluates to a Boolean true or false.

"If *dispenseRule* evaluates to true, the product is dispensed. If not, another *userMessage* object is told to engage the customer in a dialog to resolve the situation.

"Most of what I am suggesting is just moving responsibilities around among objects—to simplify things for all concerned. But it does require another user story—if Hector is agreeable—called 'update menu.' That story will be executed whenever a dispenser changes its state."

"No problem," Hector says. "In fact, some kind of story of that type would probably have been written anyway. The boss and I were discussing how we can build machines that contain different products in each dispenser and have LEDs or icons or something appear on the face of the vending machine to cue the customer about what is available inside—your menu, in essence. I'll write up the story, and we can bring it up at the next game-planning session."

"That help you two?" Ron asked Lori and Sally.

"Absolutely. We'll have this done in no time with those simplifications. We'll just stub in the menu behaviors for now until that story and object are ready. Thanks, Ron, thanks, Hector."

We have said that objects have access to all of the resources necessary to do their jobs. In the case of a software object, this means that each object is assumed to have access to all of the resources of an arbitrarily complex computer system if necessary. This is one reason that Alan Kay calls objects "intelligent virtual computers." Because we are conceptualizing each of our objects as possessing its own computer (virtual computer or thread), we have the foundation for concurrent or parallel processing systems. Objects, like the people we metaphorically equate them to, can work independently and concurrently on large-scale tasks, requiring only general coordination. When we ask an object collective to perform a task, it's important that we avoid micromanagement by imposing explicit control structures on those objects. You don't like to work for a boss who doesn't trust you and allow you to do your job, so why should your software objects put up with similar abuse?

Variations on the object-as-person metaphor include the object-as-agent metaphor. The key difference between an agent and an object is autonomy. Autonomy has at least two aspects: independence and freedom of action, which both objects and agents share; and behavioral integrity, which an object has but an agent does not. To understand what is meant by behavioral integrity, consider the source of behaviors assigned to an object and the source of behaviors assigned to an agent. In the case of an object, the behaviors are intrinsic to its nature. In the case of an agent, they are proxies of behaviors belonging to the client of the agent. An agent does the things that the client is supposed to do (would do if it had the time). This means that each agent is an idiosyncratic and highly specific reflection of the needs of a client. An agent is not composable.

An object-thinking approach to agents would lead to refactoring the agent into an intrinsic part (the behaviors that allow one to be a good agent) and a variable part (the services that the agent agrees to perform on behalf of a client), which we can call a *contract* object. Intrinsic behavior would include navigation abilities, knowledge of resources available, and general resourcefulness. A contract is itself composed of different types of objects—goal objects, rule objects, and results objects among them. Interactions between the agent object and its current contract object would also require different script objects. The result is an ensemble of objects working cooperatively instead of a single entity.

In the real world, we think nothing of people fulfilling multiple roles. People are actors, and objects can also be actors. This metaphor leads into an entire category of theatrical extensions, some of which are discussed in the next section. The metaphor means that a single object can appear quite differently in different contexts. Mel Gibson can be Hamlet or The Road Warrior, two distinctly different roles. A collection object can be used to replicate most of the behaviors of a book or a parking lot, depending on the context and the values and objects manipulated as it performs its services.

Many readers will be uncomfortable with the object-as-person metaphor. A major source of discomfort arises from consideration of characteristics that humans have that we obviously cannot replicate (and probably do not want to replicate) in software. Emotions, true intelligence, and will are major examples. The problem is made worse when descriptions of objects and their behaviors seem to allude to precisely this kind of nonreplicable characteristic—for example, "Objects are lazy."

Effective use of metaphor requires constant awareness that a metaphor is not a specification. It is often helpful to replace the metaphor—an object is a person—with a supposition: what if an object were a person? You can then ask questions about your design in this form: if an object were a person, would I write my code this way? Here are two examples:

- If an object were a person, would I directly access part of its memory without its knowledge instead of sending it a message asking for the information I need? If a developer is obsessed with performance, direct access is tempting. But reminding yourself that, as a person, you would not like someone directly probing your brain without your knowledge reminds you that this is a bad design choice. (It leads to undesirable coupling.)

- Technology exists that would allow me to make hardware connections to your brain. I could then build a control box that would allow me to raise your hand whenever I pressed a button. Eventually this same technology might allow me to make you perform a complicated dance. Again, as a person, you might not like this, and neither would an object if it were a person.

The object-as-person metaphor, and the parables you can tell using the metaphor, are simple, easy-to-remember proxies for heuristics and axioms of good design.

Software as Theater; Programmers as Directors

Engineering conveys an image of bridge or building construction. Software engineering is therefore a metaphor for how software should be constructed, that is, in a manner analogous to constructing a physical structure. Formalists love this metaphor, but object advocates find it counterproductive. A better metaphor for assembling objects to collectively perform tasks is *theater*.

Software development is analogous to casting and directing a play. The first task is to select your players, the objects that will collectively complete the expected tasks. Provide the cast with a script (cues and dialog). Test them (practice or rehearsals) to make sure you have the right actors and the right cues and dialog, and then, when you're satisfied, put them onstage and raise the curtain. If you have done your job well, the actors will proceed through the play and the audience will be provided the service of entertainment.

Most software development involves the re-creation of an *old standard*—an original play that was already cast and performed in the real world using human and tangible objects (actors). Software developers face the same challenge as stage directors: how to make a play innovative and fresh without alienating the audience by removing too much of the familiar and expected.

As fanciful as this metaphor may appear, it is deadly serious. And it reveals one of the flaws of traditional software development: too much focus on the artifact at the expense of the system in which the artifact will operate. If software (computer) objects don't simulate real-world entities in a reasonably familiar manner, and if they are unable to interact with the other objects in the real world in which they are to operate, they will fail. Software development is reality construction (or reality reconstruction), just as Christiane Floyd and her colleagues have asserted. And the theater metaphor helps us accomplish our task by reminding us "that all the world is a stage" and that our artifacts are but actors on that stage. (Chapter 7 of the Poppendiecks' book on lean software development explores this idea from a slightly different perspective.)

> **Note** Occasionally developers have a chance to create a brand-new reality. Most of what we get paid for, however, is simply reproducing standard works. Sometimes that involves replacing a single actor, like casting Mel Gibson as Hamlet instead of casting Laurence Olivier. Sometimes it involves an almost complete surface change, like the Star Trek episode that basically restages *Moby Dick* in outer space (Picard as Ahab, the Borg as the white whale). The theater metaphor adds the concept of verisimilitude (the appearance of being real) as a criterion for good software and system design.

Sometimes the script followed by our object actors will be fixed. In software, most batch processes would be considered to have a fixed script. But more and more software needs a mix of fixed and extemporaneous scripts. Extemporaneous scripts are those that are highly interactive and in which the conversation is not predictable in advance.

Visual programming environments provide an illustration of this metaphor. Object (cast) selection is accomplished by dragging iconic representations from a catalog to a workspace. Links between or among objects are established by drawing lines to connect them with one another. Each link defines a circumstance in which one object communicates with another. (Events and messages are two types of communication.) The collection of links established in the workspace is the script for that group of objects.

The play (theatrical production) metaphor can be extended a bit further. Plays come in many sizes, and the complexity of the script varies accordingly. A one-person play is relatively simple to produce (but requires an exceptionally talented actor), while a Cecil B. DeMille epic with a "cast of thousands" is considerably harder to organize. The complexity of object-oriented application software is in the scripting, not in the objects.

Note   Object-oriented programming, specifically Smalltalk, developed in parallel with graphical user interfaces. At Xerox PARC, they were aspects of the same project. Early attempts to explain OO programming tended to focus on applications having a graphical user interface (GUI). Objects dramatically reduced the time and effort required to create GUIs, which led to an inadvertent and unfortunate belief that objects were primarily used for GUI design and development. At the same time, an approach to program design, which the Digitalk Smalltalk manuals called "cocktail napkin design," gained prominence. The idea was to draw your GUI, which would be easy and obvious enough to draw on a cocktail napkin while you were discussing your program in a bar, and then design and build the model (the objects behind the interface). GUI-driven design is at least as bad as datacentric or algorithm-centric design. In each case, the developer is taking one aspect of the implementation environment and using that as the criterion for understanding and modeling objects. The typical result is a program using a lot of dumb widgets that are observed and updated by a monstrously complex behind-the-scenes controller. Object thinking requires you to understand objects in terms of their expected behaviors in a problem domain, never based on one or more of their implementation aspects.

Our tools, as application software developers, for dealing with this complexity are still quite limited. One need only reflect on the rapid accumulation of visual clutter (overlapping lines, obscure icons) in a visual programming workspace to see how limited our ability is to describe large-scale interactive scripts. As with any other complicated task, we will attempt to solve this problem by decomposing our play script into act and scene scripts.

Four additional aspects of this metaphor deserve some discussion before we move on. First, although we classify plays as being of various types depending on their complexity and scope, all theater is essentially the same, a group of actors focused on accomplishing a particular objective, coordinated by a script. With software, we distinguish between objects, components, applications, subsystems, and systems for our convenience. Close examination reveals that in each case we have a number of objects focused on accomplishing a small list of tasks while constrained by a guiding script. This tells us that we need to apply the same principles of object philosophy whether we are constructing the most specific class or a system with wide scope. We do not suddenly revert to old habits just because the job is larger.

Second, replacing actors of similar talent and skill set should not require a rewrite of the script for a play. Substituting objects capable of the same behavior should not require a redesign of the software. We should be able, in fact, to nuance or dramatically change the overall behavior of our software simply by changing players. A drama can be turned into a comedy simply by replacing dramatic actors with comedic actors. The latter receive the same cues and deliver the same basic behavior (say the same lines) but use their innate abilities to interpret the cues and respond in very different ways. This point will become important later, when we discuss application frameworks.

Third, when the curtain rises, exceptional things (not planned for in the script) will occur. It is up to the actors (objects) and their abilities, for the sake of cooperative peer communication, to recover and keep things going forward. Actors cue one another and do not have to rely on the director, nor does the director need the complexity that would allow her to anticipate and control every possible variation in a performance arising from unanticipated events.

Fourth, just as plays are categorized by genre, it's appropriate to extend the theater metaphor to software and classify systems into genres, based on typical forms of organization, or architectures. An architecture is a patterned way of organizing a set of actors, as is a genre. We generate expectations and constraints that will apply to our actors based on the genre of the performance, or the type of architecture. Architectures also provide general solutions or frameworks that make it easier to conceptualize the organization of our cast. Patterns (genres) provide "script templates" to which the designer adds detail in order to construct the actual script used by an object collective to complete its work.

> **Note** Architectural patterns will be discussed in Chapter 9, "Objects on Stage." Pipes and filters, model-view-controller (MVC), blackboards, and client/server are but a few examples of software architectural patterns that will be discussed.

Care must be taken, however, to make sure that assumptions implicit in the architecture (genre) do not contradict or contravene object thinking. It would be difficult, for example, to use the typical hierarchical control script that's embodied in the infamous program structure chart popularized by Yourdon and Page-Jones in an object fashion.

Ants, Not Autocrats

Hierarchical and centralized control is anathema in the object paradigm. It is replaced with a kind of blind coordination, as exemplified in the traffic signal example in Chapter 3, "From Philosophy to Culture." A traffic signal is blind in the sense that it does not need any awareness of other objects or their goals to accomplish its own tasks. Any sense of traffic control has been distributed to the collection of objects in the intersection and not to any single object.

The traffic signal assumes responsibility for monitoring the passage of time and cycling through a change of states at appropriate intervals (green for 20 seconds, yellow for 10 seconds, red for 30 minutes).[2] It also assumes responsibility for notifying others of its current state by broadcasting that state via an externally observable colored light. Automobile (or driver) objects assume responsibility for inhibiting or expressing their own behavior (stop on red, go on green, accelerate on yellow)[3] as a consequence of their awareness of the signal. Neither automobiles nor drivers know anything about the workings of traffic signals, just as signals know nothing about automobiles or drivers.

This kind of blind coordination seems to work well in small-scale examples such as the traffic signal, but does it scale up? The answer, suggested by ants, termites, and biological communities, is yes. "Hive communities" collectively construct extremely elaborate structures and efficiently exploit natural resources (such as food) without the need for architects or overseers. No single ant is in charge of making sure that a group of ants perform. Food foraging begins when a single discoverer ant broadcasts the discovery of food to the other ants by exuding a particular pheromone. Other ants detect the pheromone and respond by moving to the food source and then back to the hive, also exuding the same pheromone. No ant is aware of the identity of any other ant. They do not seem to care whether other ants are around. They simply detect an event (receive a message) and respond according to their intrinsic nature.

The attempt to establish centralized economies and management in the precollapse Soviet Union is a contrasting example of autocratic top-down control. It suggests that although it might be possible to construct very small-scale, control-oriented systems, it does not work on a large scale. The emerging discipline of complexity theory also provides insights into the limitations of control in large systems.

---

2. OK, only subjectively.

3. Observed but highly improper behavior.

> **Note**   If the idea of patterning software architectures on ant or termite colonies makes you uneasy, you might consider the work of Marvin Minsky (a significant contributor to OO programming as well as to AI theory) and the work of Murray Gell-Mann, Stuart Kaufmann, and many others at the Santa Fe Institute. In his *Society of Mind* book, Minsky posits the construction of intelligence by utilizing nonintelligent actor/agents (objects) that make simple decisions based on their own local awareness of themselves and their individual circumstances. These simple agents are aggregated in various ways until they form a "society of mind," which is also the title of the book in which these ideas are formulated. Gell-Mann and Kaufmann are among the founders of the Santa Fe Institute, the center for the study of complex adaptive systems. Complex systems are characterized by simple elements, acting on local knowledge with local rules, giving rise to complicated patterned behavior. And of course, you should consider the fact that XP asserts that large systems can, do, and will emerge from the creation and implementation of small local systems.

> **Note**   In human systems, the presence of strong central control has a debilitating effect. Humans lose their capability of independent action and become dependent on the presence of the controller. If that controller is removed—as it was in the former Soviet Union—it can take a long time for the "controlled" to regain their ability to function autonomously and cooperatively. Software objects designed to function in response to a master controller cannot function in the absence of that controller. This is the antithesis of design based on object thinking.

These two counterexamples provide the basis for the metaphor that objects are coordinated as if they were ants and that no object attempts to assume the role of autocrat controlling the behavior of other objects.

Two Human-Derived Metaphors

Two metaphors, inheritance and responsibility, arise from our observation of human beings. Both are important, and both are subject to some degree of confusion because the terms are used somewhat differently in different contexts.

Inheritance

Humans naturally aggregate similar things into sets (or classes). Another "natural" kind of thinking is to create *taxonomies*—hierarchical relationships among the sets. The most common example of this kind of thinking is Carolus Linnaeus's taxonomy of flora and fauna and the subsets of that taxonomy that are general common knowledge. *Fido* is a dog (example of aggregation and the subsequent identification of a set). The set *Dog* is a subset of *Canine*, which is a subset of *Mammal*, which is a subset of *Animal*. (The example taxonomy isn't complete, nor is it intended to be accurate—merely illustrative.) We could also say that a dog is a kind of canine, which is a kind of mammal, which is a kind of animal. Taxonomies are tree structures.

Another kind of tree structure—one that actually employs the term—is a genealogical chart, a *family tree*. Because both the taxonomy and the genealogy chart use the same structure, a hierarchical tree, they have become a kind of conflated metaphor.

The terms *parent* and *child*, for example, are clearly appropriate for genealogy but are somewhat suspect when applied in the context of a Linnaean hierarchy. Nevertheless, it is common to speak of the superset/subset relationship in terms of parents and children. A superclass is *Parent*, and a subclass is *Child*. From here, it's but a short step to talk about children "inheriting" from parents.

At this point, the metaphor can be helpful or potentially misleading depending on how it is used.

According to the presuppositions of the object paradigm, a child class is a behavioral extension of the parent. A dog has all the behavior of a mammal plus some additional behavior that's specific to dogs. If we say that a dog inherits the behaviors of a mammal and mean by that statement that a dog can be asked to do anything that a mammal can do, we are using the metaphor properly.

Too often, however, the metaphor is used to assert that the child class inherits the internals of the parent class, an allusion to the fact that biological organisms inherit the DNA structures of their parents. This is a poor and potentially misleading use of the metaphor.

Behavior is the abstraction that we use to differentiate among objects, and it should be the only criterion that we use to establish our taxonomy. Using any other criteria will make our taxonomy more complicated at a minimum and erroneous at worst. In the real world, errors such as racism and sexism can be seen as characteristic-based rather than behavior-based taxonomies—with the obvious negative consequences.

In the context of software objects, creating taxonomies based on internal structure (attributes or operations, for example) causes problems in numerous ways. One example is the need to create new classes of objects such as *Customer and CreditCustomer* just because one has different characteristics in some contexts than in others (a credit rating, perhaps). It can also lead to an apparent need for multiple lines of "inheritance" when an object has characteristics that are part of the structure of two or more potential parent objects.

The desire for a child class to inherit internals of its parent classes can be better accommodated if we change the notion of inheritance from DNA to assets. It has been noted that an object has access to whatever resources it needs to fulfill its behavioral expectations. If we say that child classes have access to the resources of their parents via inheritance, that is, by virtue of the parent-child relationship, our use of inheritance remains consistent with the object paradigm.

Responsibility

We know an object by what it does, by what services it can provide. That is to say, we know objects by their behaviors. We are not interested, of course, in just any old behavior. We have specific expectations of our objects and are surprised if they deviate from those expectations. Because we expect objects to exhibit certain specific behaviors, we tend to hold them accountable for those behaviors. (We experience negative reactions such as disappointment and even anger if the objects "let us down.") We expect them to "perform as advertised." Our thinking about the abilities of objects shifts from simple awareness of behavioral possibilities to expectations of service, of responsibilities. The capability is unchanged, but our perception of that capability is different enough to merit the use of *responsibility* as a label.

If an object states that it is capable of providing a given service, it should perform that service in all circumstances, and the results should be consistent. If an integer object says, "I can add myself to any integer you provide and return to you the resulting integer," it would be very irresponsible if sometimes it returned a floating-point number or, worse, if it were an integer that was other than the one representing the summing process.

Responsibility implies that an object must assume control of itself. It must be capable of assuming responsibility for its own maintenance, for notifying others of any interesting and shareable state changes that it might experience and that other objects might need to be aware of, for making sure it's persistent when it needs to be, for protecting its own integrity, and for responding appropriately to requests for service from multiple clients. Just as it's improper for one object to assume a role as controller or manipulator of another, it's improper for an object to fail to assume responsibilities that make the need for external control unnecessary.

The notion of self-responsibility will play an important role in how we decide to allocate behaviors across a collection of objects.

Thinking Like an Object

Metaphors such as those just introduced should shape our thinking about objects and about software constructed from those objects. Internalizing these metaphors and the philosophical presuppositions stated in earlier chapters allows you to start "thinking like an object." Until you are able to do so, and more important, until you can extend your thinking into new areas, you will fail to realize the full potential of objects. In large part, the internalization process will occur over time and with experience. It is possible to adopt certain techniques and use certain models to enforce the practice while you are gaining experience. Later portions of this book will explore and discuss some of those models.

Most of the models discussed will bear a striking surface similarity to models constructed using classical software modeling techniques. Syntactically, the variation between many objects and classical models is minimal. It's the semantic content of the models—derived from how we accomplish our analysis and decomposition of our domain—that will vary.

Because the models are so similar in syntactic structure, it will be very easy to revert to old habits, to use the new models in old ways. A partial defense against this tendency is the adoption of a new vocabulary. In the next chapter, we will examine a vocabulary that reflects both the philosophy introduced earlier and that is consistent with the metaphors presented in this chapter. Whenever the vocabulary definitions seem strange or unduly restrictive, remember the philosophy and the metaphors that inspired them.

5

Vocabulary: Words to Think With

Language shapes our ability to think. Words provide us with representations of particular thoughts and offer a mechanism for communicating thoughts among ourselves. The richness, variability, and subtlety of our thoughts are reflected in the size of our vocabulary. When we discover new things, we invent (or borrow) new words to express our discovery. When we want to make critical distinctions between or among similar notions, we use specialized vocabularies. The use of special vocabularies is common in our professional lives because, as specialists, we need to become familiar with unique ideas and to make important distinctions that as laypersons we might not make.

Object-oriented development has its own specialized vocabulary for all of the aforementioned reasons. The unique vocabulary of objects has another important purpose: to differentiate object concepts from traditional software concepts that *on the surface* appear to be similar. Object vocabulary is deliberately different and is focused on communicating object thinking. To ignore the vocabulary or to trivialize the differences between object and traditional terms is to make a significant error.

Perhaps the most asked question in an introductory object class is some variation of, "What is the difference between a (class, method, message) and a (module, function, procedure call)?"

In one sense, this question can be answered only with, "Nothing, there is no difference." Given this answer, the next question becomes, "Why then do you use these silly new words?" Underlying this question, of course, is the sneaking suspicion that the object advocate is a snake oil salesman trying to confuse the innocent customer with a fancy polysyllabic vocabulary.

Forward Thinking

It's Not a Code "Smell," But ...

"Every time I look at this code, it seems strange—but not strange," Jon comments to Samantha. "It's pretty ordinary for the most part, but I have this constant nagging feeling that something is different—not wrong, just different."

"Not surprising," replies Samantha. "This is probably your first real object-oriented project as well as your first XP project."

"What do you mean? I've been writing Java for several years; doesn't that count as OO?"

"Not necessarily, because what you code is dependent on how you have thought about the problem space and how you have decomposed that space into objects. Just using a particular language doesn't mean you build objects; only object thinking about decomposition assures that you will build objects."

"Huh?"

"Let me show you. Remember the 'Serene Meditation' story we worked on last week?"

"Yeah, our customer has some imagination when he writes story titles. '*Serene Meditation: The machine goes into a power-save mode until a potential customer triggers an induction field around the machine or calls the machine's published phone number. When its meditation is interrupted, the machine lights up, its selection menu is presented, and the money-accepting mechanisms are initiated.*'"

"Yeah, he does, but when we first wrote the code for that story you had two 'controller' objects, *phone* and *inductionField*, that tried to keep track of the other components and send them wake-up messages. When I pointed out the duplicated code, you quickly refactored into a single controller, but then you had to include a case statement to notify different objects depending on the actual source of the wake-up event. Only after we talked about MVC and using event dispatchers and event registration did we hit on the correct solution: let the *machine, selectionMenu, coinAccepter, billAccepter,* and *cardAccepter* objects register with the *inductionField* or *phone* object so that it's notified if it detects the unique event it's looking for. When we wrote the code, it didn't look radically different, but the organization of the code to form the methods was different.

(continued)

Forward Thinking   *(continued)*

"And last week, we were working on the form object and had really different ideas of what its methods should be?"

"Yeah, I had a whole bunch of methods, mostly setters and getters for attributes. You had only three or four methods that you thought necessary. Turns out I was thinking about attributes all wrong."

"Not all wrong, and according to some object theorists not wrong at all. When Coad and Yourdon published their first book on OO analysis, they defined objects and attributes as if they were standard data entities. Schlaer and Mellor, Rumbaugh, and a host of others did essentially the same thing. UML, which you used a lot before coming here, allows greater latitude in the definition of an attribute, but the base definition is still 'a named characteristic with a value.' You were still thinking of attributes as some characteristic of an object, the value of which the system had to remember."

"So you were thinking of a form in terms of a lot of attributes: *form-Number*, *dateCreated*, *lastRevisionDate*, title, and so on. I was defining a form as an object that contained other objects, a collection, and an object that could identify itself, display itself (with help from the objects it contained), and describe itself."

"Yeah, all the attributes I was listing ended up being inside a description object—another kind of collection, kind of like a dictionary."

"So you see, it's not the code that's different—it's the objects and the distribution of methods across the set of objects that's different."

"And the vocabulary is different too. I have to keep reminding myself that things such as functions and methods look essentially the same, but they derive from very different ideas. A method reflects a behavior expected in the domain, and a function reflects a unit of execution in the machine."

"Got it! Now back to this 'reorder product' story."

The object difference is not readily apparent at the level of implementation. As noted earlier, once software is in the machine it's "all ones and zeros." The difference is how we think about the problems and solutions. This difference is most manifest in how we do decomposition and how we decide to distribute responsibilities across a community of objects. A message and a function call might be identical, in syntax and in how they are implemented inside a machine. But who sends the message to whom, how that message is interpreted, and what kind of code will be necessary to respond will be quite different.

Object vocabulary is also different because of the underlying philosophy that motivates thinking in new terms and because we are employing different metaphors for what we are about and what we are building. Different philosophy + new metaphors = object vocabulary.

> **Important**   Object vocabulary is first and foremost a technique to help developers avoid the mistake of thinking about solutions using old mental habits.

Although numerous terms are employed in the discussion of objects, not all of them have the same degree of importance. Relatively few terms both need to be understood as fundamental and embody the majority of object philosophy. Other terms extend or elaborate aspects of essential terms and allow us to say other interesting things about objects or the way software objects might be implemented. Still another set of terms applies almost exclusively to software objects; these terms are a function of the implementation language selected for development. A fourth set consists of auxiliary terms. Table 5-1 lists the vocabulary terms in the four categories: essential, extension, implementation, and auxiliary.

Table 5-1   Categorized Object Vocabulary

Essential Terms	Extension Terms	Implementation Terms	Auxiliary Terms
Object	Collaboration/ collaborator	Method	Domain
Responsibility		Variable	Business requirement
Message	Class	Dynamic binding	Business process reengineering (BPR)
Protocol	Class hierarchy		
	Abstract/concrete		Application
	Inheritance		
	Delegation		
	Polymorphism		
	Encapsulation		
	Component		
	Framework		
	Pattern		

Essential Terms

The following terms have the greatest philosophical importance—they embody most of the philosophy that makes the object difference.

Object

Objects are the fundamental units of understanding. We define the world (and the world of software) in terms of objects. Everything is an object! An object is anything capable of providing a limited set of useful services. Metaphorically, an object is like a human agent or actor. We decompose the complex world around us in terms of objects, and we assemble (compose) objects in various ways so that they can perform useful tasks on our behalf.

Our understanding of an object is, and should be, based on that object's public appearance: its "family name" (class) and an "advertised list of services" (protocol) that it is willing to provide. Every object has a "personal name," which is a unique identifier, and a "family name," which identifies the set (class) of similar objects to which the particular object belongs. Most often we speak of the family (or class) name of the object. That name is descriptive of the object and should convey a general sense of the kind of services it might be able to provide. The set of advertised services usually takes the form of a list of syntactic phrases that we can use to invoke each behavior. Separately documented is a list of potential states that the object might be in. Not all object states are included in this list, only those that the object wants to share and those of which other objects need to be aware. Together these lists constitute our behavioral promise to the world at large. We (speaking as an object) do not share with the world any notion of our internal structure and certainly no sense of how we do what we do.

Every object has access to whatever knowledge is required to perform its advertised services. This does not mean that the object *contains* that information. Information can also be accessed by asking another object, supplied as part of a request, or calculated upon demand.

Traditionally, software was conceived in terms of passive data and active procedures. One of the more famous definitions of a program is "algorithms plus data structures." This is also called the *pigeonhole* approach to software—passive bits of data sitting in boxes (such as those seen in a post office sorting room, which are called pigeonholes) where procedures come to remove a bit of data, transform or use it, and then put it back for the next procedure to access.

Because everything is an object, there is no data. One of the principal ideas of traditional software approaches has disappeared. Everything, including characters and integers, is an object responsible for providing specific services. The elimination of passive data has important consequences for object design, a topic that will be discussed in depth later in this chapter. The consequences manifest themselves at the level of design and are felt minimally at the level of code. This should be reassuring to those (a vast majority) who are using typed languages such as Java. When you actually write code and are compelled to declare types for variables or use objects such as strings and characters and numbers solely for their ability to represent data, you won't be violating any principles of object thinking. You will find that you have fewer objects representing passive data and are much more likely to create an abstract data type to represent a *data* object instead of using constructs built into the language.

Therefore, the three popular graphic models of an object shown in Figure 5-1 are misleading and should not be relied upon. The *donut* model (what Ken Auer calls the soccer ball model because the dividing lines resemble the seams of a soccer ball) perpetuates the classic ideas of passive data and active procedures and better describes a COBOL program than an object. The *animated data entity* model also perpetuates the outdated separation of data and procedures and compounds that error by focusing on the distribution of data items—attributes—across a group of objects. Procedures are appended to the objects containing the distributed attributes. This data-driven approach to object modeling is quite popular but is not consistent with object thinking.

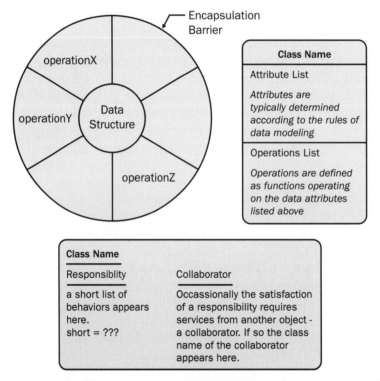

Figure 5-1   Three popular graphical object models: "soccer ball," animated data entity, and CRC card (left to right).

Another, and essential, way that objects differ from the modules at the heart of traditional software decomposition is that an object represents something naturally occurring in the problem domain, while a module represents a logical aggregation of elements appearing in the solution space. This is another reason why the foregoing graphical depictions are misleading and should be avoided. All three diagrams depict what is to be *built* instead of what is to be *modeled*. Object discovery and specification must be domain driven!

Note   What of middleware, networking protocols, persistence mechanisms (databases), and legacy systems? Are these part of the problem space, the domain, or part of the implementation space? The answer, as unhelpful as it might be, is that they can be either. You discover which they are by initially thinking of them as another domain object. Name them, and assign responsibilities to them. As you continue with your development, see whether the objects retain those responsibilities or whether all of the behaviors are reassigned to other objects. If the objects retain responsibilities, they are part of the problem space; if not, they are simply another solution space mechanism. For example, you might have a database object with the responsibilities of enabling object persistence, scheduling access to stored objects, enforcing object integrity constraints, providing backup services, and managing update transactions. It's quite conceivable that all of these responsibilities could be transferred to other objects, leaving the database without a role. (See Chapter 10 for further discussion of objects and persistence.)

Responsibility

Responsibility means a service that an object has agreed (or been assigned) to perform. Objects are charged with performing specific tasks. Each task is a responsibility. The term *responsibility* is used to aid us in discovering who (which object) should be charged with a task without the need to think about the object's structure. (We should not know its structure.) Responsibilities are characterized from the point of view of a potential client of a service. I ask, "Who would I reasonably ask for this service?" and my answer determines which object becomes responsible for satisfying that type of service request.

> **Note**   XP practitioners talk of *test-driven* development and *story-driven* development. Both are instances of domain-driven development because both assume that tests and stories reflect the domain and the input of the on-site customer. There is an aspect to testing that is not directly reflective of the domain since some tests are directed to determining whether "it was done right" as well as "it does what is wanted." The former set of tests determines the congruency of a particular solution with the dictates and constraints of the solution space.

The usual definition of an attribute is a characteristic of an entity, the value of which must be remembered by the system. In a data-driven approach, the attributes of an object are discovered first and then responsibilities are meted out as a function of which object holds which data. A behavioral approach mandates the assignment of responsibilities first. Only when you are satisfied with the distribution of responsibilities among your objects are you ready to make a decision about what they need to know to fulfill those responsibilities and which parts of that knowledge they need to keep as part of their structure—in instance variables or attributes. This is the single biggest difference in definition between data-driven and behavior-driven or responsibility-driven approaches to objects.

Responsibilities are not functions, although there is a superficial resemblance. Perhaps the easiest way to differentiate between a responsibility and a function is to remember that the former reflects expectations in the domain—the problem space—while the latter reflects an implementation detail in the solution space—the computer program. Recall the applicability graph, Figure 3-4, and its division of the world of software into two realms. Use *responsibilities* when discussing anything in the realm defined by the upper left half of the graph and *function* for things far to the left and bottom of the graph.

An object might perform any of four basic types of services. (For a more detailed exploration of types of services an object might perform, see Rebecca Wirfs-Brock and Allan McKean's book *Object Design: Roles, Responsibilities, and Collaborations*.)

Maintain and supply on request one or more units of information.

The information (everything being an object) is an object such as a string or a character or a number, the value of which conveys meaning to an observer or a user. A person object might agree to provide its identification, which means it agrees to provide you with a string, the value of which you would recognize as a unique identifier.

A more complex example would be an object, a product perhaps, that agrees to provide you with its description. In response to your request, this time the object gives you a *description object*. A description object can be thought of as a collection of labels and associated values called a *value holder* (essentially the same thing as a Dictionary in Smalltalk or a Map in Java). (See Figure 5-2.) You then ask the description object for a particular value associated with a specific label.

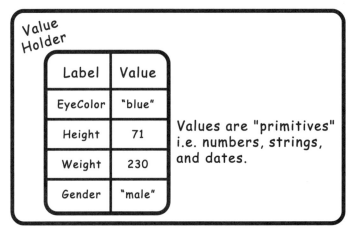

Figure 5-2   A value holder, a simple two-dimensional array with the contents of the first column restricted to labels and the contents of the second restricted to data objects such as strings, numbers, dates, and characters.

Perform a computational task.

This is a straightforward responsibility as long as you remember that computations must be performed by an object on itself. A number object, for example, can add itself to another number,[1] but it would be inappropriate for a calculator object to add two numbers together. A calculator is a kind of control object and should be avoided, both because it violates the object paradigm and because it would have to be a very large and complicated object, another trait to be avoided.

---

1. In this example, the second number does assume a kind of passive role, being subsumed by the active number doing the calculation. But either number could have been the active one, so the principle of objects acting only on themselves is preserved.

> **Note** A calculator object might still exist in your solution—but as a façade for the community of objects doing the calculating rather than the single object doing the math. Façades are quite useful because they provide a single point of reference for other objects seeking services. They can also provide a simple set of services, all or most of which are parsed and passed to objects behind the façade for actual implementation.

This notion can be generalized so that a mathematical expression, which is a specific kind of computation, should be responsible for evaluating or solving itself. An abstraction of this service is a class of objects named *SelfEvaluatingRule*. This class will be discussed in detail in Chapter 10.

Report on or update the state of the object.

Sometimes an object will change its internal nature (its *state*), and on those occasions it might be expected to report that change to others. For example, a seat object might have the state of empty, reserved, or occupied. When it changes from one state to another, potentially many other objects—potential users of the seat—would need to be notified of the change in state. The object should not, however, know anything about potential clients and should only indirectly keep a list of those objects that might want to be notified of state changes.

Every object should have the ability to accept *registrations* for event notification, even if many will never take advantage of that capability. Each registration is, of course, itself an object. Registration objects are accepted by a *Dispatcher* object, as illustrated in Figure 5-3. A registration message (please register me for event X) would be sent by an object interested in one of the states you might find yourself in and of which you have indicated a willingness to notify others. The potential client of an event notification will send your *eventDispatcher* object a registration object (see Figure 5-4) and ask your *eventDispatcher* to add that object to the queue associated with the event of interest. The registration has an internal structure consisting of the name of the object sending the registration and the message that the client object wants sent to it when the event occurs. The *dispatcherObject* stores the registration objects it receives in notification queues associated with each potential event. When the state change occurs (an event is generated), each registration object in the appropriate queue is told to send its message to its recipient.

Event Dispatcher

Event	Registration Queue
Evnt1	[object message] [object message]
Evnt2	
Evnt3	

Registration
Queues can be
FIFO or prioritized

Figure 5-3   A *Dispatcher* object. Events to be dispatched are located in the first column, whereas the second column is a queue of event registration requests.

[object message]

> object is the name or identity of an object which is sent
> the message when the event associated with the queue
> is detected. An optional priority could be added to the
> dyad if the event queue allowed priority dispatch
> instead of first in first out.

Figure 5-4   A registration request consists of a simple dyad—who is to be notified (an object) and the means of notification (a message).

Coordinate other objects.

The key here is to maintain the blind coordination principle. Examples might be a dispatcher that routes messages without any knowledge of why the messages are being sent or a queue that coordinates the sending of a group of messages and hence the activation of the objects receiving those messages but does so only because its nature is to maintain order among a collection of objects and release them from the queue at appropriate times.

The same dispatching objects (*Dispatcher* and *Registration*) are used to effect the blind coordination desired. Individual objects can coordinate with one another by exchanging registrations, and group behavior can be effected by allowing a dispatcher to have "global" visibility—again, like the traffic signal.

The traffic signal example lacks any obvious event registration and dispatching, but they are there nevertheless. "Registration" occurs when the driver of a vehicle or a pedestrian at the crosswalk gazes at the traffic light or walk signal. "Dispatching" occurs when the light from the signal is broadcast to all who can see.

Message

A message is a formal communication sent by one object to another requesting a service. A message can be imperative, informational, or interrogatory in nature.

An *imperative message* directs an object to make some change to itself. No response is expected or required. The object is assumed to have made the appropriate change. (It's quite possible, of course, for an object to offer confirmation of an imperative message by returning some specific kind of object, but care should be taken that this capability not be misused to create controller objects.)

An *informational message* is similar to an imperative in the sense that no response is expected. It differs from an imperative in that there is also no expectation that the receiving object will do anything at all in response to the message.

An *interrogatory* message is any request for a service. The object always returns an object (a typed value or a signal/interrupt in most popular programming languages) that encapsulates (embodies) the result requested. The returned object can be simple (a character or a string) or arbitrarily complex.

Messages frequently take the following form:

```
Receiver Selector (Arguments) ← returnedObject or Receiver.Selector
  (Arguments):ReturnedObject.
```

where

- *Receiver* identifies who is being sent the message. It might be a specific named object (the object *Sara*), a generic object (*aPerson*), or the name of a place where an object resides (a variable). In the case of a variable, the object in residence actually receives and responds to the message.

- *Selector* identifies the semantics of the message, the essence of the request. Selectors can be simple symbols (such as the mathematical operators, +, *, /, and so forth) or descriptive phrases (*nextObject-InLinePlease*).

- *(Arguments)* are objects sent along with the message and are optional. They're optional in the sense that some selectors do not require an object, but if a message signature indicates that an argument is required, it is mandatory. Arguments are used when the receiver of a request for service also expects the requester to provide some of the information needed to perform that service.

- *returnedObject* is an arbitrarily complex object containing or representing the result created as a consequence of receiving the message. In the case of imperative and declarative messages, the object returned is "self," that is, the object that received the message is indicating it's still available to you (usually by keeping an active pointer).

In Java, and most popular languages, imperative and declarative messages are void functions. No return is expected. If the object changed in any way as a result of receiving the message, the "self" that is returned is the newly constituted "self."

What happens when you send a message and get back the wrong object, do not get a response at all, or get an explicit error message instead of the expected object? You figure out what went wrong, determine how the object should behave in such situations, write tests for that behavior, and code a new version of your object. The real question, however, is, "Who handles errors?" The answer is to make error handling an object responsibility—one shared by every object—and to let each object respond to those error conditions that it can resolve by using the knowledge it already has in its possession regarding itself and what it is trying to accomplish.

Interface (Protocol)

The collection of messages that an object responds to and the state changes it indicates it will accept registrations for constitute its *interface*. The term *protocol* is usually reserved for that portion of the interface listing the messages that the object is willing to respond to. A protocol might include messages of the sort, "What state are you in?" or "Are you in state X?" but those messages should not be confused with the innate ability of every object to notify others of a change in its state. The list of states and the mechanism for event registration and dispatching are quite separate from the message protocol. The syntax of each message in the protocol is specified and is considered the *message signature*. Where arguments are expected along with the message, the signature specifies the class (or type in some languages) of the object expected. The class (or type) of object returned in response to the message is also part of the signature.

The preceding terms are considered essential because they embody everything you need to know about objects to successfully decompose a domain, identify and distribute responsibilities among a collection of objects, create a taxonomy of objects, and even create scripts to guide objects in the completion of specific tasks.

These terms do not provide sufficient definition for those charged with actually implementing software objects. They provide a specification only. Implementation requires concepts associated with the solution space—a programming language and an implementation platform. Also required is vocabulary for describing the "internals" of objects. A supporting vocabulary addresses these needs.

Extension Terms

The following terms, although of less philosophical importance than the essential terms, are nonetheless commonly encountered. They are useful because they nuance or extend aspects of the essential terms and because they introduce some ideas necessary to thinking about implementation.

Collaboration and Collaborator

Collaboration and *collaborator* are terms referring to a particular type of object cooperation and the object relied upon for that cooperation. Objects are social and convivial things, constantly exchanging messages with one another and cooperating to complete tasks beyond the capabilities of any single object. Collaboration is a form of cooperation that is treated a bit differently from all the other forms of cooperation.

Collaboration occurs when

1. Object A receives a request for one of its advertised services.

2. While in the process of satisfying that request, it needs to ask for a service from object B.

3. Object B is *not* an object occupying one of object A's instance variables, a temporary variable declared in the method that object A is executing in order to satisfy the original request, or an object supplied to object A as an argument of the message requesting the service—that is, it is not an object currently residing inside object A's encapsulation barrier. This definition of collaboration correlates nicely with the Law of Demeter—a general style rule (proposed by Ian Holland in 1987) for object-oriented systems.

Object B becomes the *collaborator*, a covert assistant to object A.

The exchange between object A and object B occurs inside the encapsulation barrier of the object. It's this covert aspect that makes this particular exchange different from all other object-object messaging. Collaboration is an aspect of *how* an object satisfies a request. Collaborations always involve some degree of coupling between both parties of the collaboration, so the number of collaborations should be minimized to the greatest extent possible.

Class

Class is a term with many meanings, including

■   a label for a set of similar objects

■   an exemplar object

- a storage location for knowledge (rare) or behavior mechanisms that are identical for all members of the class

- an object factory

Following is an in-depth explanation of the foregoing meanings.

- **Class as set.**   An application of the principle of aggregation, noted in Chapter 4, a class is a convenient label for a group of objects that have the same behaviors. Instead of referring to *Alice*, *Dick*, *Jane*, and *Bob*, we can refer to *Person*, meaning any one of those individuals. Objects that are included in the class set are said to be *instances* of that class.

- **Class as exemplar object.**   A confusing (for the beginner) but common practice is to use the terms *class* and *object* interchangeably, with the context indicating which is meant. For example, we talk about modeling an object's behavior, and we might even visualize a particular object (such as *Mary*), but we talk about the class, saying, "A *Person* can identify itself." When we do this, we are using the class as an exemplar of the objects it instantiates.

- **Class as storage location.**   This use of the term is relevant only in the context of software objects. The mechanisms that allow an object to fulfill its responsibilities are, in the case of software objects, blocks of implementation language code. It's more efficient, both in terms of physical storage and, more important, in terms of maintenance, to store such a mechanism in one place: in the class. Instances of the class are given access to the common mechanism when required. In the real world, this use of class does not normally occur because storage and maintenance are not usually important issues. All human beings, for example, have bits of neural tissue that, when activated, allow them to respond to the message, "What is your name?" The fact that this bit of tissue is duplicated in every human being does not bother us. It is unlikely that we will ever find a more efficient bit of neural tissue and therefore unlikely that we will ever recall all human beings for a "brain update." Conversely, in the case of software we do not want to duplicate even one line of code several billion times, and we are quite often faced with the need to update an algorithm or a bit of code. Therefore, it makes sense to store that code (mechanism) in one place. It is also possible to store information shared by all instances of a class in the class itself, and for the same reasons. This use of a class for information storage is rare because the value of the object stored in the class variable must be appropriate for all instances existing at a particular point in time, a condition that is seldom possible to satisfy.

- ■ **Class as object factory.** This is another metaphor, which states that a class has the responsibility of creating new objects, new instances of the class. To do this, it needs a specification for an instance (an object). When we define a class, we commingle what are really two definitions, one for the class itself and one for the objects it will be responsible for creating. This will be clarified later in the definition of implementation terms.

Class Hierarchy (Library)

A class hierarchy, or class library, is the taxonomic organization of a group of classes. In some implementation languages (Smalltalk), this is an organized hierarchy, while in others (C++), it might be a simple shared library with no hierarchy except compilation dependencies. A class hierarchy should, ideally, function as a kind of index to a potentially large group of objects. For example, we might be looking for an object that collects things and go to the class hierarchy to find collection classes. Upon further reflection, we might remember that things in the collection must be maintained in a particular order and find the subclasses *OrderedCollection* and *SortedCollection*. This process could continue until we discovered the class we needed or found that none was available, in which case we would create the class and add it to the taxonomy (usually at the place where our search ended).

The organization of a class hierarchy—the is-a-kind-of relationship—does not provide the only index to the classes and methods in the library. Good browser tools provide many other indexes, including senders of message, implementers of message, category of class, and category of method, among others.

> **Note**   The example presented here uses various types of collections, which might seem a poor choice because collections do not occur in most domains—as collections. If we are seeking an object, we are likely to be looking for something with a common domain name—a customer or a product, for example. Collections are ubiquitous in every domain, albeit with different names such as portfolio, bin, ledger, parking lot, airspace, and so on. It doesn't take very long before we recognize that any object that exhibits the behaviors of adding elements, deleting elements, ordering elements, returning subsets of elements, and iterating across its member elements is either a collection or uses a collection as one of its instance variables. As abstract as they are, collections soon become some of the objects you use most and are most familiar with.

Always remember that the hierarchy is based on behavior and that classes lower in the hierarchy are assumed to extend the behavior of those above them in their branch of the hierarchy.

Abstract/Concrete

Abstract and *concrete* are labels for classes that do not have instances and those that do, respectively. In creating a taxonomy, it's convenient and sometimes necessary to create a class solely for the purpose of representing (and in software taxonomies, storing) behavior common to two or more other classes. These classes are not intended to have instances. Concrete classes have instances, so by definition, all objects are instances of concrete classes.

Abstract classes are always parent classes. An abstract class should not appear below a concrete class in the hierarchy.

In languages lacking explicit taxonomic relationships among classes (in C++, for example, where the classes are simply members of a library with no explicit enforcement of the is-a-kind-of relationship, as is the case in Smalltalk), an abstract class represents a "template" for a set of related classes. Conceptually it fills the same role: a convenient place for storing specification or implementation material that applies to a group of classes, which in turn will have actual instances.

Inheritance

Inheritance is simultaneously a metaphor, a definition, and a mechanism for implementing the definition. As a metaphor, inheritance suggests a family lineage. The definition involves the establishment of an is-a-kind-of relationship between classes. In some languages, such as Smalltalk, there is a "built-in" mechanism that implements, independent of any application, inheritance automatically when the is-a-kind-of relationship is declared. In other languages, such as Java and C++, the programmer must assume more responsibility for implementing the mechanics of inheritance.

There are actually three different inheritance metaphors, two suggested by biology and one by economics. In biology, a child inherits the genes of both of its parents and hence shares some traits and capabilities based on its parentage. Biology also suggests the possibility of creating global structure that shows how the is-a-kind-of relationship connects all living things. This structure is called a *taxonomy*, and the one you are most likely to be familiar with was established by Carolus Linnaeus. The third metaphor is suggested by our practice of allowing relatives to inherit the resources of their parents.

All three metaphors have been used to explain inheritance. As discussed in Chapter 4, object thinking uses the idea of a taxonomy tree based on an is-a-kind-of relationship as long as characteristics and behaviors are used as the criteria for establishing the relationship. Object thinking explicitly rejects the idea of basing a class hierarchy based on "DNA"—the internals of an object, such as its methods or its instance variables. The definition of inheritance then becomes, "A superordinate-subordinate relationship between classes in which the subordinate (child) has the same behaviors (responsibilities) as the super-ordinate (parent) plus at least one additional."

The compiler or interpreter behind your implementation programming language needs instructions on how to actually implement the inheritance rela-tionship—how to search parent classes for methods or variables not physically present in the child class. In some languages, this mechanism is automatic and generally not accessed by the programmer; in others, it must be specified for each program. Languages with implicit inheritance built in, such as Smalltalk, have the advantage of an inheritance mechanism that has been optimized over time and as a result of experience. Languages that expect the developer to explicitly create the inheritance mechanism, such as Java and C++, will be as effective as the developer is skilled. The tradeoff is greater control.

When classes have one and only one parent, they are said to participate in a scheme of *single inheritance*. Classes may have a grandparent, great grand-parent, and so on, but the entire lineage is based on the fact that a class has only one parent on the next higher level of the taxonomy tree. *Multiple inher-itance* implies that two or more parent classes exist for a given child class. Figure 5-5 shows a fragment of a possible class hierarchy. *Person*, *Student*, and *Employee* illustrate single inheritance, while *WorkStudyStudent* is an example of multiple inheritance. The circles, *aStudent*, *anEmployee*, and *aWorkStudy-Student*, represent instances of their respective classes. *Person* is an abstract class and has no instances.

The italicized entries in the classes represent messages that can be sent to objects of that class to obtain an object holding the information implied by the message name. Send the *name* message to the *aStudent* or *anEmployee* object, and you will get back *aString*, representing that object's identification.

Inheritance can be visualized as follows. The *salary* message is sent to the *anEmployee* object. The employee object does not physically contain a method enabling it to respond, so the inheritance mechanism kicks in, and the object is given a copy of the method defined and physically stored as part of the *Employee* class structure. The *anEmployee* object then executes the method and returns the expected string object.

In another example, *aStudent* is sent the *name* message. This time, the inheritance mechanism does not find the requested method in the *Student* class, so it looks in the parent class, *Person*, where the method is found. Again, the *aStudent* object is able to execute the name method and return the appropriate value.

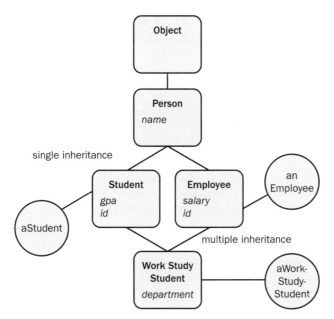

Figure 5-5   Inheritance tree fragment, showing both single and multiple inheritance.

Inheritance is assumed to be intrinsically slow because it must execute machine cycles to conduct its search for the appropriate method. The apparent slowness is eliminated through optimization in all but the most severely time-constrained applications. What happens if *aWorkStudyStudent* is sent the message *salary?* A long search chain begins with a query to the *WorkStudyStudent* class, the *Student* class, the *Person* class, and then the *Object* class, all with no results. Having reached the top of the hierarchy, the search returns to *WorkStudyStudent* and then to its second parent, *Employee*, where the method is found and made accessible. Multiple inheritance increases the potential length of the search chain and increases the time required to obtain the needed method.

An even more problematic situation arises when *aWorkStudyStudent* is sent the message ID. The needed method is not in the *WorkStudyStudent* class, so the *Student* parent is queried and a method of the correct name is found, and *aWorkStudyStudent* responds with a string representing a student identification number.

Now suppose that it's 3:00 A.M., and *aWorkStudyStudent* is in the vault at the Federal Reserve Bank. The requesting object is a security guard who wants to make sure the student is authorized to be in the vault. When *aWorkStudyStudent* returns her student ID, she is likely to be arrested. This situation can occur because classes can have identical message signatures in their protocols. (See the definition of polymorphism a little later on.)

Multiple inheritance is unnecessary. Object thinkers consider it a bad idea. It's unnecessary because there are always design alternatives (such as delegation, discussed in the next section) that remove the apparent need. It's a bad idea because it needlessly complicates the process of providing objects with access to the methods that allow them to respond to messages. It's a bad idea because it introduces the potential for error and confusion when the wrong mechanism with the correct name is used. It's a bad idea because it necessitates any object participating in a multiple-inheritance relationship to know who might send a message (for example, the *yourIdPlease* message) and to determine which of its inherited IDs (employee or student) it should return to which client. Or the client must know about the internal structure of the object it's talking to and determine whether it should ask for employee.id or student.id. In both cases, the communicating objects are tightly coupled—in other words, they must violate the encapsulation barrier in order to determine appropriate actions.

Object thinking will almost always provide alternative solutions to any design problem that at first seems to mandate multiple inheritance.

Forward Thinking

Refactoring Stories

"Hi, Hector, we need to talk about these stories if you have some time."

"Sure, glad to help. Should we stand over there by the whiteboard?"

"Yeah." Hector and two pairs of programmers head for the whiteboard. "Sally and Suroor are working on your story about updating inventory, and June and I are working on the 'menu displays available products' story," Ron introduces the subject of the conversation. "During the stand-up this morning, we started talking about the two stories and thought we saw some overlap—for example, both the menu and the *inventoryReorderList* need to know what products have been sold and if any are left. So we went out to Vending Row and tried to visualize what exactly goes on in both stories by looking at or imagining the objects involved. We want to run our ideas past you and see if they are reasonable and if they constitute some additional stories or modifications of these two you gave us originally."

"Sounds interesting. Shoot."

"OK, I'll start, and the others can jump in when they wish. Let me draw on the board." [Figure 5-6 shows the sketch Ron puts on the whiteboard.] "Here we have the central object in these stories—the dispenser.

(continued)

Forward Thinking   *(continued)*

Visualize the dispenser as a series of compartments, each one holding a product. Over here we have the menu (a list of available items), and over here we have the *reorderList* (a collection of line items, each containing the product ID, the number sold, the number to reorder, and the average shelf life information). Now, both the menu and the *reorderList* need to know stuff about the products in the dispenser, particularly about the product just entering or just leaving this first compartment in the dispenser."

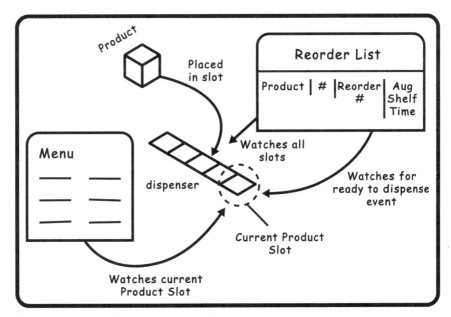

Figure 5-6   Hector's rough sketch of the objects the group is talking about, which he has made so that he has something to point to while telling the stories.

"We all think there should be some kind of 'stock dispensers' story," interjected Sally. "We watched the guy from the vendor company loading the candy machine, and we think the story would cover the reorder list watching the dispensers—all of them and all of their slots. When a new product is put in a slot, the reorder list asks that object for its *productId* and adds a line item to itself containing that ID. It also asks the vending machine for today's date and time, which it gives to the *averageShelfTime* object, which in turn will use it to calculate itself later. This story applies to all the slots in the dispenser, even the first one."

(continued)

Forward Thinking   *(continued)*

"But the first one gets contents in a second way," continues Suroor. "When a product is dispensed, the dispenser pushes the next product in line into the first position. All the other products get advanced as well. Now, the reorder list doesn't care about this event—it already has the item in its list from the time the vending machine was stocked. All it cares about is the event occurring when a product is dispensed.

"The menu, on the other hand, does want to know which new product has arrived in this spot. So it registers to be notified of any *product-Replaced* event that occurs in the *currentProduct* slot. It then asks the product coming into that slot for its name, which it adds to the appropriate spot on itself for display."

"When a product is dispensed," adds June, "the *inventoryList* wants to know as well. It actually needs to be notified of a *readyToDispense* event so it can ask the product for its ID before it's pushed off the cliff into the retrieval bin. It then tells the line item for that product to add 1 to its count of total sold. The *averageShelfTime* object also gets the system date and time at this point so it can calculate a running average of the time that that particular product ID stays in the vending machine."

Ron takes the stage again. "When the *inventoryList* is asked to transmit itself back to the home office, it tells all the line items to execute its *reorderAmountRule*. Then all the information in the four fields is ready for transmission: each product ID to be reordered, the amount sold since the last time the *reorderList* was requested, the amount to be reordered, and the average time on the shelf in that machine."

"But that's not part of our story—the two Sals are working on that one."

Hector looks puzzled for a second. "Oh, you mean Sally and Salvatore. Gotcha."

"There is another special case," Suroor says. "If a product is put in the *currentProduct* slot and it has expired, the menu shouldn't display its name; it should display a 'sold out' message or something instead. We don't think that needs to be a separate story, but we wanted to check with you to confirm our thinking about the problem."

"Seems to me you have it nailed." Hector ticks his fingers as he relates, "It seems you are suggesting five stories: stock dispensers, update menu, dispense product, update *reorderList*, and transmit *reorderList*."

"Well," Ron replies, "we already have a dispense product story; we just need to make sure that the pair working on it know about the needs of the *Menu* and the *reorderList*. And I think that the update *reorderList* is just part of the need we should convey to the dispense product pair."

(continued)

Forward Thinking *(continued)*

"OK, I'll write the stock dispensers story and put it in the hopper for the next iteration. We can just amend the narrative on the update inventory story you already have to reflect our discussion. The same is true of the update menu story. Those can stay in this iteration, then, and keep the same priority—unless you think this will radically change your estimates?"

"No, if anything, it will make it easier, so we should finish in less time than originally estimated when we didn't really know what we were going to do," Ron says as the others nod in agreement.

"And," continues Hector, "I will talk with the dispense product coders and make sure we have not changed their story so much we blow their estimate. Good work, and thanks for the suggestions. I think this better captures what happens and what we want in the final software."

Delegation

Delegation is a way to extend or restrict the behavior of objects by composition rather than by inheritance.

Consider an investment portfolio. A portfolio must be able to add and delete investments, return a subset of investments (all the bonds, perhaps), iterate across its members (asking each one its dividend date), and provide its current value. All but the last behavior can be done by a collection object. So the question arises, "Make *portfolio* a subclass of *collection?*" The answer, generally, is no—give *portfolio* an instance variable, *myInvestments*, which contains a collection object, instead, and delegate all the collectionlike behaviors of *portfolio* to *myInvestments*. When you send a message like, "*portfolio*, what bonds do you hold?" that question is delegated to *myInvestments*, which returns the bond collection to *portfolio*, which returns it to you.

Delegation is one way to address the apparent need for multiple inheritance in the case of a *workStudyStudent*. A *workStudyStudent* object could contain within itself an instance of *Employee* and an instance of *Student*. It could then define its own interface so that messages best handled by the *anEmployee* object could be forwarded to the instance variable containing that object. The same would apply to messages most appropriately handled by the *aStudent* object. Delegation eliminates the need for servers to be aware of their clients, and vice versa.

An object might want to advertise an ability to play different roles, and this too can be addressed with delegation. The *workStudyStudent* might, instead of creating its own protocol as a superset of *Employee* and *Student*, indicate that it can assume either role upon request. Its protocol would then include two messages, *asEmployee* and *asStudent*, that would tell it to assume one of those two roles. All messages sent to *workStudyStudent* after that would be directly received and responded to by the appropriate delegate object.

Delegation is used extensively in objectlike languages such as Visual Basic and is a generally useful technique that was too often overlooked when inheritance was being stressed as fundamental to object implementation.

Polymorphism

When I send a message to an object, it has complete leeway to interpret that message as it sees fit. The receiver of the message decides the appropriate response and how to respond. As a sender of the message, none of that is my concern. Because each object can interpret a message any way it wants (as long as its protocol tells me what kind of object I can expect in return when sending the message), more than one object can respond to an identical message.

Because every object has the right to define its own interface protocol, it is not unusual for two or more objects to adopt the same message signatures. A photograph and a document might both choose to implement a "print" message. The details of printing will be quite different for the two objects, as will the results. One message can yield many different responses, depending on whom it was sent to. Thinking of each response as a *form* of response, we have one message yield many forms (of response). The Greek for *form* is *morph*, and *poly* used as a prefix means *many*—hence *polymorphism* (many forms). A bit of a stretch, but that is where the term comes from.

Making the receiver of the message responsible for its interpretation gives me a great deal of freedom in how I work with mixed objects. I can talk with objects in ordinary vernacular. For example, I can ask them to print themselves using a single message, "Please print yourself," instead of remembering a different message for each kind of printable object. A graphic object in the group will hear the "please print" message and interpret it appropriately for a graphic, while a text string will hear the same message and interpret it appropriately for a text string.

Polymorphism is a completely unremarkable phenomenon in the natural world. We expect real-world objects to behave in this fashion and make jokes[2] when situations arise in which objects respond to messages in unexpected ways because they are polymorphic. Polymorphism is important in software because it relieves me of the burden of coining an infinite number of message variations so that I can satisfy the demand of a language compiler for making every subroutine invocation unique.

---

2. There's the joke about the large, leather-clad, menacing biker accompanied by his equally large and fierce Doberman who enters an elevator car occupied by a middle-class couple. When the biker utters the command, "Sit!" the couple as well as the dog immediately drop to the floor. The humor in this story (if there is any) derives from the lack of polymorphism: the couple did not exercise their innate ability to hear a message, determine whether it was for them, and react appropriately.

In the case of software objects, message signatures are supposed to capture the essence of the message so that potential senders will know how to select the appropriate message and object for their purposes. Good names are in limited supply, and many objects in quite different areas of the class hierarchy will have similar behavioral needs. Both students and employees have a need to identify themselves, so it's not unreasonable to allow them to have identical message signatures to retrieve an identification object. It's quite possible, in fact, for both to have inherited a common message signature from a shared superclass. The student object might respond with a string and the employee with an integer. Even if both reply with a string, it's likely that the string will have different values.

Encapsulation

The personal integrity of objects should not be violated. This is such an important principle that the defining term, *encapsulation*, might better be considered an essential term. I include it in the supporting terms category because of how it is used—as an explanation and justification for other terms in the object vocabulary.

Every object has a boundary separating public and private realms. This is true whether the object is a software construct or a person. That boundary is held to be impermeable: even though we know it can be penetrated, it should not be. Encapsulation defines the "insides" (structural definition and enabling mechanisms) of an object as private space, to or of which no one except the object itself should have access or knowledge.

In most ways, encapsulation is a discipline more than a real barrier. Seldom is the integrity of an object protected in any absolute sense, and this is especially true of software objects, so it is up to the user of an object to respect that object's encapsulation. For example, even though it is possible to insert wires into the brain of a human being and, by applying small amounts of electric current, make that human perform tricks, to do so would be considered a gross violation of the person's integrity. Users of software objects should demonstrate the same respect.

Encapsulation implies more than respecting the public/private boundary. Object users should not make assumptions about what is behind the barrier either. This is true whether the assumption is about a piece of knowledge that might be stored in the object or about the details of any message response mechanisms that might be inside the object. Just because an object indicates that it can provide a bit of information doesn't necessarily mean that the object has that information stored within itself—it might very well be obtained from some other object without your knowledge.

It is frequently the case that an object will be given responsibilities for maintaining and providing bits of information that it does not possess. As a typical human object, for example, I have a responsibility to remember the names and birth dates of my family members. I do a reasonably good job of remembering the names because I have memorized them: they are somehow part of my internal memory structure. I do not remember the dates. An external planner object, containing a page object, which lists my family members and important dates associated with each one, is a very valuable collaborator. To an external client, however, it would appear as if I contain both kinds of information because I can respond to requests for both names and dates.

Component

A *component* is a large-grain object made up of several basic objects. A roof truss is an example of a component. It's made up of 2 × 6 pieces of lumber and gang nails. It simplifies the process of constructing applications (in the case of a truss, a roof or a house). A component has an interface independent of the interfaces of its members.

Components, excepting GUI widgets, are frequently known as *business objects*, and an example might be a checkbook. A *checkBook* object is composed of a *checkRegister* and a collection of *numberedChecks*.

The distinction among an object, a component, an application, and a system is somewhat arbitrary, however "clearly defined" advocates may define each term. All can be called objects because all are packages of behavior with an external interface and all, even the most basic object, might contain other objects.

Framework

Framework is another term with multiple meanings. The four most common are *implementation* (for example, a set of GUI widgets); *foundational* (a partial solution to a problem encountered in multiple applications or domains), an implemented pattern (for example, resource allocation); *application*, or *vertical market application* (for example, banking); and *architectural* (for example, client/server).

■ An *implementation* framework is a collection of classes that collectively capture the behavior of a small, specialized domain. Examples might include a graphics framework or a money framework. At this level, the framework consists almost exclusively of a set of classes, a small class hierarchy that can be added to a development environment.

■ An abstract, or *foundational*, framework is both a collection of classes and the scripts that guide their typical interaction. A foundational framework offers an abstract solution to a particular problem that might be encountered in numerous applications across a variety of domains. Examples of foundational patterns include object routing and tracking, object allocation and scheduling, object persistence, and many others. An object routing and tracking framework, for example, would be useful in the construction of applications as varied as package tracking software for a parcel service and electronic network management software. Conference center room scheduling, ticket sales, and airline seat management applications could benefit from an object allocation and scheduling framework.

■ *Application* frameworks are customizable solutions to common domain needs. They are also known as *vertical market* frameworks. Examples would include an inventory control framework, an accounting framework, and a demand deposit framework. This kind of framework is a completely functional software solution but one that is easily edited (not reprogrammed) into a custom solution for a specific client.

■ *Architectural* frameworks are the most general, and might better be thought of as architectural *patterns*. Examples would include client/server, model-view-controller, pipes and filters, blackboards, presentation-abstraction-controller, and many others.

Pattern

Pattern is a term with one description and at least two meanings. The common description is, "A named solution to a recurring problem-in-context that has instructional value." The original meaning of *pattern* came from Christopher Alexander and reflected his focus on the problem space—a pattern was observable in the world, it could be described, and the description could be used to replicate the pattern when useful. The most common meaning of the term comes from the book *Design Patterns*, by the Gang of Four (GoF)—Erich Gamma, Richard Helms, Ralph Johnson, and John Vlissides—for whom a pattern is a programming design solution to a recurring programming problem.

Most of the people using the term have been inspired by the work of Christopher Alexander, an architect who proposed a *pattern language* of design parameters that would allow the construction of anything from an "independent region" to a montage of photos on the wall of a dwelling.

Alexander's goal was the discovery of the principles behind a "Timeless Way of Building," including structural, organizational, and aesthetic elements. Alexander's work tends to oscillate between the highly pragmatic and the semimystical. It's unsurprising that his work is subject to a wide range of interpretation. In fact, the intensity of argument regarding what patterns really should be is rivaled only by that of the original arguments about object programming.

Richard Gabriel, James Coplein, et al. represent those who believe that the semimystical aspects of Alexander represent the true essence of his message. For them, a pattern—and even more important, a pattern language—is quite different from what has been popularized as a pattern. The popular GoF view presents patterns as elegant solutions to discrete design problems. Numerous patterns of this sort might be incorporated into any given application.

Patterns for object thinkers are mental shortcuts or cues that direct thinking along known paths and facilitate the discovery of a problem solution. Of course, this means that the patterns themselves must be consistent with object thinking philosophy and principles, or their use will be counterproductive.

Patterns most useful to object thinkers should be derived from the problem domain, just as objects are. They should facilitate thinking about coordination and scripting of objects or about useful ways of assembling objects into components or applications. They could be considered Alexandrian patterns. Few of the patterns (about 6 of the 23) presented in the GoF book satisfy this demand. Martin Fowler's book on *Analysis Patterns* presents examples derived from a domain and is much closer to Alexander's intent than the GoF book.

Patterns that reflect the solution space are useful to the object thinker but in a very different way. If you have thought about and designed an object solution to a problem, you must still implement your solution using a programming language. Not all languages directly support object ideas, and many languages contradict object principles. If you must use such a nonoptimal language, design patterns of the sort in the GoF book provide insights that can minimize the distortion caused by the implementation language.

GoF patterns might better be called implementation patterns than design (or thinking) patterns. Other types of implementation patterns would include the coding standards that constitute one of the twelve XP practices. In particular, programming idiom or style provides a powerful pattern for implementation as well as for communication among developers. Apple's style guide for Macintosh GUIs, Kernigan and Ritchie's style for the C programming language, and Kent Beck's Smalltalk Best Practice Patterns are all examples of programmer idiom.

Implementation Terms

Those charged with the actual construction of software objects need vocabulary to support their work—and support their object thinking—while dealing with "the details."

Method

Method is the name given to the block of code that is executed in response to a specific message. Each message in an object's protocol must have a corresponding method.

As noted earlier, at this level it can be difficult to differentiate, visually or syntactically, an object method from a traditional subroutine, function, or procedure. Correct object thinking, however, will be reflected in the method collective. As an aggregate whole, object methods will vary in significant ways from a collection of routines or functions arrived at by applying traditional computer thinking while programming. For instance, there will be fewer object methods, and they will be simpler (on average) in their construction. Common control structures, such as *Case* statements and explicit looping constructs, will be absent (or if present, will be very few in number and will be used within an object and not for object coordination or scripting).

Some of the methods used by an object might be considered *private*, meaning that the object itself intends to use those methods and would prefer that they not be invoked by other objects. *Public* and *private* are concepts that apply to both methods and the messages that invoke those methods. An object will frequently send messages to itself, resulting in the execution of a private method, to obtain internally stored information or to obtain access to an object created in another method. Some languages enforce a distinction between public and private messages and their corresponding methods. Others do not, relying instead on the integrity of programmers to respect the object's design.[3]

Variable

A variable is a location or a container where an object might be located. *Class variables* are variables that are part of a class's permanent structure. *Instance variables* are variables that are part of an object's permanent structure.

---

3. Languages such as C++ and Java also allow for *protected* messages/methods. This is a way to allow outside objects to send such messages (invoke such methods) but restrict the number of outside objects having that privilege. C++ also allows for *friends*, objects that have access to the private messages/methods of other objects.

Messages can be sent to a variable, in which case they are received and responded to by the object residing in that variable location—the variable becomes an alias for the contents (object in residence) of the variable.

Late/Dynamic Binding

This is another programming term that assumes a particular importance in the world of objects. *Type* is a permanent[4] label attached to an object—kind of like a brand or a tattoo—that allows certain objects to be restricted to certain locations (variables) and allows a language compiler to enforce that restriction. In some programming languages, the concept of type is minimized so that it becomes important only when the program is actually executing. Those languages are described as allowing *dynamic*, or *late*, binding. Not all programming languages support dynamic binding, and whether or not they should is a matter of much argument.

The value of dynamic binding lies in how it allows a developer to take advantage of the natural polymorphism of objects in a direct and intuitive fashion. It is possible, for instance, to create a variable, *DisplayQueue*, that will at various times contain a text object, or a graphic object, or even a movie clip object. I can send the *display* message to the *DisplayQueue* variable, and whichever object is occupying the variable at that point in time will receive the message, interpret it (polymorphism), and display itself. I do not worry about the heterogeneous content of the variable.

A disadvantage arises from the possibility that I accidentally send an object to *DisplayQueue* that does not know how to display itself, does not respond to the *display* message. This can be prevented by asking any object seeking entry to *DisplayQueue* whether it understands the display message. If it does, it's allowed in; if not, it's refused entry.

The drawback of dynamic binding is the possibility that an inappropriate object might come to occupy the variable, receive a message that it does not understand, and cause the program to fail. In type-safe languages, erroneous assignment errors of this kind will be detected by the compiler, flagged, and corrected by the programmer before the program is allowed to execute. Unless, of course, you *cast* types and get something like a Java "class cast exception" error—the equivalent of Smalltalk's "does not understand" error.

Solving this dilemma in a dynamically bound language is straightforward. If the situation requires, I merely ask any object that seeks to occupy a variable whether it understands a particular message or whether it's an instance of a particular class, and I grant or deny residency based on its answer. This is extra work, of course, and can have an impact on performance. Deciding when I

---

4. We are ignoring, for the moment, the possibility of *casting* types.

need to employ this kind of type checking is an important part of design and of object thinking. The justification for allowing dynamic typing and inserting explicit class membership checking when needed should be empirical. Excepting the human interface, the probability of encountering a type error should be quite low. If the consequences of error are minimal, the need to insert extra code to check typing might not be needed. Simpler designs and implementations should make implicit typing so obvious that programmer error is minimized. The user interface will almost always have to enforce the equivalent of type checking for every value entered, but once a value is "in the system," it should not need to be rechecked. Typing is sufficiently restrictive that programmers will employ features such as casting to escape the restrictions. How many of which kind of errors, with what frequency, can be prevented (or caused) by employing strict typing and allowing means for avoiding type restrictions (casting)?

The merits of early and late binding are a source of considerable argument. We need not be concerned with that here. It must be noted, however, that object thinking is better reflected in an environment that allows dynamic binding. In the spirit that everything is an object, variables too are objects and should have the responsibility of maintaining their integrity instead of giving that responsibility to another object such as a compiler.

Auxiliary Concepts

The following terms do not define objects or concepts about objects. Instead, they add nuances to, alter our understanding of, or enhance our perspectives of those familiar terms.

Domain

The term *domain* refers to the arbitrarily bounded space we are simulating, in whole or in part, with the objects we design and implement. We understand objects based on how they reflect phenomena and concepts in the domain. A domain might be a business enterprise or a type of business (for example, banking or government). A domain might be nothing more than a focused community of objects collectively providing a particular set of services—for example, the domain of graphics or the domain of money.

When we are constructing a class library or a set of components, our goal should be to create a set that is capable of simulating the entire business enterprise or, preferably, the industry of which the enterprise is a member. It is almost always a mistake to define the domain as coextensive with an application program. A domain class library can be constructed incrementally as long as every class added is a simulation of behaviors expected in the domain as a whole and not just the application in which a class is first encountered. Behaviors can be added and moved via refactoring if the definition of classes is domain driven. Yet this is the level at which too many object-oriented texts provide illustrations and examples.

It is possible to define your domain as the computer—the implementation environment. This is, in theory, what object language designers do. If that is your domain of interest, object thinking should apply as much to that domain as it does to any other. Relatively few attempts have been made to apply object thinking to these domains. Of course, it is precisely this area where you might expect the greatest resistance to object ideas and the greatest allegiance to machine thinking alternatives. Perhaps this is appropriate, but it would be a lot of fun to seriously attempt the creation of an operating system that reflects "pure" objects and nothing but objects. (There have been attempts along this line, and Squeak, for example, has all operating system services built into the class hierarchy so there is no need for an operating system at all.)

This is probably a good point to insert a caveat about the material presented in subsequent chapters of this book. Almost all of the examples and discussions focus on application domains. Both an implementation domain and an execution domain are assumed.

The *implementation domain* will be a programming language and its accompanying class library. In most examples, we simply assume the existence of objects such as strings, characters, and collections. Also assumed are typical behaviors for those objects. Typical behavior is considered a superset of those behaviors included in object programming languages such as Smalltalk, Visual Basic, C#, Java, and C++. Sometimes, especially in dealing with collections, the assumptions are biased by the capabilities of Smalltalk collections (and my familiarity with that language), which are more extensive than in any other programming language.

An *execution domain* consists of the virtual machine or compiler and the operating system. Again, assumptions are made about services provided by these entities. It's also assumed that these entities are not generally object-oriented environments. Because the operating system, for example, is not object-oriented, it is frequently necessary to compromise object principles to some degree in order to make it possible for objects to interact with nonobjects.

A special kind of execution domain would be a database management system (DBMS). You could say that the very idea of a DBMS is antithetical to object thinking,[5] but such systems are an implementation necessity for most

---

5. Centralized hierarchical control and manipulation of passive data things: clearly, DBMS design, especially relational DBMS design, is not predicated on the kind of object philosophy and thinking discussed so far in this book.

organizations. Almost from the inception of object development, there has been conflict between object applications and DBMS execution environments. The problem even has its own name: the impedance mismatch problem. (See Chapter 10 for further discussion.)

Business Requirement

A business requirement is defined as any task, decision, procedure, or process that supports a business objective, goal, or mission. A business requirement might be satisfied by an individual object or by a group of cooperating objects. Those objects can be human, mechanical, or software based. If the business requirement can be satisfied by a single object, it becomes a responsibility of that object. If a group of objects is required, the business requirement is most likely to be expressed as a set of individual object responsibilities plus a script that ensures the proper coordinated invocation of those responsibilities. Most of the time we will use *story*, as used in XP, as a synonym for business requirement.

Business Process Reengineering

Business process reengineering was first defined outside the world of objects by Hammer and Champy.[6] The inclusion of the term here is simply to provide a bridge linking object thinking with business thinking. David Taylor illustrates how object thinking can be applied to the business enterprise as a whole, resulting in improved understanding and providing mechanisms for rethinking the enterprise itself. There is another important link between the ideas of business reengineering and thinking about objects. The better the object thinking, the more likely the need to reengineer the business so that it matches the simplicity, elegance, and flexibility of the new software. Object thinking almost necessarily reveals better ways to do business, even when that thinking is ostensibly directed toward software development.

Application

Application is the term used for a community of objects focused on accomplishing a well-defined set of collective responsibilities. As used here, the term *application* has almost the same meaning in object terms that it does in traditional software development.

---

6. Hammer, Michael, and James Champy. *Reengineering the Corporation*, Revised Edition: *A Manifesto for Business Revolution*. Harper Business, 2001.

Note   We have come to the end of our vocabulary list and have not included one of the most mentioned terms in object literature—reuse. There are several reasons for this. First, reuse is not a goal of object thinking; composability is. Composable objects will be reused as a matter of course, so reuse is but a byproduct of a more general goal. Second, there are ways to obtain reuse that are not related to object thinking—code libraries, for example—and the distraction is not really helpful. Lastly, reuse was once touted as the premier benefit of object orientation—a claim that proved to be highly overstated. Worse, perhaps, was the claim that maximum reuse could best be obtained via inheritance. Object thinking claims to lead to the discovery and crafting of composable objects. The goal is to create a mindset that leads to evolving flexible applications and systems that directly reflect and support an application domain. Reuse will emerge, but it is not a driving force.

6

Method, Process, and Models

Caveats to keep in mind as you read this chapter:

■ *All methods are someone else's idea about what you should do when you develop software. It may be useful, from time to time, to borrow from those ideas and integrate them into your own style. It is essential, however, to transcend any method, even your own idiosyncratic method, and "just do it."*

■ *Software development is like riding a surfboard—there is no process that will assure a successful ride, nor is there any process that will assure that you will interact propitiously with the other surfers sharing the same wave. Published processes, like published methods, provide observational data from which you can learn and thereby improve your innate abilities—just as observation of master surfers enables you to improve yourself.*

■ *No model has any value other than to assist in object thinking and to provide a means for interpersonal communication. If you can model your objects and your scenarios in your head while engaged in writing code, and if those mental models are consistent with object thinking, great! No need to write them down. If you and your colleagues use a visual model on a whiteboard as an aid in talking about scenarios and in clarifying your collective thinking about those scenarios, and you erase the board when you're done meeting, also great! If your models are crudely drawn and use only a subset of the syntax defined here (or a completely different syntax that you and your colleagues collectively agree upon), still great! Model when you must, what you must, and only what you must.*

For forty years, software development theorists focused on method, process, and modeling as the key means for improving practice, based on the belief that all software problems could be resolved if developers would give up their idiosyncratic, imprecise, and careless ways. Formally defined methods would incorporate rigorous process and modeling requirements. Following the dictates of formal methods would eliminate all vestiges of ad hoc and subjective "art." Software development would be transformed, if not into a science like mathematics and physics, then at least into a solid engineering discipline solidly grounded on a science of computing. Models would have precisely defined syntax (preferably based on a kind of predicate calculus), and all semantics would derive from formal transformations of that syntax. Properly constructed models would contain unambiguous truth, and one model (a data flow diagram, perhaps) could be mechanically transformed into another (source code, for example).

A process could be defined that would describe in precise detail each step required to move from vague idea to functional solution. At each step in the process, the developer would know exactly what to do, how to elicit required information, and how to express that information in syntactically correct models.

Methods of this sort could be expressed as automated tools. It would be possible to remove significant numbers of human developers from the process—especially those pesky and annoying programmers. Computer-aided software engineering (CASE) tools would allow a properly trained analyst to construct precise models, which would then be transformed into error-free code at the touch of a button (click of a mouse). It would, in fact, be possible to build a *repository*, an ultimate CASE tool that would allow the automatic generation of computer programs and systems in response to a change in business requirements—without the intervention of analysts or programmers.

The vision of the theorists was compelling—and highly salable to managers, who rushed to adopt the latest advances, buy the latest tools, and pay for audits that would document their compliance with the latest process standards.

Unfortunately for all, the dream was never realized in practice.

During the same period, practitioners—lacking such grand vision—focused on discovering and sharing heuristics and practices grounded in experience rather than theory. The art and craft followed by expert developers was transmitted mostly via oral tradition, mentoring, and informal mimicry. Real improvements in software development were realized—but non-self-consciously,[1] in the form of a shared culture and oral traditions.

---

1. Christopher Alexander differentiated between self-conscious and non-self-conscious processes in architecture. The latter arise only in affluent societies with universities and give rise to architectural theories whose merits are based on abstract meta-arguments rather than on any connection with practice or actual manifestations. Alexander, Christopher. *Notes on the Synthesis of Form*. 1968.

After the fact, formal methodologists adopted many of these practitioner innovations and recast them in terms of their pet theories (sometimes ignoring the origins of their "insights"). This recasting allowed the methods of such methodologists to give the appearance of supporting new innovations without initiating any substantive change. In fact, innovations were all too often redefined by the methodologists as being nothing more than some feature already present in the method: "We have been doing objects since 1960; only we called them _____." This, and similar statements, were expressed by innumerable mainstream developers and methodologists in response to innovations.

XP and the other agile methods represent the first attempt by practitioners to systematize (not formalize) practice in such a way that it could be perceived as a legitimate alternative to a formal method. So legitimate in fact, that the backlash from mainstream formal methodologists is intense. "XP is nothing more than good software engineering." "RUP (Rational Unified Process) and CMM (Capability Maturity Model) are just as agile as anything coming out of the Agile Alliance." "XP works only in certain niches (which are not really important anyway), while formal methods are required for most development." "XP is nothing more than a fad, a way for unemployed Smalltalk programmers to get jobs again."

The jab at Smalltalk programmers alludes to important relationships among XP, methodology (in general), and object thinking. To fully see the connection, it's necessary to make one last historical foray—a brief recap of object-oriented methods and models that have been advanced over the past 20 years.

Two Decades of Object Methodology

Scores of object development methods have been advanced since Alan Kay coined the term *object-oriented* and applied it to software. The first methods proposed clearly reflected the same presuppositions and philosophy that provided foundations for the Smalltalk programming language—specifically, an orientation toward understanding objects in terms of their behavior. One early method, by Adele Goldberg and Ken Rubin, originated within ParcPlace Systems (a spinoff from Xerox PARC, which developed and marketed the first version of Smalltalk). Object behavior analysis (OBA) was described in published papers but was never truly marketed as a method. An automated support product for OBA was developed but not, at that time, sold.[2]

---

2. Very late in the life of ParcPlace Systems (the spinoff that marketed the Smalltalk developed at PARC), the OBA tool was sold—under the name MethodWorks. But by that time, it had no hope of capturing any share of the development tools market. MethodWorks provided a set of forms, consistent with the OBA models, containing textual documentation about the nature and relationships of objects.

Behind the Quotes

Adele Goldberg

Adele Goldberg was a known figure in the Smalltalk world from the time the language was conceived at Xerox PARC until it was eclipsed by Java. Her concerns with education helped shape the evolution of Smalltalk, and she contributed to its leaving PARC and becoming a commercial language. When PARC spun off ParcPlace Systems, she became a board member and later president of the company. With Ken Rubin, she authored a behavioral object analysis method (object behavior analysis, or OBA) and later a guide to object-oriented project management, entitled *Succeeding with Objects*. While Goldberg was at ParcPlace Systems, a version of Smalltalk with a much larger user base—from a company named Digitalk—was acquired, and efforts were made to merge the languages and their customer bases. That effort failed, in part because ParcPlace expended resources trying to sidetrack yet another competitor—a company named OTI, allied with IBM—stopping the momentum of Smalltalk (which was threatening to become the "next COBOL") and allowing Java (a pale imitation of Smalltalk at that time) to succeed. Goldberg left ParcPlace and founded a company and product named LearningWorks, which used the Smalltalk environment to teach computing and computer programming. For a time, the Open University in England adopted the Smalltalk environment as a foundation for its programming courses.

The year 1991 was a watershed year for object methods in terms of books published. Booch, Coad and Yourdon, Jacobson, Rumbaugh, Schlaer and Mellor, and Wirfs-Brock published books describing various methods. All of these methods could be characterized as first generation. They were all produced quasi-independently and exhibited significant syntactic variation.

A great deal of argument ensued. Which method was best? Much of that argument coincided with arguments about implementation languages. It was common for methods to be closely associated with languages and praised or damned based on that association. For example, Booch's method (which was originally written to support Ada development) was preferred in the C++ community, while Wirfs-Brock was more popular with the Smalltalk crowd.

In addition to arguing with each other, methodologists took note of one another's work and recognized omissions in their own. Points of concurrence were noted. Compliments were noted. Booch, for instance, specifically noted the value of Class, Responsibility, Collaborator (CRC) cards for object discovery and preliminary definition in the second edition of his method book. Other efforts were made to extend the first-generation methods to support specific types of problems: real-time systems and distributed systems, for example.

At the same time, "The Market" demanded a single "right answer" as to which method to adopt. Booch, Rumbaugh, and Jacobson, coming together under the Rational corporate umbrella, were quick to consolidate their methods and models in order to present a unified method. Given the sobriquet "The Three Amigos," they advanced their cause. Their tool sets and methods became the foundation for Unified Modeling Language (UML) and the Rational Unified Process (RUP)—a tool and a method that dominate "official"[3] practice today.

A review of all of the methods advanced in the nineties is not possible in this space. It is possible to group the plethora of methods into three general categories (data-driven, software engineering, and behavioral) and look at exemplars of each category in order to outline the main points of divergence.

Data-driven approaches are exemplified by the work of Schlaer and Mellor, the Object Modeling Technique (OMT) of Rumbaugh et al., and the joint work of Coad[4] and Yourdon. The central focus of this category of methods is data and the distribution of that data, via the classical rules of normalization, across a set of objects. Objects in this instance are equivalent to entities in classical data models. Schlaer and Mellor, for example, describe the process for discovering objects in a manner that is indistinguishable from data modeling techniques.

OMT syntax and models allow greater variation and flexibility in relationships among objects than do the models of Schlaer and Mellor, capturing interaction among objects in non-data-specific ways, but they still define objects in terms of data attributes. Coad and Yourdon's object-oriented analysis (OOA) method essentially advocates the creation of an entity diagram, placing functions with the distributed data attributes and adding message passing to the data model.

---

3. A huge discrepancy remains between what developers officially use and what they actually use, in terms of both method and model. Licenses sold still does not equate to actual use by developers.

4. Coad's later and independent work was far more focused on behavior and patterns of behavior among groups of objects.

Data-driven methods do not bring about the object paradigm shift. Instead, they carry forward a legacy abstraction, data, and use it as the basis for decomposing the world. Followers of this type of method "think like data" or "think like a (relational) database." This obviously has the appeal of familiarity and consistency with legacy systems and provides the appearance of a quick path to objects. It's also quite consistent with the definition of an object as a package of data and methods.

It isn't consistent with decomposition of the world in a natural way because the world isn't composed of computationally efficient data structures. There are no "natural joints" in the domain that map to normalized entities. This disjunction is evident in the world of data modeling itself: just consider the differences between a conceptual data model (models data as understood in the domain) and a logical data model (models data as normalized for implementation).

Data-driven methods tend to create objects with more frequent and tighter coupling than do other methods. Class hierarchies are therefore more brittle, and changes in class definitions tend to have greater impact on other class definitions than desirable. (See Figure 6-1 for an example.) Distributing data across a set of objects in accordance with normalization rules and by following the dictum that a class must be created if a class (entity, really) has at least one attribute different from any existing class needlessly multiplies the number of classes required to model a domain. (See Figure 6-2.)

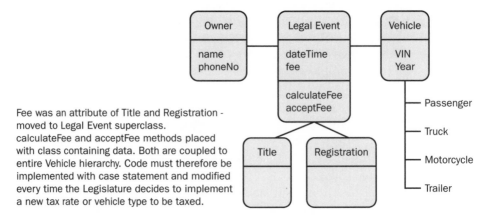

Fee was an attribute of Title and Registration - moved to Legal Event superclass.
calculateFee and acceptFee methods placed with class containing data. Both are coupled to entire Vehicle hierarchy. Code must therefore be implemented with case statement and modified every time the Legislature decides to implement a new tax rate or vehicle type to be taxed.

Figure 6-1   In this Department of Motor Vehicles example (patterned after Coad and Yourdon, 1991), data modeling rules lead the designer to place the fee attribute and therefore the calculate fee method in the *Legal-Document* class. This mandates the need for a case statement to handle fee calculations and couples *LegalDocument* to the entire *Vehicle* class hierarchy.

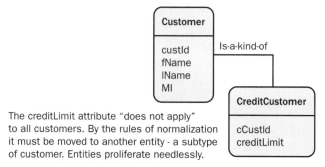

The creditLimit attribute "does not apply" to all customers. By the rules of normalization it must be moved to another entity - a subtype of customer. Entities proliferate needlessly.

Figure 6-2   In this example, the addition of a single new attribute requires the creation of a new class, allowing some customers to buy on credit and therefore have a *creditLimit* attribute, for example.

Booch and Jacobson exemplify *software engineering* methods. They openly acknowledge an intellectual debt to classical structured development and claim to be an appropriate response to the demand by management and government for a documented (formal) process for software development. They are characterized by multiple models that, when (and if) integrated, present a comprehensive specification of a desired software artifact. Supporting code generation is a frequently stated motive for these methods.

Most software engineering methods claim to be (partly) behavior driven. Jacobson's use cases are essentially identical, in fact, to the scenarios of OBA, a prototypical behavioral method. Because use cases are focused on discovering requirements to be used to define an artifact—the software—they tend to fall into thinking about an object as encapsulated data and procedures: they reflect thinking like a computer.

Nothing in these methods compels a design to reflect computer thinking. However, replication of modeling syntax from structured development and the vocabulary employed in discussion (for example, attributes and operations) reflect the artifact-centric point of view borrowed from structural development. Developer focus remains on the artifact and its design to meet specification, rather than on understanding and modeling the problem domain.[5]

---

5. Only nominal attention is paid to the process of developing a domain class hierarchy as a tangible product in most software engineering methods.

Software engineering methods (with the exception of Booch's 1991 book) fail to stress the paradigmatic differences[6] between objects and traditional modules and data structures. Even use cases, as developed by Jacobson, are less about responsibility discovery and assignment than they are about requirements gathering.

Behavioral methods, despite being first and most closely allied with the development of object thinking, have always received less attention than data and engineering methods. Proponents of other methods are quick to assert that this lack of popularity reflects fundamental flaws or lack of utility in behavioral approaches. They are wrong: other factors account for the failure of behavioralism to capture market share.

First, behavioralism was not promoted, as were competing methods. Important advocates of behavioral ideas—Goldberg and Rubin at PARC—and the originators of the most widely used behavioral modeling technique—Beck and Cunningham and CRC cards—never published any kind of method book. At a time when management almost demanded an automated tool to accompany and support any new method (this period of time was also known as the era of CASE tools), the following occurred:

- ParcPlace Systems chose not to market the tool (OBA) it had created, although it did provide the tool to those taking its object analysis and design seminars.

- Beck and Cunningham actively lobbied against the creation of any kind of automated CRC tool and, today, argue against automation of story cards in XP. Their objective was quite sound, philosophically, but disastrous in terms of marketing.

- Knowledge Systems Corporation developed a tool named coDesign, based on Smalltalk, that was highly regarded by those that saw it demonstrated. It never became a commercial product because of financial and political concerns within KSC.

- Corporate information technology organizations were actually moving to adopt Smalltalk at this time but refused to give up their relational databases, so tool vendors concentrated on object-relational mapping tools instead of behavioral modeling tools.

---

6. Booch is a notable exception to this rule. He clearly recognizes that a fundamental shift in thinking is required for object development. He also clearly recognizes the need to decompose the world based on the domain expert's point of view. He parallels Parnas's views on domain-centric (design-centric) decomposition. His method, however, does not develop or directly support this aspect of object development. Instead, his models and syntax are directly focused on what is needed to construct the software artifact.

The first, and for a long time only, book promoting the behavioral approach to objects was that of Wirfs-Brock, Weiner, and Wilkerson. Nancy Wilkinson published a small volume outlining classical CRC cards a few years later—long after the opposition had all but won the "method war."

Second, and more important, behavioral approaches were the least developed in terms of expressiveness of models and making the transition from analysis to design and implementation in a traceable fashion. It would not be misleading to characterize behavioral methods, circa 1991, as "CRC cards—then Smalltalk."

Wilkinson, in fact, suggests that the primary value of CRC cards and behavioralism is to provide an informal and rapid way to obtain input for more formal software engineering methods. Booch, OMT, and OOSE (Jacobson's Object Oriented Software Engineering) were the formal software engineering methods she seemed to have had in mind.

Third, behavioral approaches are the most alien to established software developers—even today. Thinking like an object is very different from traditional conceptualizations of the software development process. It requires, at least at the beginning, constant diligence to avoid falling into old mental habits. It is hard. Most people are unwilling to engage in this kind of hard cognitive work without a compelling argument as to why it is worth their while. That argument was never made—except in a kind of oral tradition shared by a very small community. This book is an attempt to capture several aspects of that oral tradition. As with XP, the primary justification for object thinking derives from a better fit between information technology and business and significant reductions in complexity.

In fact, behavioralism had the same reputation as XP does today—as being anti-method. There is a small element of truth in this assertion. Both OO and XP proponents oppose the use of methods as traditionally defined—especially comprehensive, highly formalized, and labor-intensive methods that prevent developers from immediate engagement with code—with programming.

This does not mean that object thinking lacks anything resembling a method. (The same is true of XP.) It merely means that the rigor and the systematization of work that accompanies object thinking is quite different from what most developers have come to associate with the term *method*.

To understand the relationship between method and XP, it's necessary to take a few moments and reflect on how method provides value to software developers.

Purpose and Use of Method

Methods come in many guises. The simplest is nothing more than the adage, "If at first you don't succeed, try and try again." Hacking, trial and error, and rapid prototyping are examples of methods based on this precept. Iterative development approaches—based on exploration, trial and error, and incremental expansion from small working systems—have been used and advocated almost since the inception of commercial computing but have never been accepted as "official" methods.

Other methods are more prescriptive, instructing the developer as to what to do and when to do it. The simplest form of a prescriptive method would be a checklist, such as that used by pilots for each phase of flight. Such checklists consist, essentially, of a set of questions of the form, "Did you remember to do this action?" Actions that need to be done in a particular order simply have their reminder questions occur in the necessary sequence.

Most software engineering methods are highly prescriptive—with precise instructions as to what and how to develop software at each meticulously defined step in a carefully arranged process. They are based on a value system that incorporates a basic mistrust of the human worker. Such methods can become highly complex and comprehensive as the checklist expands to include documentation that must be produced to confirm that each action did in fact take place, as well as syntax that specifies the exact form of the documentation so that it is known that the action was done correctly. (I have seen one such method that filled almost 20 volumes—defining each step, describing each document or artifact produced, and including algorithms for determining the correctness of all artifacts produced.)

Between hacking and prescriptive overkill is the realm of formal, informal, and aformal methods.

Formal methods tend to be prescriptive. They are characterized by a large number of models each of which requires a reasonably complex syntax, they are filled with rules and techniques that assure proper use of the method, and they are fairly strict in terms of activity sequencing. Most offer a promise of removing human developers, to some degree, from the development process—via code generation, for example.

Informal methods require fewer models with simpler syntax, demand fewer activities, and offer heuristics instead of rules and techniques. Most pick a single activity—programming, for example—and elevate it to primary status while suggesting that all other activities are valuable only insofar as they support the primary status. XP shares these characteristics and would be called an informal method.

An *aformal* method[7] would reject the idea that any task, model, syntax, rule, technique, or heuristic has any intrinsic value. Such things are valuable only to the extent that they support or assist the innate capabilities of the human developers engaged in a particular task at a particular moment in time.

---

7. *Aformal method* is almost, but not quite, an oxymoron. Some familiar aspects of method remain even in the most aformal approaches to software development.

Both formal and informal methods are seen as a kind of exoskeleton that might offer some protection, but at the cost of severely limiting the being "enjoying" that protection. Improving the innate character and capabilities of the human developer is the alternative to defining an external method, for an aformalist. Aformalism might also be considered "master practice." Craftsmen have internalized those aspects of informal method and practice most germane to their art and have transcended them.

An analogy to chess playing might illuminate the relationships among method categories. A beginning chess player follows rules and defined procedures (they are formalists), while a journeyman (informalist) relies on patterns and heuristics. A grandmaster has internalized and transcended the informal to become an aformal player.

Methods themselves are less important than the culture shared by those that embrace a method. Software engineers, for example, represent a culture enamored of formal methods (even if they cannot use them). (There are exceptions to this rule: Dave Thomas, for example, sees engineering as creative and aformal problem solving independent of any formal method or process. It is hard, however, to find that attitude reflected in software engineering texts.) Those methods are considered necessary and desirable because the method expresses the set of presuppositions, values, and worldview shared by the members of the culture. Formalists like formal methods—an obvious truism.

Managers; academics; software engineers; computer scientists; and proponents of UML, RUP, and CMM all tend to be formalists. Practitioners, as Robert Glass has shown, generally are informalists. XP and object thinkers aspire to be aformalists.

Methodological conflicts, therefore, are really cultural conflicts. When an advocate of RUP asserts that "RUP is agile," he or she is making an irrelevant statement. Of course, RUP can be agile—it is merely a tool, after all, and the practitioner has the choice of how, when, and why to use that tool. But someone from the culture that values RUP cannot be agile. (OK, technically, will not be agile. OK, OK, is very unlikely to be agile.) The same mostly nonconscious worldview that leads to adoption of RUP and UML will prevent the use of that method in any but a formal way unless a constant, conscious, and deliberate effort is made to adopt the agile worldview and cultural values at every step of development.

Formalists will advocate methods that are focused on the production of computer artifacts (software programs). Such methods will liberally employ terms such as software *engineering* and will stress correctness and both syntactic and semantic integrity. It is held that such methods are capable of producing a "correct" solution to an unambiguous requirement, prior to the expensive process of committing it to code. Code generation is then a happy byproduct of formal methods. The major drawback, of course, is that the effort required to produce the formally correct models is essentially the same as (or more than) that required to code and test. (Code, ironically, is far more amenable to formal testing than any abstract model. As Ken Auer says, "Bubbles and arrows never crash; they also never run!") This makes for a steep learning and overhead curve for those using this kind of method. They will also suffer from some degree of mismatch between the real world and the formal world they attempt to describe. The real world is far fuzzier, flexible, and illogical than any formal method can accommodate.

Informalists are more likely to focus on methods that support negotiated understanding—for example, the informal communication-oriented methods such as joint application development (JAD) and CRC. To the extent that they adopt modeling techniques, informalists see the models as a means of communication—not an artifact with intrinsic value. It is clearly recognized that such models are bound in terms of time and are meaningful for the group involved in their creation. That is why the development group must include users, managers, analysts, programmers, documenters, maintainers, and so on. They will understand the models only if they participate in their construction. Reinhard Keil-Slawik[8] shows how such models (including code) serve as a kind of external memory for the group that created them and works with them. The primary problem with these methods is the lack of technique for translating the human understanding of a solution into a "computer understanding." The computer, after all, is a formal machine and can operate only on formally defined products. This explains the tendency of informal methods (XP, rapid prototyping, open source, and so forth) to focus on programming—the actual interface between formal machine and informal developer.

Aformalists appear to reject method entirely. Observation, however, reveals patterned behavior and tasks performed in a sequential manner. Models are constructed (on whiteboards, Post-It notes, and 4×6 cards more often than with the use of an automated tool), giving those models a relatively short half-life. Aformalists do not reject method so much as they reject the idea that methods and models have any intrinsic value apart from those using them in a specific context.

In one of the *Alien* movies, Sigourney Weaver's character fought the alien monster using a mechanical exoskeleton. This exoskeleton greatly increased her human strength by amplifying her human movements with electromechanical means. Formalists tend to see method as a similar kind of exoskeleton, one to be wrapped around a human developer in order to amplify his or her skills.

---

8. Floyd, Christiane, Heinz Zullighoven, Reinhard Budde, and Reinhard Keil-Slawik. *Software Development as Reality Construction*. New York: Springer-Verlag, 1992.

Aformalists viewing this scene would be mildly impressed by the magnification potential of the exoskeleton but would be completely appalled at the cost required to gain that advantage. The human becomes a mere part in the machine and is severely restricted to a range of actions determined by the exoskeleton and its designers. They would note that continued use of such mechanical strength enhancement devices would perpetuate the physical weakness of the human and, likely, increase those weaknesses (exaggerating the importance of the exoskeleton) over time. In addition to the limitations imposed by the designers of an exoskeleton, use of one adds new complexities—how to get in and out efficiently in response to perceived need—and vulnerabilities—what to do when your exoskeleton is in the next room when the alien appears?

Object thinkers and extreme programmers reject the method-as-exoskeleton approach in favor of a method–as–weight room idea. A human uses mechanical weights and machines in a gym to increase his innate capabilities—to make his own muscles stronger and more reliable. Using a more cerebral metaphor (and one therefore more appropriate for object thinking), Kent Beck suggests using method and even XP practices as if they were etudes (musical exercises designed to help the musician internalize certain skills and techniques). Etudes are used for practice, to increase and discipline the innate capabilities of the musician so that she can then go on stage and perform music.[9]

Object thinkers and extreme or agile developers find value in method only to the extent that it helps them become better practitioners. The method itself should wither away as developer skills increase until it becomes the merest vestige required to act as a reminder or trigger for the human developer to apply his or her enhanced skills when and as appropriate. Kent Beck suggests that there are three XP maturity levels: out of the box, adaptation, and transcendence. These levels correspond nicely with the formal, informal, and aformal typology introduced earlier in this chapter. (Except XP would never have a formal level—substitute rote performance for formal in the XP context.)

This is not a new idea. The south Asian philosophy of karma yoga is grounded in the idea that right actions allow you to minimize the consequences of your actions sufficiently that you can maximize your chances of enlightenment. Aristotle suggested, "Wear the mask of a good man long enough and you become that good man." David Parnas suggested some very good reasons for faking a rational design process even when you can't actually follow such a thing. Christopher Alexander stressed repeatedly that a pattern language is but

---

9. It is true that some etudes are themselves sufficiently beautiful that they get played in concert, just like any other kind of music composition. This does not detract from the intent behind their creation.

a gate that must be passed through and left behind before you can actually practice the "Timeless Way of Building."

For object thinkers, method is never an end in and of itself. There is no intrinsic value in either method or process. Both are useful only to the extent that they provide practice in the use of, and a means of enhancement for, innate human capabilities. Within the context of this worldview, it is possible to ask whether some methods, some tools, some models are more suited to promoting object thinking than others. And the answer is yes. To determine which methods, tools, and models are the most efficacious, the following criteria can be used:

- The method, tool, model, or process cannot substitute its own goals in place of those articulated in object (or XP) philosophy.

- Each task advocated by the method and each model created using the method must contribute to the realization of basic goals.

- The models, vocabulary, and syntax associated with the method and its models must value expressiveness over correctness. Models must evoke knowledge in the head of the developer instead of making pretensions to unambiguous representation of that knowledge.

- The methods and models must

  - Provide support for "natural" decomposition and abstraction of problem (enterprise) domains. This requirement refers back to the simulation notion behind SIMULA and the object paradigm.

  - Recognize a need for two complementary processes: one focused on domain modeling and the second on application assembly.

  - Include heuristics for discovery and evaluation. Heuristics should be grounded in appropriate metaphors to facilitate learning.

  - Include heuristics or metrics that allow you to measure progress and the "goodness."

A Syncretic Approach

The preceding discussion emphasizes the differences between formal and aformal approaches to software development. It might lead one to suspect that the gulf between the two philosophies is unbridgeable—especially when considering method.

Even hard-core object purists recognize that there are many things of value even in the most formal of methods. Blending methods and approaches presents a significant challenge.[10] Incorporating valuable ideas from formal methods in such a way that the worldview and values of object thinking are preserved is equally hard.

Nevertheless, it is desirable to find some kind of common ground. Two prerequisites are required. First, the term *method* will be abandoned in favor of *approach*. This is purely a political move—to eliminate distractions caused by the "M-word" itself. Second, we will borrow a concept—syncretism—from anthropology and religious studies as a metaphorical springboard for developing a *syncretic approach*.

Syncretism refers to a particular type of blending of traditions and cultures. For example, a visitor to a Catholic church in the Caribbean or South America will almost certainly find representations (icons, statues, relics, feast days, and so on) of Catholic saints that are indistinguishable, on the surface, from "pagan" deities. These vernacular adoptions do not change the underlying principles of Catholicism; they merely make those principles more accessible (as in the use of vernacular in the mass) by interpolating a mediating form. A syncretic approach to software development would be characterized by a smooth transition from behavioral decomposition and analysis into representations sufficiently formal that they can be implemented as computer software. (In XP, this transition takes place in small steps, one story at a time.) Along the way, the user would see many elements borrowed from other sources, elements that might even be redefined in various subtle ways to maintain consistency of expression. It will be quite possible to maintain object thinking and XP practice while drafting UML models that are syntactically, but not semantically, identical to UML models drafted by a traditional software engineer.

Using the label *syncretic approach* is deliberate. Although many will take what is advocated in this book as YAM (yet another method), the intent is to create an approach to thinking about objects that nevertheless allows adoption of techniques, insights, or models that may have originated in traditional computer science and software engineering. Forms may be adopted from formalist methods, but never underlying principles or philosophies. Succeeding chapters will develop the syncretic approach more fully, but the remainder of this chapter will provide a summary of the process and a quick definition of the models (all of which are adapted from existing methods) that will be employed.

---

10. UML and RUP, it has been reported, took a lot of compromise and negotiation before they were hammered out, and the three methods synthesized there were basically similar. The elements of behavioralism in Booch were essentially discarded to make the synthesis possible. It proved much harder to combine behavioralist and software engineering approaches, although a product named Fusion, from Hewlett-Packard, made a valiant attempt.

Paradigms, metaphors, and concept definitions provide the foundation for understanding object orientation. They do not, however, tell us much about how to do object development. "How-to" requires the following:

■ The enumeration of specific actions that can be taken to reach certain goals.

■ Agreement as to a vocabulary (both verbal and graphic) and a grammar (language) for assuring mutual communication and understanding. Style, idiom, and standards are important aspects of this common language.

■ Criteria by which we can evaluate ourselves, our progress, and our products.

Object thinking imposes four additional requirements that must be addressed by a syncretic approach to development. Implicit in these four requirements (listed next) is the demand that two separate but complementary processes (as discussed in Chapter 4) be respected—object discovery and specification (Lego brick construction) and application assembly and scripting.

■ Decomposition based on discovering the "natural joints" in the domain. What goes on inside a computer, the implementation context of the software to be created, is not part of the domain.

■ Responsibility assignment based on expected behavior in the domain as observed or inferred in the domain. Preserving existing channels and means of communication is essential. Eric Evans[11] has just published an important book detailing why this emphasis on domain-driven modeling is so essential. Thinking like a computer, even when you are creating tests and writing code to realize a single XP user story, should not play a role in defining objects (decomposition of the story) or defining and assigning responsibilities to those objects.

■ Aggregation of objects into communities capable of interaction and collective solution of a task or tasks. Not only must you identify what must be done by a group of objects acting in concert, you must also identify the constraints under which they must work and any qualitative characteristics that will be used to evaluate their work. Interaction of both human and automated objects must be taken into account.

■ A reasonably direct metaphor-preserving means of adding design and implementation detail to objects based on their responsibilities.

11. Evans, Eric. *Domain Driven Design—Tackling Complexity in the Heart of Software.* Boston: Addison-Wesley, 2004.

The most tangible elements of a syncretic approach satisfying these requirements will be the set of models suggested for use by developers. This chapter will conclude with a brief introduction of a set of models and their syntax. Subsequent chapters will explore the actual use of those models.

Forward Thinking

Review

One Friday afternoon the team is getting ready to leave, when Sally looks around the room as if seeing it for the first time. "You know," she says almost to herself, "this place is a pretty good visual metaphor."

"How so," asked Ron, who was standing nearby.

"Well, there are the obvious things, like all the charts on the wall, the bulletin board with story cards; they are visual metaphors for communication."

"A lot of projects have walls full of charts and diagrams."

"Yes, but ours tell the truth. People believe them because they show both good and bad—just the facts ma'am," Sally said with a rather bad imitation of Jack Webb as Sergeant Friday. "Our documents are not fancy or polished, but they are useful—pragmatic aids to communication, not valuable artifacts in themselves."

"They're playful, too," suggested Ely as he joined the conversation, "like those object cubes that Dan made by taping three-by-five cards together. Remember the way that Suroor and I were juggling them as we talked through that problem last week?"

"And they can be stacked up—a metaphor for how you can build things with objects. As useful as they were, the old CRC cards could not do that easily. Building a house of cards is a lot harder than a house of blocks."

"A cube is a pretty simple shape—and XP prizes simplicity."

"It would take a videotape to show it, but the way our walls came to be covered in paper would contribute to the metaphor as well. When we started, the walls were bare; it was only as our knowledge of what we were doing increased that we had a need to externalize our group memory with the diagrams and object cubes."

Most of the team had joined the discussion by now, and Sally was looking around the group. "There is something else, maybe the most important thing of all—you. If you look at the people in this room, you see something very different than you would in any other software shop.

(continued)

Forward Thinking   *(continued)*

It's in everyone's body language and expressions and interactions. Hard to describe but very obvious. Everyone here has confidence—we all have internalized a lot of knowledge, not just about our project, but about object thinking and XP practices. It's a part of us as individuals."

"I know what you mean, and it's not just because we learned a few new programming tricks, or gained some experience, or even because this project is wildly successful. Somehow we have learned a new way to think about problems, a new vocabulary to think with, and a new way to perform—to work."

"And joy and serenity along with the confidence."

"Hah, sounds like we are all enlightened somehow."

"I think we are, at least in one important aspect. We have learned a lot about thinking, and we have applied it and we have somehow transcended it—as with Christopher Alexander's pattern language, we have passed through the gate and are living object thinking."

"What should we do with this enlightenment?"

"When the Zen monk was asked how he exhibited his enlightened state, he replied: when I am hungry I eat; when I am sleepy I sleep."

"And how does that apply to us?"

"Well, when Monday comes we will all come in and write software."

Models

Models are valuable only to the extent that they facilitate communication among human beings. (A model that can be "understood" by a computer is a programming language.) This implies that the effort required to construct the model must be less than the communication value that arises from its use. The dramatic failure of CASE can be traced almost entirely to the fact that the effort required to learn and use the tools far exceeded the ability of resultant models to facilitate communication.

Unfortunately, a learning curve and some degree of overhead will always be associated with the use of any set of models and any automated tool supporting the construction of those models. It's the balance between benefit and cost that's critical in determining whether models and tools will be useful.[12] In that spirit, none of the following are essential in the sense that you cannot do object thinking without them. None of the models have fixed syntax or content— what is presented is suggestive. All of the models can and should be simplified as the developer internalizes object thinking skills—until, as with the Cheshire cat, only the model's "smile" remains to evoke the knowledge in the head of the developer and of the development team.

Semantic Net

A semantic net consists of little more than nodes, arcs, and text labels (see Figure 6-3), with nodes representing things and arcs representing relationships among those things. Nodes are labeled with a noun or noun phrase and relationship arcs with a verb or verb phrase.

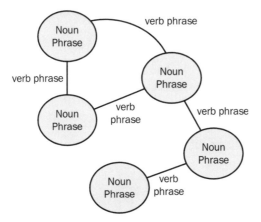

Figure 6-3   A semantic net, a brainstorming tool for discovery of potential objects in a domain.

A semantic net can be useful to jump-start a discussion of objects in the same way that underlining nouns and verb phrases in a written problem description. In both cases you are attempting to quickly identify potential objects and typical—in the domain—interactions among those objects. The primary utility of a semantic net is to serve as a brainstorming tool that can be used by a group of people simultaneously. (A good-size whiteboard is very useful.)

---

12. Booch clearly recognized that developers had an upper limit on the amount of time they were willing to expend learning a method or syntax. He advocated the use of a subset of his full modeling set, called whimsically "Booch Lite," as the kernel that was most useful most of the time.

The model produced need not persist beyond the point when the objects, responsibilities, and constraints identified have been transferred to other models (such as the object cube). The LIMT sidebar illustrates a typical use of a semantic net.

LIMT—Low-Income Mortgage Trust

The Legislature has created a $2 billion dollar fund—the LIMT—to help young couples acquire a home they ordinarily could not afford. Mortgages are granted to qualified couples. The trust subsidizes monthly mortgage payments when necessary, collects payments, and invests whatever capital is not tied up in mortgages.

To qualify for a mortgage:

1. A couple must have been married at least 1 year but not more than 10 years.

2. Both spouses must be gainfully employed. At the time of application, proof must be submitted of full-time employment for at least 48 of the previous 52 weeks.

3. The couple meets the LIMT definition of financial need by meeting one or both of the following requirements:

    ❑   Installments on a fixed-rate 30-year 90 percent mortgage for a qualified home exceed 28 percent of their combined gross income.

    ❑   They lack sufficient savings to pay 10 percent of the cost of the qualifying home plus $7,000 (the estimated closing costs).

A mortgage may be issued to qualified couples if

1. The price of the home to be purchased is below the published median price of homes in its area for the past 12 months.

2. The price of the home to be purchased is less than $150,000.

3. LIMT has sufficient funds to purchase the home.

    LIMT calculates weekly its pool of available mortgage funds as follows:

1. Expected annual income from investments is calculated and divided by 52.

(continued)

LIMT—Low-Income Mortgage Trust   *(continued)*

2. Expected annual operating expenses are calculated and divided by 52.

3. Total income from weekly mortgage payments is calculated.

4. Total of expected payment grants is calculated.

5. Pool amount is then equal to line 1 plus line 3, less line 2 plus line 4.

6. If the cost of homes to be purchased is less than the amount calculated in line 5, LIMT is deemed to have sufficient funds.

7. Unspent funds each week are invested.

If a mortgage is granted, the couple must

1. File an annual copy of their income tax form to confirm preceding-year income.

2. Submit copies of pay slips to confirm monthly gross income each week.

3. Make weekly payments on the mortgage as calculated. Payment amount may vary from week to week.

Weekly payments are calculated as follows:

1. Capital repayment is 1/1560 of the purchase price of the home.

2. Interest payment is 1/52 of 4 percent of the current mortgage balance.

3. Escrow payment is 1/52 of the sum of the annual property tax and the homeowner's insurance premium.

4. Total mortgage payment is the sum of lines 1 through 3.

5. The couple will pay a maximum of 28 percent of their weekly gross income. If the mortgage payment calculated exceeds the 28 percent limitation, a payment grant for the amount of the difference between the mortgage payment and the income limitation is provided by LIMT. This grant amount is not added to the outstanding debt.

(continued)

LIMT—Low-Income Mortgage Trust   *(continued)*

Processing requirements are as follows:

1. All data requirements must be updatable.

2. Annual return on investments is updated frequently by the brokerage firm.

3. Expected expenses are updated quarterly.

4. Available funds are computed every week. A report is printed showing the computation details and results.

5. A listing of all or a selected subset of investments is printed on demand.

6. A listing of all or a selected subset of mortgages is printed on demand.

7. Weekly mortgage payment notices (with payment grant amounts where applicable) are sent to mortgagees following calculation of the mortgage payment and payment grant amounts.

The required reports and queries are as follows:

1. List of mortgages by specified price range

2. List of past-due mortgage payments, with indication of which are fewer than 7 days, 8 to 14 days, 15 to 21 days, 22 to 28 days, and more than 29 days late

3. List of total grant amounts by month

4. Status of specified account

5. Combined details of mortgage application, mortgage information, and payment details

Figure 6-4 shows a semantic net based on the foregoing example. Remember that this is not intended to be "correct" or complete. A semantic net is a brainstorming tool, and one rule of brainstorming is to record everything, even if wrong, and save analysis and criticism for later. There will be nodes and connections on the net that will require clarification and modification. For example: a couple does not really have an employer—only individuals do, so it will eventually be necessary to indicate that a

(continued)

LIMT—Low-Income Mortgage Trust   *(continued)*

couple consists of individuals and individuals have an employer. Directed arcs—arrows—would definitely improve the readability of the semantic net, and you are encouraged to use them in flagrant violation of the syntactic specification for such a net. (Be more daring yet: if the relationship seems bilateral, use a double-headed arrow.)

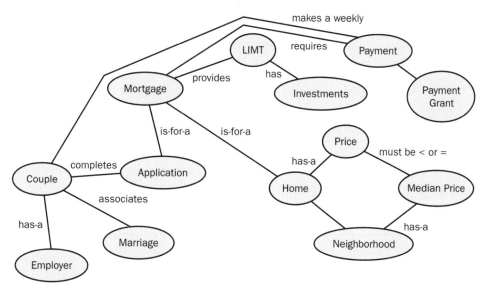

Figure 6-4   Semantic net for the LIMT example.

Object Cubes

An object cube is derived from the CRC card as invented by Beck and Cunningham and elaborated by Wirfs-Brock (particularly stereotypes). Object cubes offer single, consistent, metaphor-preserving model objects. The model is used to aid thinking about decomposition as well as design and some aspects of implementation. Each of the six sides of the cube, illustrated in Figure 6-5 through Figure 6-10, captures one critical aspect of the conceptualization of an object.

■　**Side 1**   (class, responsibilities, collaborations, the classic CRC card) contains the name of the class to which the object being modeled is an instance, a list of its responsibilities, and identification of any required collaborators.

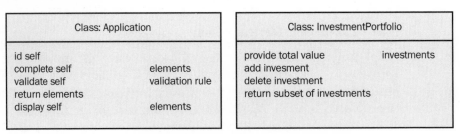

Class: Application		Class: InvestmentPortfolio	
id self		provide total value	investments
complete self	elements	add invesment	
validate self	validation rule	delete investment	
return elements		return subset of investments	
display self	elements		

Figure 6-5 The classic CRC card view of an object (LIMT example).

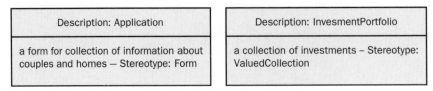

Description: Application	Description: InvesmentPortfolio
a form for collection of information about couples and homes — Stereotype: Form	a collection of investments – Stereotype: ValuedCollection

Figure 6-6 Object description and stereotype (LIMT example).

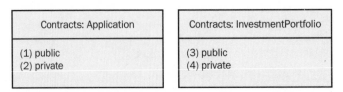

Contracts: Application	Contracts: InvestmentPortfolio
(1) public	(3) public
(2) private	(4) private

Figure 6-7 Contracts: categories of methods or responsibilities (LIMT example).

Knowledge Required: Application		Knowledge Required: InvestmentPortfolio	
id : aString	Variable	myInvestments : aCollection	Variable
myElements : a collection	Variable	invstmntToAdd : anInvstmnt	Argument
myRules : aCollection	Variable	elmntsRqstd : aSpec	Argument
elemntsReqstd : aSpec	Argument		

Figure 6-8 Knowledge required by an object (LIMT example).

Draft Message Protocol: Application	Draft Message Protocol: InvestmentPortfolio
id	add: anInvestment
id: aString	delete: anInvestmentId
instantiate	return: aSpecification
validate	totalValue
rules	
rules: aCollection	

Figure 6-9 Message protocol.

Events Generated: Application	Events Generated: InvestmentPortfolio
funded -- notifies of change in status	bankrupt -- portfolio reached zero value

Figure 6-10 Events generated by an object.

- **Side 2** includes a text description of the nature of the objects represented by the class. Stereotypes (as defined by Wirfs-Brock) should be included on this side and any notations helpful for implementation.

- **Side 3** provides a list of named contracts, the most common of which will be *public*, *private*, and *protected*. Contracts[13] are intended to reveal the intent of the class creator as to who should be able to send particular messages. Some programming languages enforce this intent (Java), and others do not (Smalltalk). Each contract lists the messages (entire signature or just the selector) that should be included in that contract.

- **Side 4** identifies the discrete pieces of information that an object will require if it is to fulfill its assigned responsibilities. Each piece of information is given a descriptive label, a code indicating the source of the knowledge, and the name of the class that will embody or contain that knowledge.

- **Side 5** lists all of the messages that an object agrees it will respond to. Each message listed here will identify the message selector, or message name; indicate whether any arguments are required (and if so, the class of each argument); and identify the class of the object returned in response to the sending of the message.

- **Side 6** names and describes any events (changes in the state of an object) that other objects might want to be made aware of.

Interaction Diagram

Interaction diagrams are versatile: they're used to aid discovery as well as to capture implementation specifications. They model the communication among a group of objects engaged in a particular task. Most behavioral object thinkers

---

13. Historically, contracts could be used to aggregate messages by the class of potential senders. Contracts can also be used to reflect the "method categories" that appear in some IDE browsers for some languages. Care should be taken in this case to avoid contracts that are language or programming tool specific.

employ the term *scenario* for interaction diagrams or a nested set of such diagrams. Each scenario is bounded by a precondition (what must be true and what message must be sent to initiate the scenario) and a postcondition (what is to be returned when the scenario completes normally). Figure 6-11 illustrates the syntactic components of an interaction diagram. Figure 6-12 uses the syntactic elements of Figure 6-11 to capture a specific conversation—filling in and validating an application for a mortgage.

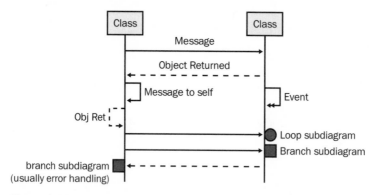

Figure 6-11   In this set of symbols from an interaction diagram, symbols whose labels appear in italics are additions to standard UML.

Use cases, as advocated by Jacobson, are a nested set of scenarios (interaction diagrams) whose precondition and postcondition are defined by a single exchange between a user role and the target system.

A text equivalent of an interaction diagram (see Figure 6-13) is a simple table with the preconditions and postconditions noted as headers and columns named Client, Request, Server, Object Returned, and Comments. The Client, Server, and Object Returned columns contain text labels for objects. The Request column contains a text description of the request. It will eventually map to a message sent to the server by the client. The Comments column contains any explanatory text or commentary found to be useful.

A still simpler form (see Figure 6-14) can capture the same information as a top-level use case diagram: the requests and responses between a user role and the system. These might also be used to exhaustively list all requests that might be made by one object of exactly one other object. The model has a header that identifies the Client object and the Server object. Columns are available for listing the requests that the client makes, the object returned as a result of a given request, and comments.

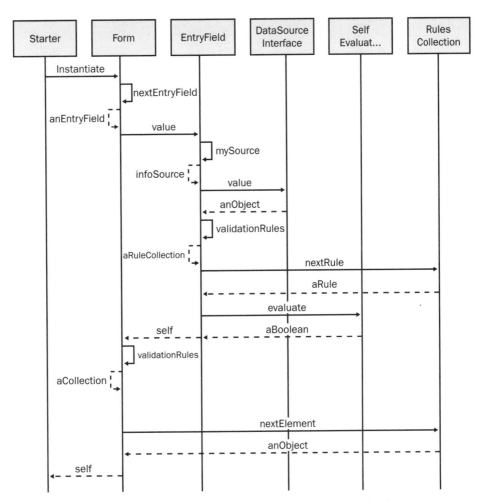

Figure 6-12   This interaction diagram illustrates the conversation required to fill in and validate a mortgage application.

Pre: blank form				Post: form filled-in
Client	**Message**	**Receiver**	**Object Returned**	**Comments**
Form	Next field	self	An entry field	
Entry field	Value please	Human user	A value	
Human user	value is (x)	Entry field	self	Iterate until all fields have values

Figure 6-13   Text-only equivalent of the previously modeled interaction diagram.

Client: aUserRole		Server: anObject
Request	**Object Returned**	**Comments**
Daily report	A report	Example of message that might be sent to the "System Object" a la a use case.
First element	An object	An example of a specific message sent to an arbitrary collection object.

Figure 6-14   This text-only binary use case model captures the same information as a top-level use case diagram.

These models are useful in defining the high-level responsibilities of an application in the same way as a traditional context diagram (one system bubble, several external entities, and connecting arcs labeled with highly generalized data flows) or a graphical use case model (one system bubble with stick figures representing user roles, and connecting arcs labeled to reflect generalized requests and responses). The intent is to define user/system interactions at a high-enough level of abstraction to ensure discovery of an exhaustive list. This type of model might also be used in cases in which an exhaustive list of potential interactions between two objects is required. I have seen this type of use in a medical device specification.

It is unlikely that you would use binary use case models to capture all interactions in a system. The number of models required to do so is $n!$ (n factorial), where n is the number of objects in your system. Even simple systems would require a huge number of binary use cases to capture all possible interactions. Most developers will reserve the use of this particular model to capturing interactions with objects or systems external to your immediate development focus, or to low-level interactions among a subset of objects involved in critical conversations—wherein every possible interaction must be identified and dealt with appropriately.

Static Relation Diagram

The static relation diagram is probably the most familiar to any software developer of all the models presented here. Static relation diagrams depict relationships, relatively static in nature, among a group of classes. Here are three common examples and their uses:

- **Class hierarchy**   A simple diagram showing a single relationship: is-a-kind-of. The root (topmost class) of the hierarchy is labeled, by convention, *Object*. Many class hierarchy diagrams will be focused on a subset of an entire domain and might not have *Object* as root. Figure 6-15 is an example of a class hierarchy diagram.

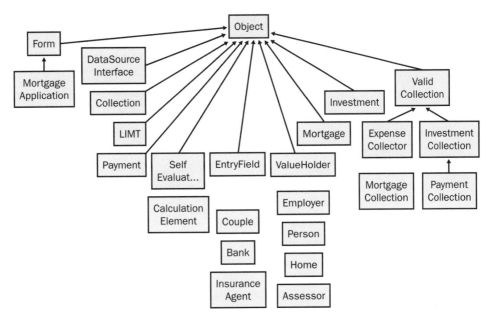

Figure 6-15   A class hierarchy diagram showing single inheritance only.

- **Gestalt map**   The most appropriate use of such diagrams is to provide an overview, or gestalt, of a system or an application while minimizing the amount of detail. A semantic net is a simple example of a gestalt map. Gestalt maps, an example of which is shown in Figure 6-16, provide a convenient shared reference point that reminds developers of the objects involved in an application and important ways in which they are related. Some very common types of relationships captured on a gestalt map include is-a-part-of, is-a-collection-of, is-composed-of, uses, coordinates, associates, and is-a-kind-of. (These types of relationships often have their own graphical syntax representation instead of requiring a text label.) Notice the absence of labels such as *Manages* or *Controls*, relationships that should not exist from an object thinking point of view. Decorations and annotations added to a gestalt map enable the capture of constraints or business rules.

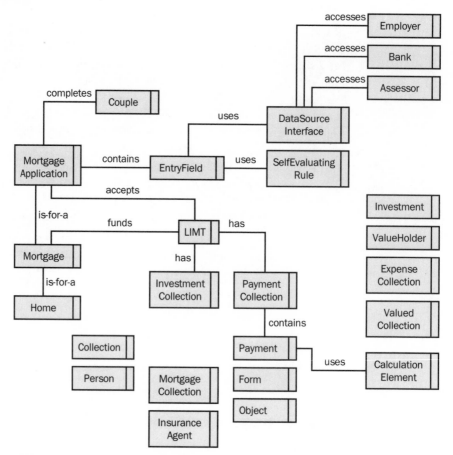

Figure 6-16   A gestalt map provides an overview of the objects and their static relationships.

The more you add special annotations and decorations to the syntax of a gestalt map, the more likely you are to abuse its intent by showing too much detail. A gestalt map is not a set of blueprints, using the analogy of a building; it's the 3-D model that shows what the building will look like in its planned setting without the minute details.

In Chapter 10, a very different kind of gestalt map, an "evocative" map, is introduced. This kind of gestalt map is more appropriate for XP development because it doesn't fall into the trap of being exhaustively representational.

■ **Collective memory map**   A specialized static relation that shows how knowledge is distributed among a community of objects and that provides structural and definitional metadata relevant to that knowledge. Specifically, it notes the distribution of objects—stored in instance variables of other objects—whose primary purpose is to represent some piece of data (strings, numbers, dates, or the like). Special-purpose structures—for example, *valueHolders* (a simple indexed collection, with each element consisting of a label and a value associated with that label)—are composed entirely of these data representation objects. Any constraints and relationships that exist among this subset of objects are noted on this diagram. The most typical examples of such constraints or relationships are analogous to the key/foreign key relationships found in a standard relational data model and to class (type) or value domains typically defined in data dictionaries or schemas. Figure 6-17 shows a collective memory map.

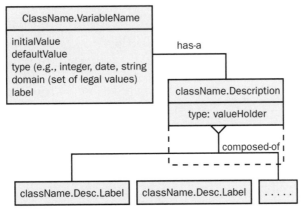

Figure 6-17   A collective memory map, a static view of the "data" in a system.

Collective memory maps constitute a nod to anyone deeply concerned with data representations and who miss their entity relation diagrams. The utility of these diagrams is easily overstated, and judicious and conservative use is encouraged.

Object State Chart

David Harel revolutionized state modeling with his *state charts*. Almost all object modelers now use at least a subset of his notation to capture state-dependent information about objects. A typical subset of Harel state chart notation is shown in Figure 6-18.

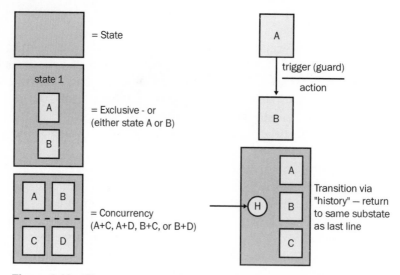

Figure 6-18   The most commonly used symbols borrowed from Harel.

Properly defined and designed, most objects will have an exceedingly simple state. Therefore, the use of this kind of diagram to model object state is seldom required. Object state charts are extremely useful for modeling state-driven interactions among objects, such as the interactions that occur in a typical GUI.

I'd like to conclude this chapter by repeating one of the caveats presented at the beginning: no tool has any value other than to assist in object thinking and to provide a means for interpersonal communication. If you can model your objects and your scenarios in your head while engaged in writing code, and if those mental models are consistent with object thinking, great! No need to write them down. If you and your colleagues use a visual model on a whiteboard as an aid in talking about scenarios and in clarifying your collective thinking about those scenarios, and you erase the board when you're done meeting, also great! If your models are crudely drawn and use only a subset of the syntax defined here (or a completely different syntax that you and your colleagues collectively agree upon), still great! Model when you must, what you must, and only what you must.

7

Discovery

It is said, "A journey of a thousand miles begins with a single step."
—Anonymous

This adage is usually quoted as a motivation: "Get started, and the rest will follow." The adage misses the potential problem, however, of what happens if that first step is in the wrong direction. It isn't necessary to be a fan of chaos theory to recognize that even the smallest change in initial conditions (the first step) can have enormous impact on the eventual results.

For instance, suppose you are in Albuquerque, New Mexico. (Bugs Bunny was famous for making a wrong turn here.) You want to go to Washington, D.C., following a direct line slightly north of east. Unfortunately, you were celebrating your coming departure last night, you arose much later than usual, and, thinking it was morning and the sun was rising in the east, you headed off in the direction of the sun. You might still get to Washington, D.C. (the Earth is round, after all), but your journey will be rather tortuous and take an inordinate amount of time.

Beginnings are just as critical in software development, and initial mistakes are a lot more common than one might suppose. A truism of software development is that the most costly mistakes are made the first day. Two major factors make beginnings so perilous in software. The first is simply a lack of knowledge. We know the least about the what, the how, and the why of our development project at the beginning. This should be so obvious that it need not be stated, but surprisingly, we insist on making critical decisions about projects (such as overall design, timelines, and costs) at the very time we are least prepared to make them.

Management usually takes the heat for this mistake. An oft repeated statement (that I heard in a keynote speech at a conference, but is really a paraphrase of a famous Santayana quote[1]) is, "Insanity is doing the same thing that failed last time and expecting it to work this time." Management, it is said, is guilty of precisely this and therefore should be considered insane. But it is not insanity at work here—it is culture. If the rationalist philosophers had been correct and the formalist software engineers had been correct, it would have been perfectly reasonable to assume that we *should* be able to define perfect specifications and derive working software from those specifications with mechanical transformations. Computer scientists, software engineers, and rationalist western culture in general have been selling management a bill of goods.

The second most common source of error, especially by experienced developers, is to anticipate how the computer is going to implement your software before trying to understand how the software should simulate some part of the domain in which it is going to be used. This is *computer thinking*, as described in earlier chapters. If you start the development process, as is almost always done, focusing first on what you are going to tell the computer to do and how it is to do it, you have started your thousand-mile journey with a 180-degree misstep. There may have been a time when computers were so hard to use, limited in capability, and expensive that it was expedient to use them and their requirements as a lens through which the rest of the world was "cut and measured," but that is clearly not the case today.

> **Note**   The argument in favor of computer thinking almost always revolves around the issue of efficiency or performance. But as the developers of SIMULA discovered, if you get the modeling and simulation correct, you get a surprising amount of performance as a byproduct. One of the axioms of XP admonishes making things work and making them right before attempting to make them fast. Even classical software engineers are adamant about the need to save performance issues for the very end of development. But it isn't just performance— it's the focus on the machine as the ground for understanding the software development project that constitutes the wrong first step.

Sometimes it is necessary to foreshadow implementation (programming). You might need to ask yourself the question, "Can I build this?" Thinking about

---

1. Original quote from George Santayana: "Fanaticism consists in redoubling your efforts when you have forgotten your aim."

implementation can give you a general answer. When you are first thinking about writing tests and code, you will think about how you are going to implement a specific story. You will have already done the design, the identification of objects, visualization of the basic conversations among those objects, and the assignment of methods to those objects involved in your story—quite possibly in your head or via discussion with your pair programming partner. Thinking about the code at this point provides useful feedback. You might discover you have a bad design, bad language, or code that needs refactoring.

It's never appropriate to tell yourself, "This is what the code will look like, so I need an object to hold these parts of the code, and another to hold these parts, and another to make sure these two do what they are told to do when they are told to do it," which is precisely what structured development tempts you to do.

Perhaps the greatest benefit of object thinking is that of helping you start off in the right direction. Object thinking does this by emphasizing the need to *understand the domain first*.

Domain Understanding

Understanding the domain involves five types of mental discipline reinforced by object thinking principles and ideas:

■   Extract your understanding of the domain from the domain; use the metaphor of domain anthropology to guide this effort. The goal of software development is to create artifacts, with each artifact consisting of an admixture of hardware, software, processes, and interfaces allowing interaction with other artifacts or with people. Deciding which artifacts are needed and how they will be required to interact with existing (and planned) artifacts as well as with people is a result of understanding the domain—as the domain is understood by its inhabitants. (See the sidebar in the next section of this chapter, "Domain Anthropology and Management.")

■   Decompose the problem space into behavioral objects, and make sure the behaviors assigned to those objects are consistent with user expectations. This requires understanding why users make distinctions among objects and the *illusions* they project on those objects. User illusions (following Alan Kay) consist of how people recognize different objects in their world and, having recognized an object, what assumptions are made about how to interact with that object and what its responses will be.

■ User illusions should be maintained; your software objects should not violate them unless you can construct a plausible alternative story that shows a different set of domain entities interacting in different ways or having different capabilities. Business reengineering involves exactly this kind of activity—using domain language and user illusions creatively to craft new stories, some of which might lead to new software.

■ Decompose your problems (applications) in terms of conversations among groups of objects. Everything of interest in the domain is currently accomplished by groups of objects (people and things). Any artifact you construct must participate in a natural way in these same groups. Perhaps your artifact is simply replacing an existing object in the domain with a computer-based simulacrum, in which case it must know how to respond to and supply some relevant subset of recognizable and intuitive interaction cues. Perhaps it is an entirely new object, in which case it will need to be "socialized" to conform to the existing community.

■ Model your objects as simply as possible consistent with the needs of the development team (which should include users, à la XP) to communicate their collective understanding of the objects and the domain. Only after you have completed this kind of modeling should you even begin to think about how to implement any new or replacement objects your domain understanding leads you to believe are desirable.

This chapter will discuss how object thinking influences your understanding of the domain, its objects, and the models useful for clarifying and communicating your understanding. Chapter 8, "Thinking Toward Design," will outline how to move toward implementation without abandoning object thinking or our understanding of the domain.

Domain understanding involves using another metaphor, domain anthropology, to provide the mental perspective used when discovering objects and their interactions. The same perspective is useful for identifying and assigning discrete services to specific objects. A number of heuristics can be employed to facilitate object discovery and definition. I will now discuss each of these factors in turn.

Domain Anthropology

The software developer must confront a strange world with the goal of understanding that world in its own terms. A close approximation of this task is the work of a cultural anthropologist confronting a strange (to her or him) society. Domain anthropology provides a very useful metaphor—providing both cautions and insights that will guide the application of object thinking to the early phases (requirements definition, object identification) of development. Software expertise does not trump domain expertise. The longer a software developer works in a domain, the more effective her software work will be.

I begin with a caution: anthropologists have their own culture—with its associated explanations, values, assumptions, and so forth—and they must zealously guard against the mistake of interpreting everything in the new society in terms of their own (often unconscious) culture and values. This kind of cultural relativism should be respected—the software developer does not have a "special" viewpoint that allows him to judge or alter the culture he is working with.

Software developers, on the other hand, are fair game for evangelistic efforts. Most developers are steeped in the "way of the computer," with abundant assumptions about how a computer works and the best ways to make a computer perform its tricks. You could say that developers have internalized a culture of computing. The fact that this book—as well as the object and XP movements in general—is trying to change developer culture does not imply that developers have a corresponding right to change user or organizational cultures. Developers, traditional or reformed, must set aside their professional culture (just as the anthropologist sets aside his or her birth culture) before they attempt to understand users and user domains. Following this injunction is inconsistent with the goals and intents of the stereotypical "computer geek" who has invested a lot of time and energy to think like a computer.

> **Note**   To be totally honest, this book is attempting to influence more than just the culture of software developers. To begin with, I hope it affects all members of an XP development team, which includes both users and managers, and that it promotes change of the organizational culture-at-large in ways that make it more amenable to iterative, extreme object development. Even more grandiose hopes fill my mind from time to time—that I will make a small contribution to a movement that redefines software as a craft performed by human beings on behalf of other human beings. Beneath the staid exterior of the practitioner-academician beats the heart of a wild-eyed evangelist.

A developer attempting to understand a new application or problem domain is not unlike an anthropologist confronting a new culture for the first time. She is surrounded with experts in that domain, but they speak and act in "strange ways" that she needs to understand. You need to learn from them how they view and make sense of their world.

> **Note**   As an "anthropologist" and an outsider, you do have a perspective that the domain experts lack. Much of what the domain experts actually do and think about is invisible to them in the same way that a human is rarely aware of the culture to which he or she belongs. You will be able to observe important aspects of the domain that the experts will fail to report to you or talk about because they are "so obvious" that they are below the threshold of consciousness. But do not confuse this kind of objectivity with projections of your own cultural values (computer knowledge) onto the domain you are supposed to be observing.

When a cultural anthropologist confronts a new culture, the first task (after allaying suspicion and obtaining some kind of rapport) is to learn the language. The object developer needs to learn the names of things in the domain that have been accorded object status by the natives—made distinct from the domain and from other things in the domain—by virtue of having been given a name. Naming things is how domain experts (and the indigenous peoples studied by the cultural anthropologist) naturally decompose their domain.

> **Note**   Software developers must also allay suspicion and establish rapport. An anthropologist does this in two ways, by convincing the "natives" that he is basically harmless and an amusing curiosity and by being a source of minor valuables—services such as a ride, small amounts of money, or goods desired by the people he is studying. These techniques work reasonably well if the people do not have extensive experience with anthropologists. They don't work very well when there is an adverse history of interactions. Native American people, for example, are extremely leery of anthropologists (excepting sometimes anthropologists that are also Native American) because they have been exploited too many times in too many ways. The world of software suffers from this same kind of adverse history. The whole reason there is so much emphasis on requirements and specifications is to provide the basis for a contract between two groups that basically distrust each other. Perhaps the most useful pointers and techniques for overcoming this mistrust can be found in the work of Larry Constantine and even the domain-driven design ideas advanced by Eric Evans.

Most books and methods addressing how to do object development recommend that the object discovery process begin with underlining the nouns (names) in a domain or problem description. While it is true that many of those nouns will indeed turn out to be viable objects, it is unlikely that any written description will be sufficiently complete or accurate to meet the needs of domain anthropology. Cultural anthropologists do not base their understanding of a culture solely on written reports by people in that culture. They go and live with the people, observe them, and talk with them. Domain anthropologists must do the same thing.

Domain Anthropology and Management

Anthropological investigation of a culture is not an easy task. The anthropologist will spend months, if not years, preparing to go to the field. That preparation includes digesting all that is already known about the target culture (and other similar cultures) as well as techniques for observation and information elicitation. Once in the field, the anthropologist will spend a minimum of a year, optimally two years, living and interacting with the people he is studying.

A domain anthropologist should do no less! Observation for a complete business cycle (including the annual financial cycle), which includes the major events and rituals (new employee to company picnic) that occur in the domain, will yield important information relevant to the design and success of any new software system.

However, management is unlikely to provide the necessary time for this kind of activity—at least not as overhead for any single project—if domain anthropology is seen as a new "phase" of software development that must be completed "up-front" before any code is written. XP, fortunately, builds domain anthropology into its practices. Early and frequent releases, short feedback cycles, and open communication all work together to simulate the participant/observation experience of a domain anthropologist. As with the anthropologist, these activities begin with fairly simple day-to-day activities (and the new software to support them) and evolve, as the developers gain experience with the domain, into more sophisticated systems. There are other parallels, such as the on-site customer playing a role quite similar to that of the cultural informant relied upon by anthropologists.

Given that management will likely not allow time for a complete ethnography, some kind of conversation about the domain with both users and developers participating is desirable. Constructing a semantic net (see Chapter 6, "Method,

Process, and Models") is a useful way to gather information about potential objects and expectations of those objects. While constructing this net, the domain anthropologist must operate, somewhat, as if she were a naive child—constantly asking

"What is this?"

"Why is this considered to be a _____?"

"How do you distinguish between this and that?"

"Why?"

The answers to these questions not only reveal potential objects but also start to reveal the expectations that domain experts have of those objects. Begin the object discovery via the semantic net technique by asking for one or two sentences about the domain in general, such as two sentences that describe what your company/department/team does. Select a couple of nouns and verb phrases, and write the first elements of a semantic net (see Figure 7-1) on a whiteboard. Ask everyone present to brainstorm new elements (circles, nouns) and new connections (arcs, verb phrases). This exercise should be a stream of consciousness—brainstorming—session, with analytical discussion to follow later.

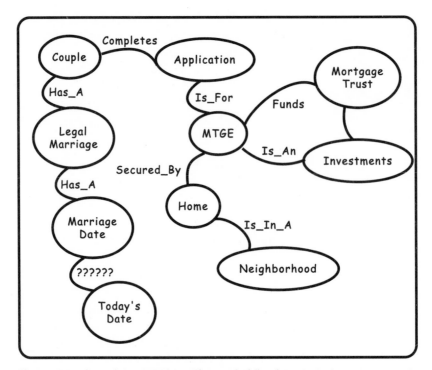

Figure 7-1   A partial semantic net for a subsidized mortgage company.

It usually takes but a short period of time, five to ten minutes, to produce a fairly large diagram. The circled nouns provide a rich set of potential objects, and the relationships provide an equally rich set of potential responsibilities (expectations of those objects). This semantic net can then be placed on the wall as a common reference point as the discussion proceeds to more detailed levels.

Subsidized Mortgage Company

The partial semantic net in Figure 7-1 is based on the following conversation about a company that provides subsidized mortgages to qualified couples.

Please give me a brief description of your company.

Our company provides mortgages to qualified couples, subsidizes monthly mortgage payments when necessary, collects payments, invests whatever capital is not tied up in mortgages, and otherwise manages its assets. (This yields an initial net consisting of bubbles for mortgage, couple, payment, investment, and asset. Initial arcs include investment is_an asset, couple receives mortgage.)

I assume the mortgage is for a home?

Yes, a home that must have a purchase price less than or equal to the median price of all homes in its neighborhood. Oh, and the home cannot have a purchase price greater than $100,000.

What qualifies a couple for a mortgage?

Couples must have been married for at least 1 year, but not more than 10, and be gainfully employed. They will not have the required 10 percent down payment required by other lenders, and the monthly payments on a $90,000 mortgage will exceed 28 percent of their joint gross income.

What do you mean by gainful employment?

At the time of application, proof must be submitted of full-time employment for at least 48 of the previous 52 weeks.

We also have to have funds available that are sufficient to cover the mortgage.

How do you know if you have funds available?

We calculate our expected income from investments and divide by 52 (we calculate available funds weekly); we figure our annual operating expenses and divide by 52; we total weekly income from mortgage payments (oh yes, we also collect mortgage payments weekly); and we calculate any grants we expect to give out this week. Expected annual income from investments is calculated and divided by 52 and added to the pool of funds. We then compare the cost of the mortgage or mortgages applied for with

(continued)

Subsidized Mortgage Company   *(continued)*

---

the amount of money in the pool and fund all we can. Any leftover money is invested.

People have to apply for the mortgage? (Note the naive question.)

Of course they fill out an application, and when the information on the application is verified, the application is deemed fundable. If we have money, we grant the mortgage and the application is given funded status. If we do not have the money this week, the application stays fundable until it is funded or some other event causes it to be canceled.

One reason for reducing the object discovery process to simple questions and observations is to eliminate preconceptions. If a cultural anthropologist were to begin an analysis of kinship with the preconception that everyone lives in a nuclear family (mother, father, and 2.5 children) and that everyone practices monogamy, her analysis of human kinship patterns would be so incomplete and distorted that it would be worthless.

An analogous result will occur if the domain anthropologist begins her task with preconceptions about data, functions, processes, how things must be implemented in COBOL, or how computers work. These preconceptions about implementation will blind the domain anthropologist to what is going on in the domain and what is required of the new software artifact. For instance, a software expert is likely to see any kind of form as an ordered collection of static text objects and entry field objects because that's the way that a form will be implemented. If this knowledge disposes the expert to ask users only those questions dealing with choices of text and entry fields and the values that can be placed in an entry field, the expert will miss potentially important behavioral requirements. Behavioral requirements for a form might include identifying itself, modifying itself, presenting itself (with the implication of multiple views), completing itself (making sure every entry field contains appropriate values), and validating itself. These are behaviors that will not be discovered by asking about contents.

The initial focus of domain anthropology is on identifying stories and some potential objects in the domain. Stories reveal both potential objects and some of the "social relationships" among them. Human cultures have rules for interaction among their members. People engage in a complex web of mutual obligations that change with time and circumstance. People participate in relationships, some fixed (such as biological parentage) and others temporary (such as employer-employee). Similar social relationships exist among objects, and they too must be discovered.

Note   Another warning: We have "trained" users over the years to anticipate how software developers think. It is not unlikely, therefore, that they, at least initially, will try to tell you what they think you want to hear. They will couch their responses to your questions in terms of data, attributes, algorithms, and functions. When this happens, they must be questioned further to discover the behavior involved.

The metaphor of an object as a person is important for developers to begin to understand objects. It is equally useful for domain experts and should be discussed with them preliminary to any question-and-answer session. Both the developer and the domain expert can then use a common language in their discovery dialog. For example:

"*Well, there are customers.*" (User offers a potential object.)

"What do you expect of a customer?"

"*It should tell me its name, or identify itself.*"

"What else?"

"*It has a unique identification number.*"

"Do you want it to tell you that number?"

"*Yes.*"

"Then we can say it must report or tell you its unique identification number."

"*Yes, and it should tell me its address, phone number, age, gender, birth date ...*"

"Wait a second, you mean it should be able to describe itself and tell you how to contact it?"

"*Yes, yes, exactly.*"

Details, and in some cases discovery, of some relationships will occur only as attention shifts to defining tests and writing code (and the implicit design that occurs simultaneously). The domain anthropologist (embodied in the on-site customer working with technical developers) focuses on how and why objects interact and, in some cases, why they do not interact—in other words, what rules prevent a specific object from certain types of interactions with other objects.

How objects interact is mostly a matter of recording actual and possible (desirable) conversations among objects. Why is mostly answered by seeking the task or tasks that motivated the conversation. There are different ways to organize the work required to solicit all the conversations and tasks relevant to our understanding of the domain and of the objects we might have to build to operate in that domain.

One way to organize this work—fairly traditional in a software engineering sense—would be to isolate a subset of the objects in the domain, draw an arbitrary boundary around them, and label the collective the *NewSystem* object. You could then ask each remaining object in the domain to identify the services it might require of the *NewSystem* object. The set of nonduplicated services constitutes the responsibilities/behaviors of *NewSystem*. These, in turn, will need to be examined to expose the actual multiobject conversations required to provide the identified service. Conversations might have subconversations. Eventually this process will yield a set of nested conversations, each nested thread being a *use case* as that concept was developed by Ivar Jacobson and incorporated into UML. Alternative, and probably better, ways to approach this work can be found by reading Alistair Cockburn's work on use cases and Larry Constantine's discussion of "essential form."

Each threaded conversation can be modeled, using UML syntax, with a high-level diagram (similar to the context diagram of structured development) that represents each service consumer (user role) as a labeled stick figure and the *NewSystem* object as a labeled circle. (See Figure 7-2.) The making of a request by a service consumer defines a precondition for some conversation among objects within the *NewSystem* circle. The return of an object to the service consumer constitutes a postcondition for that same conversation. The conversation itself can be modeled with an interaction diagram. (The syntax used to construct interaction diagrams is covered in Chapter 6, "Method, Process, and Models.") Interaction diagrams can be nested, although UML graphical syntax provides no way to represent the presence or absence of a subscenario. The extended UML syntax shown in Chapter 6 does provide for branching and looping subscenario notation for the interaction diagram.

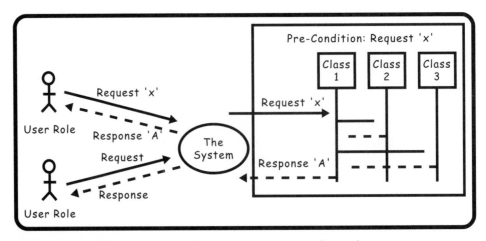

Figure 7-2   A UML-style, top-level (analogous to a context diagram) partial use case.

> **Note**   Use whichever syntax (graphical or textual) you prefer. Remember, object philosophy questions the utility of any representation or model beyond its immediate assistance to those involved in making the model. Don't get caught up in trying to make your model "complete," "accurate," or "true."

This same information about the objects in a domain and their interaction can be modeled textually. The system request table (Figure 7-3) replaces the stick figure diagram of UML, and the conversation table replaces the graphical interaction diagram (Figure 7-4).

Requester: (User Role) Control Tower		
Request	**OBJ Returned**	**Comments**
where is airplane x?	a location	sent to airplane
what planes are in my airspace?	a collection of planes	
are any planes in danger of colliding?	an alert	implicit question, for error handling
remove plane x from my airspace		no object returned, but blip disappears
add plane x to my airspace	a blip	

Figure 7-3   In this system request table, the service requester is identified at the top. (*NewSystem* is assumed to be the service provider.) Each line identifies the service requested: the message sent to *NewSystem*, the object returned as a result of that request, and notes for explanations if needed. Each line of the table constitutes a precondition/postcondition for a conversation.

PreCondition: BlankForm			PreCondition: allFields	
Client	Request	Provider	Object Resumed	Comments
form	nameField	self	aField	
form	instantiate	aField	self	
afield	valueplace	aDataSource	aValue	
afield	validate	self	self	
...				
...				

Figure 7-4 In this conversation table, preconditions and postconditions are noted at the top of table. Each line of the table shows who is making a request, the nature of the request (message), the service provider, the object returned, and a comment if necessary. The conversational order is assumed to be top down.

There is nothing necessarily wrong—or non-object-thinking—with the systematic approach just outlined. To be systematic, however, it presumes a concerted effort to identify all use cases up front and is based on defining the requirements for *NewSystem*. An alternative approach, one much more consistent with XP ideas and techniques, would be to define stories one object (or a small number of objects) at a time. All the same elements of discovery are present that would be in a systematic approach—it's simply a philosophic preference to do things in the small.

We begin, this time, by looking at the semantic net constructed earlier and noting the relationship (completes) between couple and application. We then write a simple story about this relationship:

A couple requests an application for a mortgage and fills in all necessary blanks.

This story gets expanded into a sequence of interactions:

1.   The couple glances at the application to make sure it is the right one (implicitly asking the application to identify itself).

2. The couple looks for the first blank spot (implicitly asking the application for the next space needed to be filled in).

3. The couple asks what information needs to be placed in that spot (implicitly asking the blank space for its label, on the assumption that the label will describe the information needed).

4. The couple enters a value in the blank spot.

5. Steps 2 through 4 are repeated (next blank spot replacing first blank spot in the description of step 2) until there are no more blank spots.

This conversation can be graphically depicted with an interaction diagram, as shown in Figure 7-5.

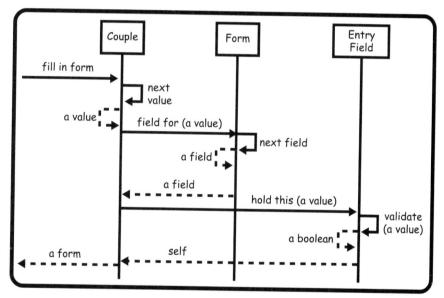

Figure 7-5   This interaction diagram depicts the user-driven conversation required to fill in a form.

This conversation assumes an *active* couple object and a *passive* form object. In one sense, this reflects reality: a paper form is pretty passive, and a couple is made up of live human beings capable of action. Nevertheless, it isn't as reflective of object thinking as it might be. Consider the alternative story card:

A couple requests an application. The application, the couple, and entryField *objects collaborate to make sure every* entryField *needing a value contains one.*

This leads to a conversation with the following steps (graphically depicted in Figure 7-6):

1. The couple requests an application from *SubsidizedMortgageCompany*. (Our conversation reveals a new object capable of providing an application.)

2. The application presents itself to the couple. (Implicit identity verification plus ability of the object to display itself.)

3. The application identifies the next *entryField* (or fields, since both a paper form and a GUI-based computer screen allow multiple *entryField* objects to request input simultaneously) requiring content by asking itself for the next field (or fields) and then notifies that *entryField* (those *entryField* objects) that it/they now has/have the opportunity to obtain content.

4. The *entryField* asks the couple for input. (Implicit request, manifested by asking a *blinkingCursor* to display itself in the area of the *entryField* or by highlighting itself in some other way.)

5. The couple provides a value.

6. The *entryField* notifies the application that it is satisfied.

   If it is not satisfied, an exception condition exists, and a story describing how to handle that case must be defined.

7. Steps 3 through 6 are repeated until the supply of *entryField* objects associated with the application is exhausted.

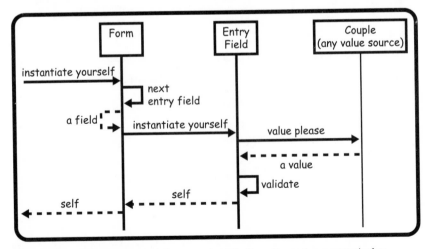

Figure 7-6 This interaction diagram depicts the alternative scenario for filling in an application.

Differences in the conversation are minimal, but they reflect the behavioral parity of all objects—that every object, including humans filling the role of information provider, are defined in terms of the services they can provide others. Each object is an active entity in control of its own destiny. The alternative way of thinking about the conversation also reveals objects that might not have been discovered or thought about in the original model of the conversation.

More important, the thinking behind the alternative conversational model is more general—more abstract—and therefore applicable regardless of the means of implementing the application. Behavioral expectations of the application and its parts are consistent whether implemented with paper or as a software application. True, the software versions of the objects have more interesting or dynamic ways of exhibiting behavior. An example is the *entryField* object using the services of a *blinkingCursor* instead of simply displaying itself as a blank space.

The alternative model is also more consistent with user expectations of the objects involved, which is the real goal of domain anthropology. If we are to build digital versions of forms and entry fields, they should reflect the expectations of their naturally occurring counterparts. For example:

- We expect application forms (any form, for that matter) to "present" their constituent parts (labels and entry fields) to us in an organized and reasonably clustered way. In the digital manifestation of the form, this is accomplished through interaction with a cursor or, more crudely, by presenting the entry fields to the user one at a time. In the paper implementation, the form still presents the elements to us in order but does so implicitly—taking advantage of cultural conventions.[2]

- We expect entry fields to ask us to enter a value. The digital version does so by using a blinking cursor assistant object to remind us that it is waiting and refusing to go away until it is satisfied. The paper version does so by nagging us simply by remaining blank. Nature abhors a vacuum no less than a human abhors a blank spot on a form.

The value of applying object thinking to conversation discovery and modeling will become more evident as we consider responsibility assignment and discovery in more detail. Here's a preview: allowing *entryField* objects and form objects to validate themselves in collaboration with another object (a rule object). A paper-based entry field seeks validation by displaying its content to a human and asking for confirmation or replacement of its displayed contents. A digital version could do the same thing by asking a rule or rules to evaluate themselves (to true or false) using the value held by the entry field as one of the rule variables.

---

2. Reflects U.S. and Western culture. Other cultures use right-to-left and down before left-to-right conventions.

A reader note earlier in this chapter suggested that a domain anthropologist brings to bear a certain sensitivity or objectivity by virtue of being an outsider. Seeing the implicit behavior of forms and entry fields, just noted in immediately preceding paragraphs, is an example of applying this kind of objectivity. It would not occur to a typical user to volunteer how they interact with forms and entry fields because that interaction is based on cultural conventions that are nonconsciously applied. The conventions are nevertheless real and need to be identified and exploited in order to develop and design the most robust objects and applications.

Object Definition

Semantic nets and stories (scenarios, use cases, interaction diagrams) provide input, but the most critical aspect of discovery is object definition. Each object must be identified in terms of its actual or intended use in the problem space— the domain. The metaphor of domain anthropology continues to shape our thinking about each individual object and what we expect of it in terms of services (behaviors, responsibilities).

Each circle on the semantic net is a potential object. We can select any one of them and attempt to identify all of the services such an object might provide in its domain—*in its domain, not just the application or specific problem where we first encountered this object.* It is true that object thinking is biased in that it expects most objects to have limited and simple behaviors—which makes it possible to model them in terms of an entire domain rather than an application. This bias is supported by experience, but it is an inductive conclusion, and the exception or exceptions may yet be found. Typically we would use the first two sides of the object cube model to record our thoughts about the object and its behaviors.

Our goal during discovery is object definition, not object specification. Definition means we want to capture how the object is defined by those using it, what they think of that object, what they expect of it when they use it, and the extent to which it is similar to and different from other objects in the domain. Specification will come later (maybe 30 seconds later if you are doing XP and working on a single object), when we allow ourselves to consider how this object might be implemented (simulated) in software. Specification will involve making some design decisions and capturing the information necessary for someone to actually build the software version of the object.

Object definition involves capturing three bits of information: a short prose description of the object (in the words of a domain user), an enumeration of the services it is expected to provide (and, if other objects are used as helpers for any given service, the kind of object to be used), and, when appropriate, a stereotype—another object or other objects that the one we are working with resembles in terms of similarity of services provided. Wirfs-Brock and McKean identify several stereotypes, including information holder, structurer, service provider, coordinator, controller, and interfacer. Peter Coad has also written about a wide variety of stereotypes. Ivar Jacobson uses the idea of stereotypes with emphasis on model (service providers), views, and controllers.

Side 2 of the object cube is used to record the description and any stereotype; side 1 is used to record the list of responsibilities and collaborators. To this point, we are engaging in exactly the same thinking and recording process advocated by Beck and Cunningham and their CRC cards. It would not be unusual to actually use 3 × 5 index cards for discovery because they are cheap, easy to modify, and shareable (you can pass them around); and they provide a good visual reminder that well-defined objects have limited responsibilities.

Where to start? Pick an object or two from the stories selected by the customer for the first development iteration. This will provide a starting point. For example, *Application* and *entryField*. We ask the user (domain expert) for a definition, and the user responds, "An application is a kind of form used to collect specific facts about the people applying for a mortgage and the home they want to purchase." We record this information on side 2 of the object cube (or on the back of the 3 × 5 card). The definition, conveniently, provides us with insight into a stereotype for the application object—it's a "kind of form." So we record that fact on side 2 as well. (See Figure 7-7.)

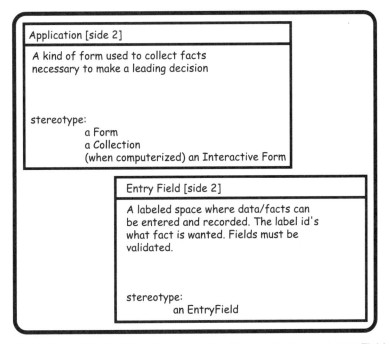

Figure 7-7 Side 2 of the object cube for the *Application* and *entryField* objects contains a simple record of the description and stereotype obtained from the domain expert (user).

We do the same thing for the *entryField* object, obtaining the information shown in Figure 7-7.

We now turn our attention to the services we expect from our *Application* and *entryField* objects. We have several choices of how to think about the services. We can look at the arcs connecting the application circle to others on the semantic net to see whether they suggest services expected of the application. We can go over the story about filling out the application to see what was expected of the application in that story. Either of these options is likely to expose services that our application must satisfy, but those services might be couched in specific language reflective of the limited context in which we discover the service rather than the domain as a whole. We will take care to generalize any such discovery so that the service reflects the needs of all of the objects that might use our application.

A third way to approach the enumeration of services is simply to ask the question, "I am an application; what services can I provide to others?" To help us answer this question, we can look at an actual physical example of the application form, and we can begin to collect those stories involving the application that have been provided to guide our immediate development activities and phrase the question in the context of each of those stories. "In this story, what services do the other objects expect of me?" As your project evolves and as the application object is discovered in other projects with other stories, you revisit your thinking about the essential services that your object is to provide.

We notice that the application has a funny string of characters at the bottom (something like AF001rev10/03), and we also notice a line of print at the top in larger font size than the other contents. We surmise that these character strings identify the form in some way. We also recall that the stories told about the application implied that users of the application looked at it to confirm that they had the right form. From this we conclude that the form has a responsibility to *identify itself*. We record this information on side 1.

Visual inspection reveals several examples of short text strings and several examples of blank spaces. We might give these things names—*textString* and *entryField*, respectively—and then create a new object cube with those names on them. We will want to explore those objects later to determine what their responsibilities might be.

Our attention is on the application, however, so we wonder whether the application has any responsibility in connection with these newly discovered objects. It's obvious that the application holds these elements in an organized manner. We might arrive at a responsibility that the application holds elements. We reject the phrasing *holds elements* because that does not describe a service; instead, it describes something the application must do to provide a service. If we say *holds objects*, we are implying an implementation decision: how an object is to do something rather than what it is to do. A bit of thought, and we come up with the responsibility *provide access to elements*. Implicit within this responsibility are variations such as *provide access to a subset of elements* and *provide sequential access to elements*. We might record these variations on side 1 so that we don't forget them, even though we aren't sure they are appropriate responsibilities.

Note   Abstraction, generalization, classification, and essentialism are three quite different but apparently similar concepts. Abstraction is the act of separating characteristics into the *relevant* and *irrelevant* to facilitate focusing on the relevant without distraction or undue complexity. Generalization also involves separation but more in terms of *shared* and *not shared* characteristics. Classification involves (depending on the linguistic theory you prefer) either separation based on conformance to a set definition or similarity to a prototype—the separation being in the class or not. Essentialism is an attempt to separate *accident* and *essence*—to identify the characteristic that is essential to being considered an instance of some class.

Unfortunately, abstraction and generalization tend to be used as synonyms for all four terms as well as for each other. I am as guilty of this as anyone else—hence this note and its attempt to deal with an apparent contradiction between object thinking and XP.

Kent Beck says, "Keep things simple by not providing abstractions until the abstractions provide simplicity," one expression of his consistent warning against "premature" abstractions. He, and most followers of XP practice, believe that abstraction should arise from refactoring rather than from activities typically associated with the analysis and design phases of traditional development.

Object thinking suggests you should take care to generalize responsibilities so that they can be used in any context. This is not abstraction of the type chastised by XP. It is much closer to essentialism—finding the specific traits or characteristics that make a thing a thing. Sometimes this is as simple as removing adjectives from a service description (method name). At other times, it is subtler and a bit closer to generalization: instead of "Provide unique identification number" as a responsibility that reflects how an object identifies itself in a context, use "Identify self." A significant part of object thinking is devoted to providing the philosophy and metaphors and definitions required to accomplish this paring of things to their essential nature. I believe that the apparent contradiction between object thinking and XP is just that—apparent—and derives from nuanced use of common terms.

We can see the application, so we know it can display itself. We would record *"display itself"* on side 1. It's necessary to think a bit about what's involved in displaying the application because more than one object is visible: the application, of course, but also the *textString* and *entryField* objects. It's inappropriate for one object to assume responsibility for the actions or behaviors of others. The text strings and entry fields must display themselves. The application might be the recipient of the display request, but it must be careful to delegate some of the display behavior to its elements. We can capture this information by recording that *myElements* is the collaborator used by the application to make sure all objects are displayed.

> **Note**   As you tackle more stories involving forms, you'll discover additional abstractions or recursive use of the same abstractions. For example, a complex form might have sections or pages that are themselves forms with their own elements—an example of recursive organization. This kind of organization reflects the *composite* pattern. Some forms will have check boxes or other means of collecting information. At first, these appear to be something other than an *entryField*, which in our discussion so far appears to be a box for collecting a string. A bit of reflection reveals that a check box—and almost any other widget you might find of use in simulating a form—is, in terms of its behavior, just an *entryField*. Different widgets have different appearances, and thinking about that fact might lead you to positing a view object, charged with providing a visual presentation of an object. An object that exists in different view contexts would have multiple view objects at its disposal, one for each context. An apparently simple responsibility of the form object—display itself—turns out to be quite complex when we start to think about writing the code that enables that responsibility. But we want simple code as well as simple responsibilities. To obtain simple code, we must refactor—which means thinking about how we can break up the code and distribute it to other objects. In this case, part of the responsibility gets delegated to the elements that the form comprises and still further to objects that specialize in visual representation tasks—view objects.

Usually we want to record only one collaborator on a line. To accomplish this heuristic goal, we might stereotype both *textString* and *entryField* as displayable objects. We can then record *displayableObject* as the collaborator. It would be nice to be a bit more specific about instances of *displayableObject* that we are collaborating with, so we might refine our label (which identifies a new class to be thought about) to *displayableElement* instead. This implies that any elements the application contains that are displayable are the ones we collaborate with to complete the application's display responsibility.

The fact that the application is a container of other objects also suggests to us a second stereotype for application. It has behaviors similar to a collection—another type of container object. We should add this observation to side 2 of our card.

One more responsibility needs to be considered. In one of our stories, it was suggested that the application form needs to be verified or validated. The information entered on the form—the information contained within the *entryField* objects—must be confirmed. This would suggest a responsibility *validate application form*. But who should this responsibility be assigned to? According to the precepts of object thinking, the application must be responsible for validating itself!

So we add one more responsibility to side 1 of the object cube, *validate self*. Exactly how this is done we do not know. But a bit of reflection indicates that part of the validation is done on the values stored in each *entryField*. The application should not be validating the *entryField*; the *entryField* must be responsible for that itself. Just as was done with the display responsibility, the application will delegate to each *entryField* its share of the validation workload. We list *entryField* as a collaborator for the *validate self* responsibility of the application.

Alas, our thinking may be leading us astray a bit in our consideration of validation. Perhaps it is not one task but two similar tasks, one of which belongs to the application and the other to the *entryField*. To be sure we are doing the right thing, we need to ask what is meant by *validation* as that term is used in the domain. So we might ask a user, "How is an application validated?" The user then provides a simple story about validation:

"Well, the data in each field is checked to see whether it's the right kind: a name, a date, a dollar figure, things like that. Then we verify that the value is accurate and permissible. By permissible we mean things such as the number entered in age has to be between 25 and 40, or the number of years married must be between 2 and 10. By accurate, we mean that the income figure is verified with the employer. Also, the bank balances, things like that. Finally, we check the application for consistency. Say they enter a city name and a postal code. We check to see that the postal code matches the city."

Thinking about the story suggests that the application, as well as each *entryField*, is validated by applying a rule or rules to the value stored in an *entryField*. In the case of the application, the rule might have to look at values stored in more than one *entryField*.

Our first attempt to implement this story might utilize a lot of *If* statements and the hard-coding of a lot of values in the conditional checks of those *If* statements.

There is significant potential for inappropriate coupling of our objects—for example, if we had a "validate" method for a form with code that looked like the following:

```
Validate
If form.city concatenated with form.zip is found in zipcodeDirectory return
    "TRUE" Else return "FALSE."
```

If the names of fields on the form change or if the rule changes in some fashion, we will have to fix the code. There is insufficient flexibility and too much reliance on conditional code to pass the XP "smell test." Applying the object thinking principle—everything is an object—in thinking about how to refactor our code should lead to the discovery of another kind of object—a rule object. A rule object is given the responsibility to evaluate itself to some value (either the TRUE or FALSE of this example or any other value). We can then provide the form and each of its *entryField* objects with a rule (or rules) that it can use to effect its own validation. So we change both object cubes to reflect the newly identified collaborator. We would also make a new object cube for the *validationRule* object.

When we are done, we probably have the object cube—sides 1 and 2—for *Application* and for *entryField* completed as shown in Figure 7-8. Once we complete sides 1 and 2 of an object cube for every object identified in our semantic net, and once we have assured ourselves that we can tell any story the user can tell us about using those objects, we are done. The overall result for the subsidized mortgage company will be similar to Figure 7-9 (side 1) and Figure 7-10 (side 2).

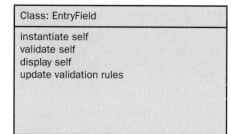

Figure 7-8   Sides 1 and 2 of the *Application* and *entryField* object cubes. "(Indented lines on side 1 of Class: Application are collaborators for the immediately preceeding responsibility.)"

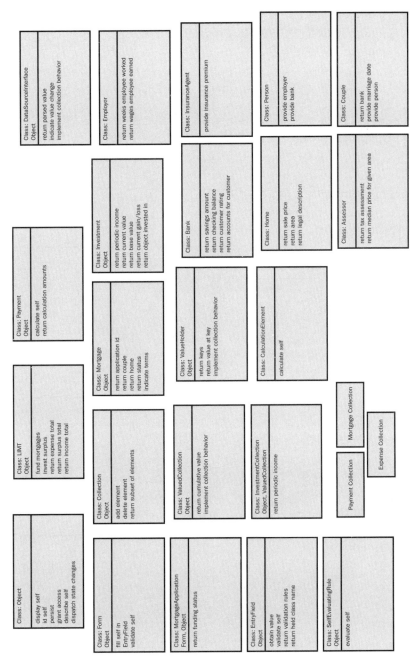

Figure 7-9   Objects identified in the subsidized mortgage example (side 1 of the object cubes).

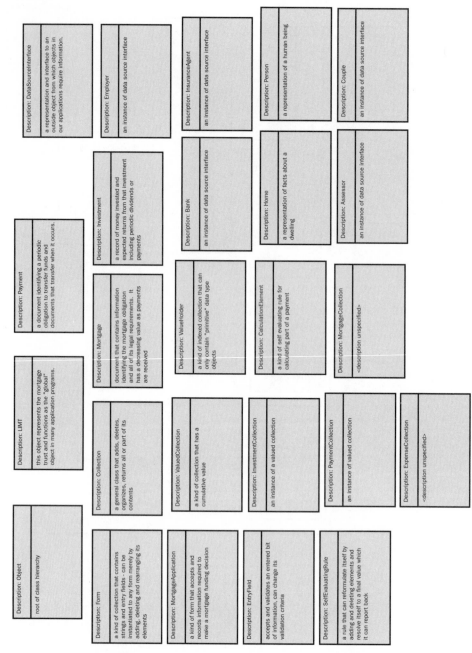

Figure 7-10 Objects identified in the subsidized mortgage example (side 2 of the object cubes).

As you look at the figures, you'll see objects that we have yet to discuss in the text—objects that have come to light as other developers worked on their stories. As the team works, objects will be proposed and developed by different pairs, and you might not be aware of much more than the names of the objects until you have the opportunity to work on a story involving those objects.

Object discovery provides us with a set of named objects and a set of responsibilities assigned to each one. We might also have a short prose description of the object and a stereotype. In one sense, we are ready to code the objects we have discovered, and that would be the expected activity of the XP programming pair (coding tests first, of course).

Object thinking can still help you as you think about the code and start to make implementation decisions. For example, we can use the stereotype to suggest an existing object that might be modified or employed to help fulfill the responsibilities of the one we are working on. This kind of implementation decision will give rise to a taxonomy of classes—a class hierarchy. Such a hierarchy has several benefits for programmers: providing already written and tested code that we can employ for our own ends and, because of the taxonomic organization, a kind of index we can use to look for code that might be useful to us.

Chapter 8 will introduce some additional aspects of objects that we can think about to facilitate our implementation—aspects that might be characterized as design considerations. In Chapter 10, we'll look at class hierarchies (taxonomies) in a bit more detail.

Another Example
Some Objects from an Air Traffic Control (ATC) System

Imagine we are working on modeling the world of air traffic control. We will have identified a number of objects in that realm, including passengers, airplanes, control towers, flight routes, controlled airspaces, and many more. We will also have captured a number of stories about how objects interact in this world. The following is a brief illustration of how a few objects might have been modeled in such an example. We will focus on the airplane and some objects that come to be identified as we consider the airplane and its responsibilities. We will use the story of how an airplane fulfills one of its responsibilities—reporting its location as the background—for our process of discovery.

Figure 7-11 includes a depiction of side 1 of the object cube for an airplane. By *identify self*, we mean that the plane can provide its registration number. *Describe self* entails giving a requester of that service an object

(continued)

Another Example   *(continued)*

containing the characteristics of the airplane (type, manufacturer, seating capacity, and so on). *Report location* means the airplane will provide a location object containing all the pertinent information for a location (altitude, latitude, longitude, vector, and so forth). *Move to new location* means the airplane will actually relocate itself in space.

The only one of these responsibilities that looks complicated to code is move to new location. A fair amount of calculation is required to determine the combination of acceleration and attitude that will be required to get from "here" to "there," and then directives need to be issued to the objects capable of effectuating those changes.

There is another, subtler, complexity in the plane's ability to report its current location. Although the explicit responsibility is to provide a current location, there is an implicit responsibility to report the *correct* current location. A location is a composite of several values—all of which are dynamic—and the only way that the plane can assure itself of the correctness of the location it is providing is to have one constructed in response to the request it receives from the control tower.

We probably do not want to add a responsibility to the airplane of the sort, *construct location*. Instead we acknowledge the need for construction in the original *report current location* responsibility by adding a collaborator to that line. We then expect the collaborator to assume the task of construction. Object thinking mandates that objects do things to themselves, so the obvious collaborator is a location object.

The airplane can ask its collaborator, the *aLocation* object, to instantiate itself (obtain and remember all the appropriate values for altitude, latitude, longitude, airspeed, and so forth) immediately upon receiving the control tower's request for a location. The location object then interrogates the necessary instruments to get the values it needs. But which instruments? How does (or how can) the location object find the instruments it needs to instantiate itself?

The airplane provides the context for the request, so we want to interrogate the instruments associated with (that are a part of) the airplane; therefore, we ask the plane for those instruments. The location could ask the plane for each instrument in turn, but our code will quickly reveal this to be a less than optimal design. For one thing, the plane is busy, and we would be an annoying disruption. For another, we would have to add a lot of responsibilities to the airplane of the sort, *provide access to altimeter*. Instead of creating a *provide access to* responsibility for each instrument,

(continued)

Another Example   *(continued)*

we introduce yet another object—an *instrumentCluster*—and add a *provide access to* instrumentCluster responsibility to the airplane.

An *instrumentCluster* is basically a collection of instruments. As with any collection, we can ask it for a subset of its members and ask it to iterate across its membership. The location can then ask the *instrumentCluster* for the next instrument in the collection and ask that instrument for its value.

Remember, the thinking and design activities that we just discussed take place as part of the activity of writing tests and code. It need not be an explicit separate step in the development process. It's reflective of the thinking that goes on as each pair interprets their story, identifies the objects needed, thinks about which object will do what, and how that object will actually do what it is expected to do.

If the development team chose to actually draw models to assist them in this chain of thought, they might look at Figure 7-11 (side 1 of the object cubes for *Airplane, aLocation, instrumentCluster,* and *Instrument*) and Figure 7-12 (an interaction diagram confirming the report current location story).

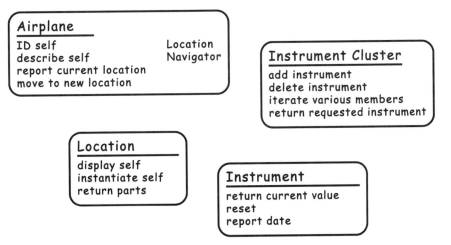

Figure 7-11   Side 1 for airplane, location, *instrumentCluster,* and instrument objects.

(continued)

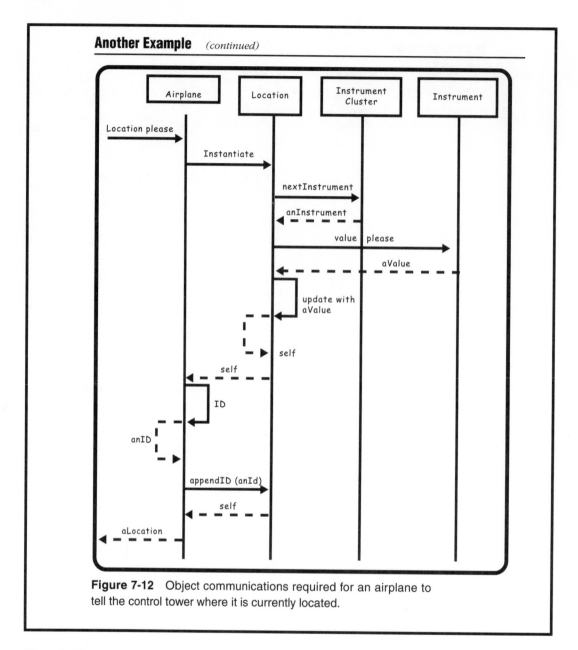

Figure 7-12 Object communications required for an airplane to tell the control tower where it is currently located.

Heuristics

Implicit but perhaps not obvious in the preceding section (and in the sidebar) are a number of heuristics for discovering and assigning object responsibilities. There are also some points where the developers' thought processes might have proceeded in a different direction: there are different and equally valid object designs. Some hints of why the examples shown are as they are can be incorporated into the discussion of the heuristics.

Heuristic: Let objects assume responsibility for tasks that are wholly or completely delegated to other objects in cases in which the responsibility reflects natural communication patterns in the domain.

For example, the question might arise as to why the control tower asks the airplane for a location instead of talking directly to a location object and having it talk to the airplane's instrument cluster. After all, it is the location that actually does the work. If you are familiar with modern aviation, you know that control towers have the ability to talk to at least one instrument carried by an airplane—the transponder. This question raises a general issue of when an object should or can assume responsibility for work actually done by others.

In the case of *Airplane*, it seemed a natural call. After all, the control tower already has to talk to the planes (actually the pilots) about all manners of business, so it doesn't seem illogical for it to do so for location as well. The plane is already "visible" to the control tower, and the plane provides the context of meaning for the values that will be accumulated by the location object. It does no harm to let the plane front for location, and it does a lot of good. Similarly, there is value in letting the location object front for the *instrumentCluster* and *Instrument* objects. If at some point in the future we have a more abstract *FlyingThing*, we can use the same interface to obtain locations for any specializations of that class, such as the airplane. If the definition of location (the type and number of values it contains) varies, the interface remains the same. If new types of instruments are invented, they can be added to the *instrumentCluster* without any need to know details about them—as long as they can respond to the *currentValue* message.

Heuristic: Delegate responsibilities to get a better distribution and increase reusability.

An example of this heuristic arises from the answer to the question of why the *Airplane* needs the instrument cluster. We can arrive at the answer by enumerating all the responsibilities that are involved with keeping track of and using a set of instruments:

- Know which instruments are included in the set.
- Assemble a location by asking the correct instruments, in the correct order for their values.
- Remove an instrument from the set if it is bad.
- Keep track of which instruments belong in which kind of airplane.
- Add new instruments when available.

- Monitor the status of all the instruments.

- Replace an instrument with an improved model when asked.

- Make one or more instruments available when asked.

This seems like a lot of work for an airplane to undertake, especially when we would like the airplane to concentrate on moving safely from one place to another. Safe flying requires a lot of responsibilities in its own right, responsibilities quite dissimilar to those just enumerated. It will also increase reusability of both the airplane and instrument cluster objects by keeping separable responsibilities separate.

When an object accepts responsibility for work that it cannot do alone, it does so to meet expectations expressed in its environment. As the programmers write the tests and code for that kind of responsibility, each segment of code represents their thinking about specific tasks that the object must complete if it is to accomplish what is expected. Each of those tasks—code segments—might be moved (via refactoring) to other objects better prepared or better suited to fulfilling that specific task. Delegation arises from refactoring code. But it's expected that programmers learn from experience and that the next time you think about a test or a block of code, you might recognize immediately that it belongs in a different object—a kind of anticipatory refactoring that is grounded in your own programming experience.

Delegation can lead to the temptation of management. This is to be avoided. If you delegate, delegate. Do not try to retain any control over how your delegate does its job. Do not attempt to second-guess your delegate's work by adding all kinds of elaborate result-checking code. When you actually code the delegate object, give it the ability to evaluate its own work and correct its own mistakes, and then rely on it to do its job while you concentrate on yours.

Heuristic: Use anthropomorphization and foreshadowing to determine whether an object should assume a given responsibility.

Experience doing object development allows you to anticipate (or at least think about) what might happen as a guide for current activities. Foreshadowing is a necessary part of iterative development. It allows you to learn from prior experience and apply that learning to avoid doing "wasteful" or "inappropriate" things right now. The future you anticipate might be the next test, the next line of code, the next object or task in the story you are working on, or even the next story.

Foreshadowing will frequently take the form, "If I give this object this responsibility, later I will find that it requires this and this piece of information and will require an ability to do this thing in this manner." You can then decide that the responsibility should or should not, in whole or part, be assigned to the object under consideration. If your immediate thinking about a method seems to be leading you in the direction of constructing a complicated and long method, stop! Think ahead a bit and reevaluate what you are doing. There is no need to write ugly methods if a bit of foreshadowing can help you refactor as you write. Decisions regarding responsibility assignment and method code are seldom final; they are just a way to help you distribute responsibilities in a way that minimizes, to some degree, future work.

Foreshadowing is not a substitute for refactoring and emergence; rather, it's a way to learn from experience and to apply XP and object thinking principles as you work. For example, as you start writing the twentieth line of code for the method you are currently working on, you should be hearing alarms—"This is too hard"—that cause you to pause and see whether you can mentally imagine what the entire method will look like and refactor the image of the code instead of the actual code.

Anthropomorphization assists us in thinking about responsibilities and other objects in several ways. We can think of objects as being "lazy" and wanting to do only a limited and closely related set of activities. We find the responsibilities that need to be delegated to other objects by foreshadowing what might be involved in fulfilling a responsibility. We can think about how much the object might need to know, whether it will need to know the "wrong" kinds of things about other objects (that is, anything not evident in the object's interface), and what it might need to do.

Heuristic: Responsibilities should be distributed among the community of objects in a balanced manner.

No object should have a disproportionate share of the responsibilities. How is it determined whether an object has too many or too few responsibilities? If you use a 3 × 5 lined index card to record your responsibilities—one to a line—you will find you are limited to six or seven entries. This is an excellent heuristic for the maximum number of responsibilities that an object can or should assume. The lower bound is that an object must have at least one unique responsibility, or there is no justification for making it a separate kind of object.

A balanced distribution of responsibilities across a group of objects is the goal. Also implied is a balance in the distribution of knowledge among those objects. An object should not do too much or know too much. You can determine the knowledge distribution, roughly, via foreshadowing, as previously noted.

Heuristic: Always state responsibilities in an active voice describing a service to be performed.

A common tendency for new object developers is to list as responsibilities things that an object must "know." An airplane must "know its current location." While this may be true, it can be misleading. It implies too much about how the object might be implemented because "knows" implies an instance variable. It's also quite possible that an object will know things (a private key for decryption, perhaps) that it will not be willing to share with others and that therefore will not be included in the interface for that object. *Provide private key* would not appear as a service, although the message *privateKey* might be in the object's protocol with the designation that it is a private message. *Decrypt message*, on the other hand, might be a listed responsibility. Always state your responsibilities in terms of a service, with an awareness of a possible client for that service.

Heuristic: Avoid responsibilities that are characteristic specific, that focus on providing a potential user with the value of a single characteristic of the object.

It would be a mistake to list responsibilities such as know age, know height, know eye color, and know weight. (See the preceding heuristic.) It's also a mistake to list report age, report height, report eye color, report weight. Even though the latter are in an active voice, they are characteristic specific and should be avoided. The source of the problem is that an object might have a lot of characteristics, and you have room for only six responsibilities. It's better to look for an umbrella label for the responsibility, such as *describe yourself* or *identify yourself*. Important advantages will be gained by following this heuristic, that is, keeping the conversation at the right level: what, not how or how much.

> **Note**   As a developer, you try to get basic behavior first. Obviously, when you get to the details, the actual details will be necessary, but not now. For example, you might have a responsibility called *describe yourself* or *provide access to demographic information*. You might ask the on-site customer a couple of questions:
>
> "When you say 'demographic information,' do you mean name, address, phone number, and so on?" "Yes," she might reply, "that, and hair color, eye color, and the like."
>
> "Are they all used just for informational purposes, or are some of them prominent in other behavior?"
>
> "They are mostly informational, except ... ," an answer that may lead to a new responsibility or a natural grouping.
>
> Sometimes you get domain people who want you to know every characteristic. Assure them that "you'll get the complete list when we are getting ready to implement this behavior."

One advantage is flexibility. If you make the interface to your class dependent on the characteristics it might need to report and someone decides on a new characteristic, you will need to redefine your class. The alternative is to have a responsibility *describe yourself*, which results in giving the requester a description object. This description object might be a simple collection of key/value pairs or an arbitrarily complex object with its own domain-driven (not just this story) set of behaviors. Even the simplest case provides significant flexibility. The description object can be asked for one or more of the values it contains so that the client gets the information it needs. However, when you decide to add a new characteristic to an object, you can do so by simply sending a message to its description object telling it to add a key/value pair reflecting the new trait. (Again, assuming a very simple form of description object.) No redefinition or recompilation is required.

Foreshadowing implementation for a moment reveals another advantage arising from the fact that different clients might need to ask about different characteristics. If the characteristics are defined in the interface, a situation requiring multiple object types (classes) is created. For example, it's likely that a credit department will need to know characteristics of customers that are not shared by other departments in a company. The temptation, when characteristics are part of the interface (or when a data-driven approach to design is used), is to create a small class hierarchy with *Customer*, *CashCustomer*, and *CreditCustomer*, with *Customer* defining common characteristics as attributes and *CashCustomer/CreditCustomer* adding at least one unique attribute each.

If the characteristics of a customer are held in a description object, only the *Customer* class is needed. All clients can ask the customer for its description and then ask the description for those characteristic values in which it's interested. Cash or credit becomes just an additional characteristic of the object, not a determinant of class structure or other implementation details.

There are some obvious exceptions to this heuristic. Almost all objects will need to identify themselves on occasion. The object returned when the "ID please" message is sent might vary significantly from object to object: the object might be as simple as a string or as complex as a passport. Depending on the context, both types of identification object might be required. It's quite likely that if a simple identity string is a characteristic of the object, that same string will likely be part of the more complex object, the passport. Deciding whether a characteristic merits a separate responsibility will be revealed in the collection of scenarios in which the object is involved. If an object has 10 characteristics, for instance, and 1 of them is asked about frequently and by a number of clients, it should probably be a separate responsibility. If the other 9 are the subject of only occasional inquiries or are almost always asked for at the same time and in the same circumstances, they should be grouped in some fashion, and the responsibility becomes to return the group.

Heuristic: Create proxies for objects outside your domain that are sources of information required by objects within your domain.

In the process of completing both the binary use cases and the scenarios, a number of objects that are outside your domain will be identified. Legacy systems and human beings are the most obvious examples. They continue to be of interest and importance because they are sources of information or behavior that your objects will require. These requirements will be exposed in the scenarios as messages sent to these outside objects.

> **Note**   Some objects that appear frequently in your stories may turn out, in fact, to be external objects or representatives of external objects. For example, the airplane object in the air traffic control example earlier in this chapter is really a kind of proxy for objects that are not directly part of the ATC system itself. Real airplanes (their pilots, really) are customers of the ATC and a source of information that the ATC uses in fulfilling its responsibilities.

For instance, if I were an order object I might need to obtain information and decisions from a human being. I will want them to describe themselves to me and tell me where they live, and what items from our inventory they want. Since you cannot build a human being object, you can create a *HumanInformation-Interface* object or a *HumanProxy* object that will be your interface to the real-world human. A generalization of this heuristic is a class *DataSourceInterface*, of which *HumanProxy* is an instance. So common is the need for this heuristic that there is actually a pattern—Proxy—that documents its structure and use.

Heuristic: Look for components.

A component will look exactly like an object at this stage of development; that is, it will have a name and a set of responsibilities. When you foreshadow those responsibilities, however, the object starts to look complicated and will seem to need a lot of collaborators, usually a sign of a need for further decomposition and redistribution of factored responsibilities.

If the set of responsibilities are strongly coherent and if domain experts seem aware of but unconcerned by an internal complexity—the way people are aware that an automobile has a complex internal nature but ignore that in favor of using a car as a car—you probably have a potential component. You should identify your object as a component and plan to do detailed analysis of it later, as if it were a small, separate piece of application software.

8

Thinking Toward Design

Discovery involves applying object thinking to the problem of decomposition (finding the objects that reside in the domain) and the problem of requirements (the behaviors expected of individual objects and aggregations of objects as they interact in that domain). Tangible results of discovery probably include partially completed object cubes and a set of stories. These results take tangible form because they have value as a kind of external memory for the group of individuals involved in development.

The CRC card method of Beck and Cunningham moved directly from discovery into implementation. Once you had a set of cards and stories, you started to write code, doing some design-oriented thinking about the code as you went along. XP follows the CRC card method closely: pick up a prioritized story card, grab a partner, and start writing code. XP does require you to write code to be used in testing your work before actually writing the code to implement your objects and stories. Design, in XP, is not a separate process; it's infused in the process of writing tests and code. (Actually, discovery is infused in the same activity: you identify your objects as you begin thinking about implementation—tests and code—of your user story.)

Moving directly to the coding process may work for those whose brains are already saturated with object thinking, who have internalized the ideas and ideals to the point that object thinking is automatic and largely nonconscious. For those just learning object thinking (or XP), there is a potential pitfall: the metaphors and definitions that served you well in discovery cease to provide valuable guidance as you think about design and implementation. Even worse, the "good" metaphors are replaced with "bad" metaphors, metaphors reflective of computer thinking as discussed in Chapter 1, "Object Thinking." One of the roles of an XP coach is to provide direction and help novice developers learn the skills of object and XP thinking.

Thinking toward design suggests the continual application of object ideas and metaphors as the developer's focus shifts from story to specific object, to specific method, to test, to code. Attention shifts from *what* to *how*, and how involves making decisions about design and implementation that are not required when the focus is on the domain and what is expected from objects participating in that domain.

Thinking toward design implies that it isn't necessary to actually construct formal, documented designs—only that your actual activities should continue to be guided by object ideas and metaphors. Tangible documents and models suggested in the rest of this chapter are intended to illustrate object thinking about design and implementation and provide a convenient means of sharing ideas among a group of developers. As you internalize object thinking, the use of tangible documentation becomes less critical while remaining useful as a kind of checklist you can use as a substitute for perfect memory (both individual and collective). An XP test is another form—the preferred form, usually—of external memory and the only form that's intended to persist past the point of its immediate creation and use. Tests remain even after the whiteboard full of diagrams is wiped clear and the deck of story cards has found its way to the recycling bin.

Object Internals

Discovery has provided a decomposition of a domain into objects, an assignment of responsibilities to those objects, and a description of how objects might communicate and cooperate with one another to complete tasks beyond the capabilities of individual objects. This is usually not sufficient information to actually build computer software simulations of those objects and of those interactions.

Here are some examples of why this is so:

- Sides 1 and 2 of the object cube (and the classical CRC card) capture only behavioral expectations of your objects—they tell you nothing about the internal construction of those objects and nothing about the means used by those objects to fulfill their responsibilities.

- Assignment of responsibilities to an object tells you nothing about how to invoke that responsibility and nothing about what form the response will take.

- Identifying a need for collaboration tells you nothing about how the client object uses its collaborator, nor anything about how it knows of the collaborator's existence and location, nor anything about the form of communication with that collaborator.

There is a clear need to think about how your objects will be simulated, to make decisions about construction (design). Those decisions must be guided by the principles of object thinking and based on the intrinsic needs of the object. *An intrinsic need is defined as the means for fulfilling an assigned responsibility.* It's necessary to discern additional information about our objects and their needs. It's inevitable that the process of determining this information will involve making decisions about implementation, normally an activity associated with design.

There are innumerable ways to implement even the simplest object or object responsibility. Take, for example, obtaining the string that uniquely identifies an object. Different languages provide different implementations (*object.id*, the dot notation of Java and Visual Basic versus the *id getter* message convention of Smalltalk); different groups set different naming conventions, which necessitate different syntax; and even the nature of the "id" itself might vary, in some cases being an object, in others a type.

While necessary, design decisions can impose unwanted limitations on the ability to use an object in different contexts. This is reflected in the immense difficulty involved in creating libraries of reusable components and the need for extensive middleware anytime objects created in one context need to be used elsewhere.

Keeping the object's domain-assigned responsibilities in the forefront of your thinking while making design decisions ameliorates design-based limitations. For example, if you are designing an object for use in a database environment, you might be tempted to implement the object so that its internal structure mirrors the table structure of the database. This will limit the use of such an object to that specific implementation environment—unless you employ middleware or other kinds of interpreters and translators.

If, on the other hand, you continue to let your design be guided by the domain and the behaviors allocated to an object by that domain, you can avoid making decisions that will inhibit the natural composability of that object as it exists in the domain. The following discussion attempts to illustrate the importance of domain-driven design while providing some guidelines for how to accomplish it.

Knowledge Required

If we think of an object as if it were a human being (anthropomorphism) and we give that object a task, it's appropriate to think about what that object may need to know to complete its assignment. We can use our understanding of human beings and what they need to know to perform tasks as a metaphorical guide for our thinking about object knowledge.

For example, suppose we ask Sara to ride her bike to the store and bring home some milk. She will need to know

- How to ride a bicycle.

- Where the store is located.

- A route between home and the store.

- Perhaps, if more than one store is nearby, which store we want her to go to.

- The actual quantity of milk required—disambiguate the word *some*.

- If timing is an issue, when we want her to perform this service.

Actually, the list of things required is potentially very large. A lot of the items on our list are assumed to already exist—for example, how to ride a bicycle. We have criteria (usually tacit) that limit our listing of what Sara needs to know to a few details. We have similar criteria for considering what an object needs to know to fulfill its responsibilities.

If we ask Sara to ride her bike, we probably already know she has claimed that ability and we trust her in making that claim. If an object says it can identify itself, we assume (trust) that the object has a method—a block of computer code—that actually performs the identification service. We do not need to explicitly list such abilities as required knowledge. (We will explicitly name the methods themselves when we specify how an object's responsibilities are to be invoked, that is, when we specify a message protocol.)

We will usually assume that Sara knows which store to go to and the route to take *unless* she has more than one option *and* it matters to us which option she selects.

We will also assume that now means now and that the service is to be performed immediately upon receipt of the request—again, *unless* we want the option of requesting the service at a specified time or in a particular set of circumstances.

Most of the time, we are interested in recording the information— knowledge—required by the object in order to fulfill its advertised services. Information is perilously close to being what we typically think of as data. It's therefore very easy to fall into the "computer thinking" trap of assuming that knowledge required equals object data structure or object attributes. Object thinking will help us avoid this trap.

The responsibilities recorded on side 1 of the object cube drive our thinking about the knowledge required. Look at each responsibility, and ask what the object will need to know to fulfill this task. List your answer—as a descriptive noun or noun phrase—on side 4 of the object cube. Figure 8-1 shows sides 1 and 4 of the airplane object cube introduced in the "Another Example" sidebar in Chapter 7, "Discovery."

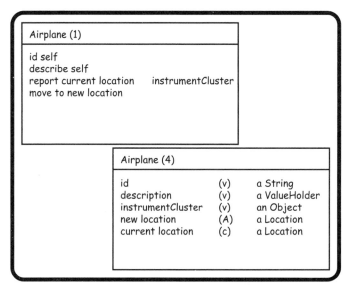

Figure 8-1   Sides 1 and 4 of the *Airplane* object cube, showing the relationship between responsibilities and knowledge required.

How did object thinking lead to the results recorded on side 4 of the object cube for the airplane?

■ The airplane is responsible for identifying itself. It therefore needs to know its ID. We record the noun (actually an abbreviation) *id* on side 4. (See the "Object Cube Idiom" sidebar coming up for additional explanation of why things are recorded the way they are in the examples.)

■ It needs to report its current location—hence *currentLocation*.

■ It needs to move to a new location on request—therefore, *newLocation*.

■ Because side 1 of the object cube indicates that serving a request for current location requires collaboration with the airplane's instrument cluster, it needs to know of the instrument cluster itself—so we record *instrumentCluster* as a piece of knowledge required.

In most cases, the list of knowledge required will be fairly short and reasonably obvious. In some cases, a single responsibility might yield more than one piece of required knowledge.

Completing a list of items to be known is but the first step in thinking about the object's knowledge requirements. We have two other decisions to make about each piece of knowledge recorded in our list: how it is obtained and what form it takes (what class will be used to encapsulate that knowledge).

Object Cube Idiom

A number of factors play a role in deciding the actual form—the actual words and symbols—used to record information on an object cube. Paramount among these is the need to be explicit and avoid ambiguity. For example, the expectations of an object should be obvious from the phrases selected to record those responsibilities; the name of a piece of knowledge should unambiguously describe the semantic understanding of that knowledge; the names given to classes and methods should reflect the essence of those classes and methods. (In this regard, we are very Confucian in our insistence that "only if things are given the proper names will all be right under Heaven.")

Countering the need for explicitness is the need for brevity. Eventually most of the names will be used in writing program source code. No coder really likes to type long descriptive names.

Another factor is the syntax of the programming language that the development team is most familiar and comfortable with. Smalltalkers will be quite comfortable recording *id: aString* as a method name or using *Integer* as a class name, but C++ programmers are more likely to use *id(string)* and *int* in similar circumstances.

This author, like everyone else, is a victim of his past: the idiom I am most comfortable with derives from the use of the Smalltalk programming language and its associated style and idiom. Although I will try to be as non-language-specific as possible in my illustrations, be forewarned that some idioms and conventions will inevitably creep in.

Another example of idiom is naming conventions such as the one that suggests that the method names for retrieving the object in a named variable and for placing an object in that variable are the same as the variable name itself—with the addition of an argument in the case of the *put* method. For example, the airplane has a piece of knowledge named *id*. A method for retrieving the object encapsulating that ID (usually a string) would be simply *id*. The method name for replacing the *id* string with another string would be *id(aString)*.

The proper idiom for use on object cubes, in code, and in any other phase of modeling or development should reflect the community doing

(continued)

Object Cube Idiom   *(continued)*

---

the development. It's the responsibility of the developers in your organization or your domain to determine appropriate idiom and to train new members of your development community in the use of that idiom. XP practices of coding standards, pair programming, and collective ownership of code support the creation and dissemination of appropriate idiom.

An object has any of four different ways to gain access to the knowledge it requires:

- It can store that knowledge in an instance variable.

- It can ask (in the specification of a message signature) for that knowledge to be provided along with the request for service (the message).

- It can obtain the knowledge from a third party—another object.

- It can "manufacture" the knowledge at the point when it is required.

Upon deciding which of these options is most appropriate, we will record that decision by noting an appropriate symbol next to each piece of knowledge. The symbols used are arbitrary, but in the examples in this book we will use V for variable, A for argument, C for collaboration, and M for method. Here are several of heuristics for deciding which option to use:

- Objects are lazy. Every time you decide to store a piece of required information in a variable, the object must assume responsibility for maintaining that variable; it must add the capability to retrieve and to update the contents of that variable upon request. So whenever possible and appropriate, use argument (A) and method (M) instead of variable.

- Collaboration is a form of dependence. Deciding to use a collaborator to obtain required knowledge makes you dependent on that collaborator. Objects strive for independence, so collaboration should also be minimized to the greatest extent possible.

- Remember the definition of collaboration—requiring the service of an object not found inside your own encapsulation barrier, which will eventually require direct or indirect coupling with that collaborator object. (With direct coupling, you know the actual name or ID of the object used as a collaborator, whereas with indirect coupling, you know where to find the object—in a global variable, perhaps.) Coupling of this sort is just as undesirable in object thinking as in any other development method or approach.

■ In addition to knowing who your collaborator is (for example, the *instrumentCluster* piece of knowledge recorded on side 4 of the *Airplane* object cube example), you will also need to know the message that will be sent to the collaborator in order to invoke its help. That message might require arguments and, if so, those will have to be added to your knowledge required list. Using collaboration therefore increases the intrinsic complexity of the object using collaboration as a means of access as well as establishing an undesirable coupling between objects.

■ You might want to add the symbol G as an option for recording your decision to access a piece of knowledge. G would stand for collaboration with a global variable. Starting down this road, however, might lead to making a distinction between a global in an application (G_a); a system global—the system clock (G_s), for example; or some sort of intermediate, such as the pool dictionaries in Smalltalk (G_p). If making such distinctions helps you and your group, there's no harm in using them. Take care that your object cube does not reflect a particular implementation context to the point that the general utility of the object is lost.

A final decision about knowledge required is that of determining the kind of object that will embody (encapsulate) the information. A class name will be recorded for each piece of information listed on side 4 of the object cube. (Using a class name rather than a program language type is preferred for this purpose because some information is complex—that is, not a simple primitive.) There should be one encapsulating object per knowledge item.

In some cases, you will discover an entirely new kind of object when making this decision—the location object, for example, used to encapsulate the various components that make up an airplane's location: altitude, latitude, longitude, and vector.

Discovery of the location object is a direct result of applying object thinking to the question of knowledge required. As you think about what a location really is, you discover the various component values that make up a location. You apply the "lazy object" principle and find out that both the airplane and the instrument cluster find that keeping track of the location components is too taxing and needs to be delegated to someone else. The other candidate is an instrument, but no instrument should know or try to keep track of any value except the one specifically generated by that instrument. Since none of your known objects is a suitable home, you will likely decide to create a new object with responsibilities for recording and maintaining the values that make up a location.

Figure 8-2 shows sides 1 and 4 for the objects in the air traffic control (ATC) example from the "Another Example" sidebar in Chapter 7. Except for the location object just discussed, the selection of an encapsulating object is pretty much a matter of common sense coupled with knowledge of the existing or planned class library for your domain.

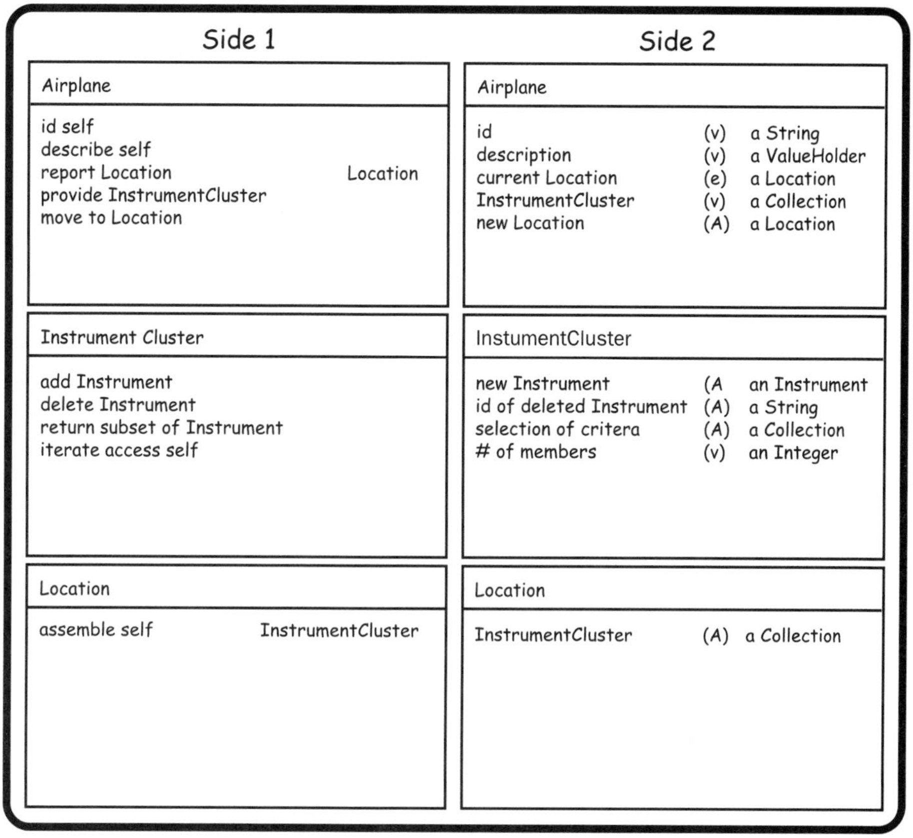

Side 1		Side 2		
Airplane		**Airplane**		
id self		id	(v)	a String
describe self		description	(v)	a ValueHolder
report Location	Location	current Location	(e)	a Location
provide InstrumentCluster		InstrumentCluster	(v)	a Collection
move to Location		new Location	(A)	a Location
Instrument Cluster		**InstumentCluster**		
add Instrument		new Instrument	(A	an Instrument
delete Instrument		id of deleted Instrument	(A)	a String
return subset of Instrument		selection of critera	(A)	a Collection
iterate access self		# of members	(v)	an Integer
Location		**Location**		
assemble self	InstrumentCluster	InstrumentCluster	(A)	a Collection

Figure 8-2   Sides 1 and 4 of the objects (classes) introduced in the ATC example from the preceding chapter.

Figure 8-3 shows side 1 of the objects in the mortgage trust application discussed in Chapter 7, and Figure 8-4 shows the knowledge required for those objects.

Message Protocol

Side 1 of the object cube tells us what an object can do but reveals nothing about how to ask for the advertised services. We know from object thinking in general that services are invoked by the sending of a message to the object providing the service, but what form must the message take? This is not a trivial question because the form of the message is arbitrary, but it must be exact, or the receiving object will ignore it. (Actually, it will cause an error if the message is wrong—a variation of "I haven't the foggiest notion what you are asking me to do.")

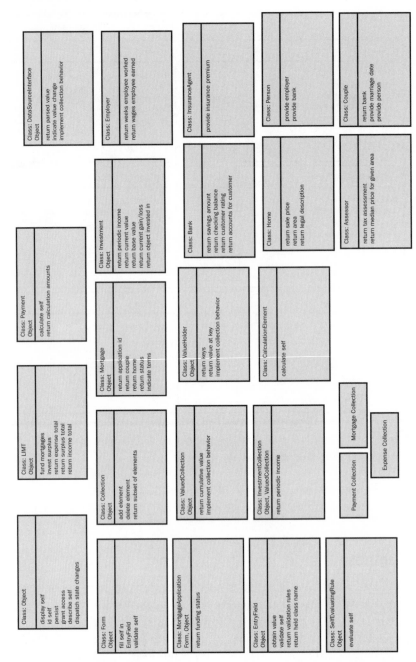

Figure 8-3   Object classes from the mortgage trust application introduced
in the preceding chapter.

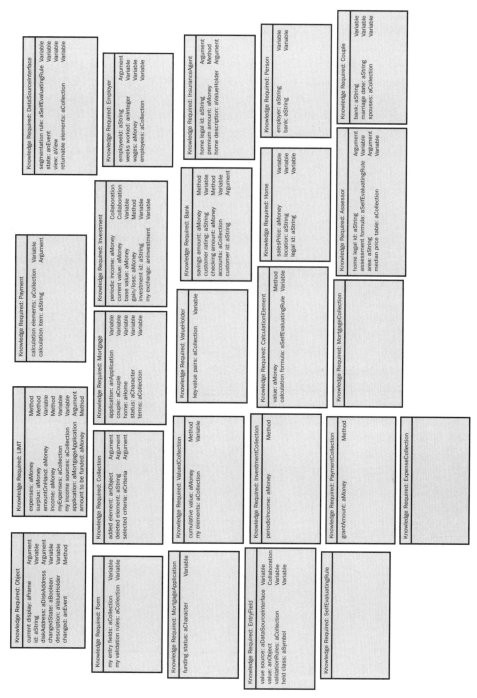

Figure 8-4   Knowledge required for objects and responsibilities identified
for the mortgage trust application introduced in the preceding chapter.

We also have no clue about the way the object will respond to any request sent its way. Will it provide us something in return? In many cases, we hope so. If it does, what will be the nature of the returned item?

To answer these questions, we use side 5 of the object cube to record a message protocol—a list of messages and their associated responses. As with knowledge required, we refer to side 1 to elicit the necessary list of messages. We also apply whichever idiom and convention for message syntax that's employed in our development environment. As individual messages are recorded, care must be taken to maintain consistency with decisions made elsewhere on the object cube—notably the names and encapsulating objects noted on side 4 (knowledge required).

Figure 8-5 shows side 1 (responsibilities) and side 5 (draft message protocol) for the objects in the ATC example. Figure 8-6 and Figure 8-7 show, respectively, side 1 and side 5 for the objects in the mortgage trust example.

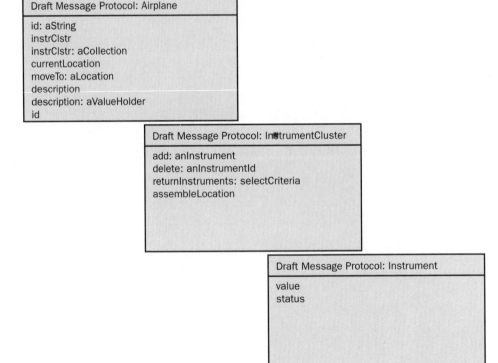

Figure 8-5   Sides 1 and 5 of the objects in the ATC example introduced in the preceding chapter.

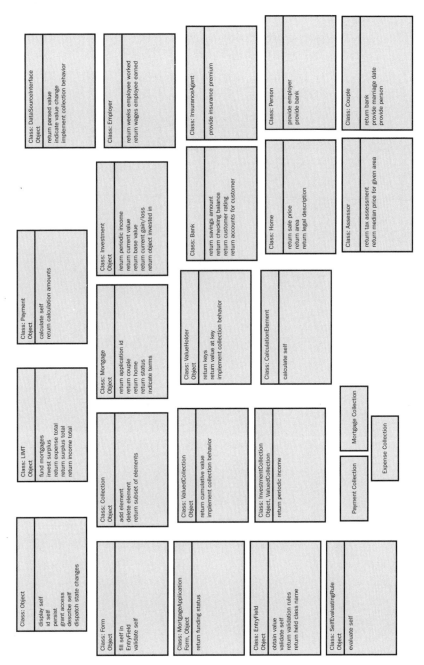

Figure 8-6   Responsibilities for the objects in the mortgage trust application (object cube side 1).

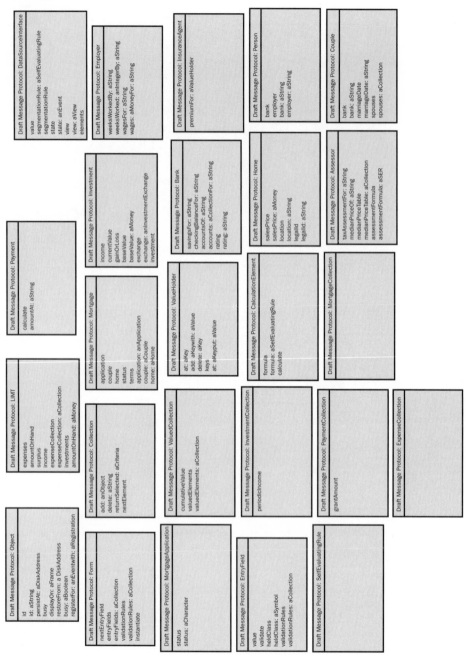

Figure 8-7   Message protocol for the objects in the mortgage trust application (object cube side 5).

Completing side 5 is usually straightforward. The following heuristics help with any nuances involved:

■   A full message signature includes three elements: the message selector (the actual message name), arguments (if any; arguments are optional), and the nature of the object returned to the sender of the message. For example, *includes (anObjectSpecification) aCollection.* Parsing this message signature results in identification of *includes* as the message selector, *(anObjectSpecification)* as the argument, and *aCollection* as the object returned. Because we are recording the messages received by the object whose cube we are completing, we omit the name of that object when drafting the message protocol; only the last three elements of the message signature are recorded on side 5.

■   Messages must be descriptive of the nature of the service (behavior) being invoked. It should be possible for a naive user of your object to immediately discern what is likely to happen if the indicated message is sent to the object. This includes specification of arguments—it should be obvious what kinds of objects are being passed as part of the message.

■   Messages must be relatively terse (programmers will get tired of typing long messages), a requirement that is at odds with and less important than the descriptiveness requirement. Programs are read for understanding more frequently than they are typed.

■   Messages should reflect the syntax of your chosen implementation language and any standards or conventions, such as naming, adopted by your development group.

■   If you have decided, on side 4, to store an object encapsulating some bit of information in an object instance variable, you must add two messages to your protocol: one to obtain the object in the variable (a getter message) and one to replace it (a setter message). Either or both of these messages can be categorized as private (see the next section about message contracts), or you can decide to make the variable immutable. It is also possible (relevant if either the getter or setter is considered private) that your language allows access to a variable by reference instead of via an explicit message. (Languages that allow access by reference from outside the object are suspect in terms of object thinking principles and philosophy.) Nevertheless, it is a good idea to record both getter and setter on side 5, even if you elect one of the other implementation options. Two common conventions for getter/setter message style are to use the variable name itself as the getter and the variable name plus argument as the setter; and to append the word *get* or *set* to the variable name. (Example for the *id* variable: *id* and *id: aString*—or *getId* and *setId*.) The argument, if any, will reflect whatever decision we made on side 4 as to the nature of the encapsulating object for that variable.

■   Some messages are imperative commands: "Don't bother giving me anything back; just do this!" In those cases, no object is returned. A Smalltalk convention is to note *self* as the object returned. For those more familiar with C++ and Java, it is perfectly appropriate to put the term *void* in place of *self*. The meaning is equivalent, although there are still technical differences as to what, if anything, is actually returned.

Message Contracts

Side 3 of the object cube has not been forgotten—it's only now that it will make some sense to talk about what's recorded on that face of the object cube. That side 3 is not swapped with side 5 is a historical artifact: the idea of contracts precedes the idea of object cubes. A contract is a concept introduced by Rebecca Wirfs-Brock and her coauthors as an extension of the information recorded on the original CRC cards invented by Beck and Cunningham. The idea was to aggregate responsibilities—later, messages—into groups to reflect the users of those methods. This particular use of contracts did not gain wide acceptance, and the idea of contracts became rather obscure. Even so, the programming concept of interfaces and templates has much in common with the idea of contracts.

A concept from programming—message scope or visibility—provided renewed use for contracts. In a programming language such as Java, methods (and their invoking messages) could be designated public (anyone can send that message and invoke that service), private (only the object itself can send the message to itself), and protected (only a designated group of user objects can send the message). Other languages, most notably Smalltalk, did not make explicit provision for such method/message declarations. Using contracts to at least specify the intent of the object developer as to the proper use of messages was a natural extension of the notion of contracts. If the implementation language supported message scoping, side 3 provided a specification to the programmer. If not, side 3 documented the intended use of the categorized messages—and no good object programmer would misuse private or protected messages. (Smile.)

As class libraries grew in size and the messages associated with individual classes grew in number (something that should be minimized if object thinking guides the design of those classes), it proved useful to create subcategories of classes and of methods to simplify the search for an appropriate class or method in the library. A typical browser in an integrated development environment (IDE) might show the following four lists: categories of classes, class list, categories of methods, and method list. A user would select the desired class category and see only those classes in that category displayed in the second list. Then the user would select a method category and see only those methods included in that category displayed in the last list. Typical method categories include accessing, displaying, updating, and calculating. Such categories can be captured on the object cube as contracts on side 3.

The layout of side 3 (shown in Figure 8-8) is simple: a contract name followed by an indented list of the messages intended to be included in that contract. A message can appear in more than one contract unless the contracts reflect programming specification of public, protected, and private.

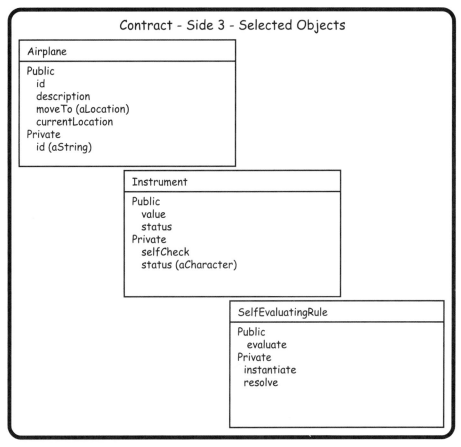

Figure 8-8   Contracts for all classes in both the ATC and mortgage trust application examples (object cube side 3).

State Change Notification

"Objects encapsulate state." When this claim is made, it's usually a reference to changes in the objects occupying an instance variable. This idea reflects the common definition of state—a change in value of any aspect or characteristic of a thing—colored by the way state is used in data-driven object design.

If an object is properly designed, it is typically so simple as to have very little interesting state. Some examples of state might include the following:

- An object in an instance variable has been replaced with another object; the object (or value of that object) matters far less than the fact that the change occurred, so we would characterize the new state as *changed*.

- An object might be in the process of responding to a message and therefore unavailable to receive a new message. State = *busy*.

- An object might be defective in some sense, out of calibration or completely inoperative, yielding the states *faulty* and *dead*. (In the latter case, we are not looking for *dead* so much as "I'm dying, gasp, gasp … the butler did it" written in blood with the object's last exhalation. Or, less colorfully stated, *failing*.)

- An object might be uninitialized: none of its instance variables contain objects other than *Nil*.

- An I/O device might have a *ready* state.

- A state based on the value of an instance variable: the *pressure* variable of a *steamEngine* object and the *danger* state that would occur if the value of *pressure* exceeded some limit.

- From the world of persistence (databases), a variation on the *changed* state can be surmised: *dirty*, which means a change that has yet to be reflected in the persistent persona of the object. There is an inconsistency in value between the cell of a database table and the object stored in an instance variable.

Although it is possible for an object to have numerous states, only a few of those states are likely to be of any interest to anyone outside the object itself. In those cases in which other objects might be interested in a state change, it is appropriate to list and describe those states on side 6 of the object cube. The syntax for side 6 is very simple—a descriptive name of the state and a short description of that state. Figure 8-9 shows side 6 for all objects in the ATC and mortgage trust examples.

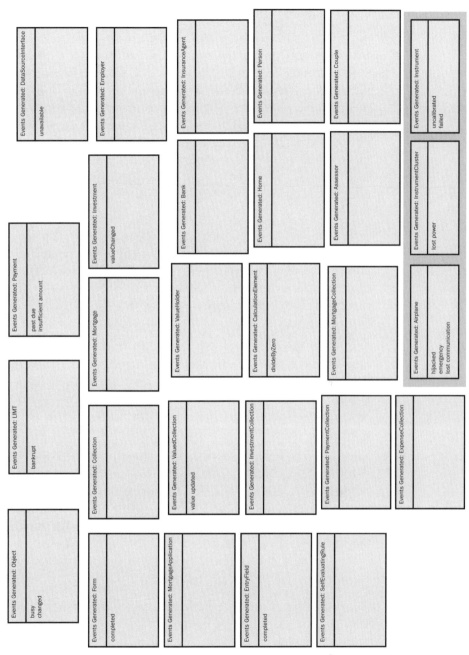

Figure 8-9   Events for objects in the ATC and mortgage trust examples (object cube side 6). Note that most objects have no events. In some cases this is because they are inherited (MortgageApplication from Form), but usually it just reflects that most objects are not willing to share much state information, except for the almost universal "changed" state inherited from class Object).

Here are some important caveats concerning object state and side 6 of the object cube:

■   Side 6 records only those states that the object is willing to make visible to other objects. In this sense, side 6 is akin to side 1 in that it publishes part of the object's interface: the part of the object visible to others. Some state changes might be kept private to better reflect the domain being simulated by the object. For example, a *selfCalibrating-Instrument* might have a state, *out of calibration*, that it does not make visible to the outside world. Instead, it detects that state itself, takes steps to correct that state, and only if it fails in such attempts does it generate a public state, *failed. Failed* would appear on side 6 of the object cube, but *out of calibration* would not.

■   State changes are visible only to the object experiencing the change. Many objects will choose not to allow anyone to be aware of their changes, and even if an object does make a change public by listing that state on side 6, it does not imply that you—or any other object—can see that change, only that you—and all other objects—can request to be notified when the object detects the change in itself.

■   Side 6 of the object cube does not capture and is not intended to capture state-related constraints on an object's behavior. That kind of information is captured in a static diagram—specifically a state chart—and will be discussed in Chapter 9, "All the World's a Stage."

■   Advertising a willingness to notify others of state changes implies that the object has a mechanism for keeping track of who is to be notified, how, and for what. At first this implied requirement might seem to violate object-thinking precepts, but it's quite possible to satisfy such a requirement in a manner consistent with object thinking. The mechanism is an *eventDispatcher* object. Every object capable (and willing) of notifying others of its state changes must contain an *eventDispatcher* to effect that notification.

An *eventDispatcher* object can be visualized as a simple two-part table, as shown in Figure 8-10. The first column of the table contains events, one per row. The second column of the table contains a collection of *eventRegistration* objects. An *eventRegistration*, in its simplest form, is a two-part object consisting of a *receiver* and a *message*.

Event Dispatcher	
Event	Registration Queue
event 1	[REG1] [REG2]
event 2	[REG1]
event 3	[REG1] [REG2] [REG3]
event 4	
event 5	

Registration

[receiverObject message]
Registration (if priority allowed)
[receiverObject message priority]

Figure 8-10 An event dispatcher table and an event registration tuple.

Creation of an *eventDispatcher* object increases flexibility by centralizing but not controlling the awareness of which events exist and who is to be notified when they occur. If an object decides to publish a new event, a simple message to the *eventDispatcher* requesting the addition of a new row to the table is sufficient to effect that change. An object's *eventDispatcher* can be queried as to which events are available, and it responds with a collection (a list) of the contents of the first column. Such queries are almost always made by the programmer as she decides what objects and scripts need to be created to realize a story. Only if you were building a complex-adaptive system (artificial life, for example) would you expect other objects to query a dispatcher about its event list at run time.

If *objectA* wants to know about a state change in *objectB* (one that *objectB* has advertised as public), it sends a registration of its own construction to *objectB*'s *eventDispatcher*. The *objectA* object decides what message it wants sent to effect the event notification, which means that *objectA* can change its mind—use different messages in different contexts—simply by asking that its earlier registration be replaced with a new one containing a new message. This capability provides significant run-time flexibility, allowing changes without necessitating any changes in code and subsequent recompilation of *objectB*.

One other possibility to be noted: suppose we need to notify objects in a particular order—for example, some objects need to be notified immediately and the needs of others are less urgent. We can change (probably subclass) *eventRegistration* to be a triple—*receiverId*, message, priority.

We can then allow the collection that makes up the second column of the *eventDispatcher* to be a sorted collection. As *eventRegistration* objects are added, they are sorted according to their priority values. (Event dispatching as described here is consistent with the observer/publish-and-subscribe patterns published elsewhere.)

Object Appearance

It would be difficult to talk about objects without talking about the graphical user interface (GUI). The Star project at Xerox PARC simultaneously advanced local area networking, GUI design, Smalltalk (object-oriented programming), and alternative input-output (I/O) modes (notably the mouse). Networks and I/O were sufficiently esoteric and close to hardware design that they went their separate ways, post-PARC. GUI design and objects, however, emerged so tightly coupled that it's often assumed that the primary (if not exclusive) use of object design and object programming is the construction of graphical interfaces.

Visual development environments (such as Microsoft Visual Basic) managed to convey the impression that objects were the same as the GUI widgets that appeared in the interface design toolbox. Once you had those widgets in place on your form object, you did real programming—sans objects. (Yes, it's true that the objects are still there, but they are not emphasized or enforced, with the net effect that most Visual Basic programs tend to be event-driven procedural in nature and not OO.) Even Smalltalk IDE tools such as Parts (an extension for Digitalk Smalltalk) and VisualAge (IBM) emphasized the utility of objects for GUI building with far less emphasis on the objects behind the interface.

A worse error was propagated when many of the early tutorials on object programming introduced a misconception by suggesting a "method" colloquially referred to as "cocktail napkin design." It was suggested that the correct way to design an application was from the interface in; that is, sketch your interface on a cocktail napkin and then find the objects necessary to implement that interface. The GUI became a straitjacket to which objects had to conform. This, in effect, meant that object design and implementation were little more than the hard-coded reflection of the specific and idiosyncratic design of a set of visual interfaces. Change the visual interface, and you had to change the object. Not only did this make for a lot more work, it meant that objects were not reusable in different contexts if those contexts defined visual interfaces in an alternative fashion.

> **Note** "You can't emphasize this point enough," suggests Ken Auer, speaking about the danger of "GUI-in" design. "In my early days of OO, if you talked to someone who had been using Smalltalk for 1 to 3 years, you could almost rely on the fact that they 'got it.' After the advent of Parts, VisualAge, and (to a slightly lesser extent) VisualWorks, I had many interviews with programmers who had been 'programming with Smalltalk' for 2 or more years and didn't realize there were supposed to be some objects other than the GUI and the database. Even the ones that recognized this tended to have a poor handle on how central the domain objects should be because they probably spent a good two-thirds or more of their time dealing with GUI and/or DB issues." Ken's comments support a basic premise of this book: object thinking is most easily corrupted by reverting to old, familiar forms of thought. Laying out widgets on a form and objects as data entities are but two examples.

Object thinking acknowledges the special relationship between an object, *X*, and some group of other objects whose role is to represent, visually or otherwise, object *X*. At the same time, it suggests some important differences in the way that relationship is discovered and implemented.

Occasions Requiring an Appearance

While engaged in the task of discovering objects and responsibilities, we told stories about object interactions. Among the interactions in those scenarios were instances of an object displaying itself to a client. An example might be a character displaying itself on some medium for the benefit of an observing human being. What actually appears on the medium is not the character object; it is a representation of some aspect of that object (its visual appearance but not its behavior, or dynamics, or "soul"), just as your photograph is not you but a representation of some part (the surface part) of you.

The converse of displaying oneself to a client is to display the void at the core of your essence when you have yet to be instantiated. This time you display the void as a kind of request for service, asking a human user to please provide substance (a value) that will make you a fully instantiated object. An *entryField* widget consisting of a simple white rectangle and perhaps a blinking cursor within the bounds of that rectangle is an example of an object displaying its "void" and requesting the human user to fill that void with a value. A hybrid of both display and request is a display of your current value with the implicit request to change that value if appropriate.

Even the simplest object might have multiple representations of itself, just as you probably have more than one photograph of yourself. A character, for example, might have a boldfaced appearance and an italicized appearance. In cases in which an object has multiple appearances and can be asked to switch from one to the other, it's necessary to add messages to the protocol that make this ability evident. For example, a date object might have two messages in its protocol—*displayUS* and *displayEurope*—the difference between the resulting display being a transposition of the day and month values.

Most objects are compositions of simpler objects. Remember that every instance variable an object might have contains another object. If an object with instance variables has a gestalt (view of the whole) appearance, that gestalt is necessarily a composite of the appearances of itself and all of its contained objects.

It's easier to illustrate ideas about an object having multiple appearances by using visual metaphors. But visual representations are not the only appearances an object might have. Imagine an object that needs to store itself in a relational database. The relational database management system (RDBMS) cannot accept the object in its natural glory, so the object must marshal[1] itself into a stream of bits that can be accepted and held by the RDBMS. The resultant stream of bits constitutes an appearance of the object but is not the object itself, any more than a visual representation is.

Glyphs

The application of object thinking to the issue of text characters, numbers, and graphical symbols should lead to the recognition that all of these are really just instances of a single kind of thing: a glyph. A glyph object would have one major responsibility: to display itself. To fulfill that responsibility, it would need to know

- Its origin, a point used in the definition of its extent and in placement of its value on a medium.

- Its extent, an area (not necessarily a regular area, but likely some sort of polygon).

- Its scaling factor, an analog of point size, some constant that would allow it to occupy greater or lesser extent.

(continued)

---

1. Marshaling involves the object taking itself apart, asking each part to convert itself into bits, and then asking each part to line up in some kind of order. The process is analogous to a modem converting an analog signal to digital (and eventually back again).

Glyphs   *(continued)*

- Its orientation, a radian (used if the glyph is to be laid out other than horizontally).

- Its value, something as primitive as a bitmap or, more likely, an algorithm (vector) that results in the generation of colored pixels on a medium that is the actual appearance of the glyph.

- Its ASCII value, a bit stream.

- Its EBCDIC value, a bit stream.

- Its Unicode value, a bit stream.

The message protocol for a glyph would include the display message (the glyph would use values in all the appropriate variables to create the bit stream sent to a printer or graphics card that actually generates the display) and getter and setter messages for each of the instance variables listed in the foregoing list.

If glyphs existed in typical information system applications, it would not have been an issue when a certain rock star changed his name to a Celtic-Egyptian symbol.

The separation of objects and views or appearances of objects is essential. This separation of objects and views has also been addressed—but incompletely—in a number of different ways in programming languages and architectural patterns (for example, model-view-controller).

Object thinking would suggest that every object will have a collection of appearances, will advertise (as a responsibility/service/message) its ability to appear in different guises as well as variations (point size, for instance) of a single guise. Each object will transfer to its appearance object (for example, a glyph, as described in the sidebar "Glyphs") responsibility for acquiring and maintaining the information required to effect each appearance.

An elementary object, such as a character, might have a small set of appearances each of which is a simple glyph. The appearance of a more complicated object, such as a string, a date, or a number, would be a composite (an ordered set of appearances of each of its constituent parts): each character in a string, each number and symbol in a date, each integer and symbol in a number. A still more complicated object, such as a form, would be a composite of its own appearance (a boundary perhaps) plus the composites of each of the elements appearing on the form plus the composites and glyphs of each member of each element that appears on the form.

Keeping track of this apparent complexity is relatively straightforward: you simply apply the composite pattern. *Composite* is one of the 26 patterns in the first pattern book, *Design Patterns*. Applied to appearances, the composite pattern asserts that every appearance is made up of glyphs or appearances. A glyph is defined as a leaf node in the hierarchy; an appearance is defined as an instance of appearance, which in turn is made up of appearances, glyphs, or a combination. To display an appearance, you use recursion to traverse the hierarchy, displaying all glyphs and decomposing all appearances into glyphs and appearances until you reach a level containing nothing but glyphs.

Widgets, Forms, Reports

Visual programming languages typically provide a number of different widget types to be used in collecting and displaying bits of information. A character widget, a number widget, a date widget, and a currency widget are examples. Object thinking suggests that there is a need for only one type (class) of data entry widget. A *dataEntryWidget* would have an appearance, the simplest form of which would be a simple rectangle or a bit of underlining. It would have behavior that would include signaling whenever it has been changed (a person entering a value in the box or on the line). It would also possess a set of rule objects that it could use to validate its own contents. An example of a rule might be *valueEntered* is a date; if true, return True; else return False. Another example: *valueEntered* is between *minValue* and *maxValue*. Because the rules are objects and because each widget has a collection of rules that it can apply to itself—a collection that can be modified at any time with add, delete, or replace messages—creating any type of specialized widget is trivial. (See the discussion of self-evaluating rules in Chapter 10, "Supplemental Ideas.")

A form, in light of object thinking, is nothing more than an ordered collection of elements. An element might be a string or a *dataEntryWidget*. A form would have responsibilities to display itself, collaborating with its elements; update itself (add and delete elements); effect different instances of itself (fill itself in, collaborating with its *dataEntryWidget* objects); and validate itself, working with its own collection of rule objects. Form validation rules exist for ensuring consistency among the values stored in *dataEntryWidget* objects (each of those widgets having already validated its contents according to its own set of rules). For example, a form validation rule would ensure that the value stored in the Zip Code widget is consistent with the value stored in the State widget.

(continued)

Widgets, Forms, Reports   *(continued)*

A report is similar to a form in that each comprises a collection of elements. The form adds and deletes elements to become different instances of the form. The form displays itself by asking each element to instantiate itself (obtain a value for itself) and display itself. Each element has its own set of appearance rules, which it uses to display itself. An example of an appearance rule is "My point size is 1.5 times the default point size for this report."

Both reports and forms make use of the glyph and composite patterns discussed earlier in this section.

Object State, Object Constraints

Readers familiar with typical treatment of object development might be curious as to the absence, so far, of any discussion of object state other than the willingness to notify others of state changes as recorded on side 6 of the object cube. Some definitions of objects suggest that they encapsulate state; and modeling methods and tools, such as Unified Modeling Language (UML), provide sophisticated models for capturing state-of-the-object information.

Object thinking shows little concern about state when objects are discussed specifically because a properly designed object has very little interesting state. What state it might have should be private—behind the encapsulation barrier—except to the extent that the object is willing to make public the fact that a state change occurred.

Most discussion about object state is really about state-based constraints to be imposed on an object. Such constraints are not intrinsic to the object itself; they are an aspect of the situation in which the object finds itself employed. This kind of state modeling is important but not important in advancing our understanding of individual objects. For this reason, discussion of state modeling involving objects will be taken up in Chapter 9.

All other constraints that might be imposed on an object are also reflective of a situation, not of the object per se. Table manners, for example, reflect a set of rules that promote or inhibit intrinsic human eating behavior—fingers and communal bowl in an Ethiopian ethnic restaurant; a plethora of special-purpose utensils and prescribed behaviors at a formal state dinner. It's a mistake to attempt to incorporate this kind of variation into an individual object's specification. This type of rule-based constraint will also be addressed in Chapter 9.

9

All the World's a Stage

Chapters 7 and 8 focused on individual objects and problem domains. The discussion focused on discovering—identifying—the objects that already exist in a domain and understanding what is expected of them in that domain. The focus was on an entire domain—either an enterprise (Woodgrove Bank) or an area of commerce (banking industry) as a whole—to avoid defining objects in terms of their idiosyncratic behavior in narrowly defined applications.

Our goal of object discovery was facilitated by telling specific stories about small groups of objects engaged in resolving specific problems or, collectively, providing a specific service. We did this to illustrate, to explore, and to discover the *intrinsic* capabilities and expectations of that object. No single story defined the nature of an object. The *set* of stories we used to discover and model objects was broad enough in scope to ensure a proper balance of specificity and generality: specificity so that the objects could be built and built simply; generality to ensure that the same objects could be used in multiple contexts without modifying their essential nature.

A number of concerns that typically arise in software development were not mentioned or were mentioned but set aside for later discussion. Deferred issues fall into four broad categories:

- Static relationships, associations, affiliations, compositions, and interaction channels that are assumed to be, but seldom are, permanent

- Scripting, providing the cues to be used by a collection of objects while completing specific collective tasks

- Constraints, keeping objects from doing things that they are capable of but that we want to prevent in certain circumstances

- Implementation, providing detailed information about the inside of our objects; algorithms to be used and detailed specifications about formats and values of information

The first three categories were deferred because they do not inform us about objects, only about contexts in which objects must operate. Implementation issues are deferred in accordance with the long-standing development rule, "Figure out what must be done before you concern yourself with how it is done."

We are also being consistent with the Lego brick metaphor: separating the problem of *creating* bricks from the problem of building things *with* bricks. To reintroduce another metaphor, we separated our discussion of actors and their intrinsic talent from the discussions of casting, screenplays, and direction. Our goal was to create actors (objects) with the versatility required to assume many different roles in a wide variety of genres and to avoid creating objects that were typecast—doomed to play the same role, in the same screenplay, over and over again.

Generally, we do not try to solve all the problems of the world in one fell swoop. Instead, we arbitrarily set a boundary that delineates our focus and separates it from the rest of the universe. We call this bounded space our "system," or our "application," or our "program," or our "object." Unfortunately, we also tend to be a bit sloppy in our use of terminology and frequently use the terms *application*, *system*, and *program* more or less interchangeably. In the rest of this section, I will use the term *application* as a label for the domain and our artificially bounded portion of that domain and the term *application artifact* for specific instances of executing code—programs or objects. (To see the difference between *application* and *application artifact*, see the sidebar "Systems and Artifacts.")

Systems and Artifacts

Structured analysis was, in its own time, a new paradigm for software development. As popularized by Larry Constantine, Ed Yourdon, and Meillor Page-Jones, an initial task was the creation of a model of the "existing system." Developers were instructed to create a model—data flow diagrams, entity relation diagrams, context diagrams, and even program structure charts—to document their understanding of how things were currently done. This effort was supposed to facilitate understanding and modeling of a new "system" to replace the existing one. In practice, this step was seldom completed: its value was not understood, and its cost was significant. Later editions of books on structured analysis tended to eliminate this step altogether.

Modeling the existing system has a parallel in object thinking: domain-centric analysis. There is an implicit assertion in both: you cannot begin to understand what must be until you understand what is. This assertion has two corollaries:

- Almost all of the objects you will ever need are already defined, and already have behavioral expectations associated with them, in the domain.

- Almost all of the requirements of new development arise from a misalignment of behaviors and objects. Misalignment results when the wrong object (or group of objects) is providing a particular service, a service is more appropriately provided by a silicon-based object simulation instead of a carbon-based biological object, or, occasionally, no existing object is capable of providing the needed service.

Christopher Alexander (*Notes on the Synthesis of Form*) offers another expression of the need to understand the problem and the problem (domain) space in detail before proceeding with development. Design, according to Alexander, is the process of adapting a solution to a problem. The problem defines the needed solution, and understanding the problem therefore reveals the required solution.

Systems and Artifacts   *(continued)*

Object thinking and structured analysis share a common belief that the existing system must be understood before one proceeds with development. They differ, however, in a very significant way. Structured thinkers, like software engineers, tend to think of the system in terms of a bounded artifact, a piece of software executing on hardware. Object thinkers view the system as *The System*: the complex whole of the domain and all its parts (objects), explicitly including all the human objects and all of the patterned interactions of those objects. It is this System that we seek to understand before attempting to intervene with any development project.

Understanding an entire System is seemingly a daunting task, one reason why most software engineering texts suggest a much narrower focus. Paradoxically, expanding our focus actually provides significant benefits and has the effect of simplifying our work. The dictum "Everything is an object" provides us with a single metaphor/model and a means of partitioning even the most complex domain into a relatively small number of objects with easily understood behaviors.

This perspective also has the effect of redefining what is meant by *artifact* and *application* as those terms are used in development projects. Artifacts are objects or methods—nothing more. Applications are simply scripted assemblies of objects, some objects being software simulations, others being physical entities, and still others being human roles.

A side effect of this perspective is a kind of minimal-intervention principle. Recognizing that introducing any change into a complex system will have widespread, frequently unforeseen, and too often deleterious consequences, we seek to minimize those effects by making the smallest possible change. Examples of applying the minimal-intervention principle include introducing a single new object, adding a new behavior to an existing object, reassigning a behavior from one object to another, simulating as faithfully as possible an existing object with software, and assembling and scripting the least number of objects necessary to fulfill a single story, as XP defines user stories.

We do need to understand more about the application—the context in which our objects will perform and the precise tasks we expect our objects to perform—before proceeding with development. Specifically, we need to determine the relationships, constraints, and interactions that will be required of our objects in each specific circumstance. (Although we might discover new things about our objects while engaged in our study of the application and might be required to modify the intrinsic nature of our objects as a result, it's a major mistake, from an object thinking perspective, to define objects in terms of an application instead of a domain.)

Static Relationships

There are an open-ended number of possible relationships among objects. Some are so common as to have special notation invented for them in modeling tools (UML, for example): *using*, *is-a-part-of*, *is-a-kind-of*, and *contains* are examples of common relationships.

From this large set of possible relationships, only two tell us anything about the intrinsic nature of our objects. All of the others provide information about the context—the application—in which our objects operate; they are *situational relationships*. The two relationships that describe intrinsic aspects of objects are *is-a-kind-of* and *collaborates-with*.

Is-a-Kind-of Relationship

Classes are not essential to object thinking, merely a convenience. From a cognitive standpoint, the use of classes allows us to think about an entire group instead of all the members of that group—something we have been doing throughout this book.

Combining the idea of classes with the is-a-kind-of relationship yields a taxonomy, a particular kind of structural organization, that can then be used as a kind of index to help in finding an object with a particular set of behaviors. Figure 9-1 is a class hierarchy diagram—specifically, a taxonomy of the classes in the mortgage trust example introduced in Chapter 7.

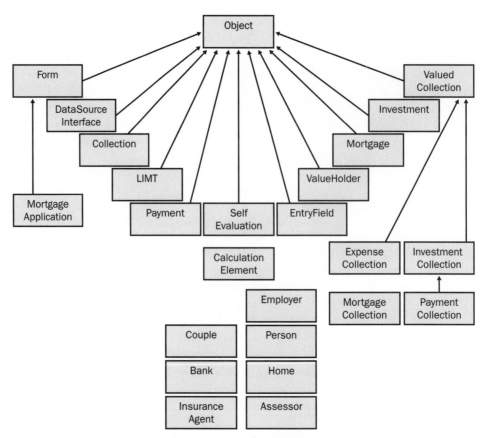

Figure 9-1   The is-a-kind-of relationships among the objects (via their classes) in the mortgage trust example.

Using a taxonomy requires only a general notion of the behavior or behaviors you need in an object as a starting point. You can find an object with that (or some of those) behaviors and then move up or down the taxonomy to find an object that matches your needs in a more precise manner. If no existing class of objects meets your needs, you can still use the taxonomy to simplify your creative work by finding the object that best matches your needs and saying that your new object is-a-kind-of the one you found. You then create a subclass and give it the precise behavior you want, and you use, via inheritance, behaviors that already exist in the superclass.

From a cognitive point of view (we will discuss an alternative point of view in just a minute), your taxonomy *must* follow two rules:

■   Exhibit a single line of descent (single inheritance) based on nothing but the behaviors of the objects. Ideally, you should create your taxonomy (class hierarchy) as soon as you have completed side 1 of the object cube. That way, you are not tempted to create a hierarchy based on object internals, that is, methods or instance variables. Single inheritance is important to avoid "abominations" that break the taxonomy—the way the platypus breaks the Linnaean taxonomy of fauna. (Linnaeus noted certain attributes of animal species such as "warm blooded," "lays eggs," "live birth," and "covered with hair" and used them as the basis for classifying fauna. The platypus, a furry mammal that lays eggs, breaks the classification rules and is therefore an "abomination.")

■   Subclass only by extension—by adding behaviors. A subclass should be able to do everything its superclass (or superclasses) can do, plus at least one more thing. This means that you can substitute an object from a subclass in any situation calling for an object from its superclass and still get the behavior you expect. If you define a subclass by subtraction (taking away a behavior) or by redefinition (overriding a behavior), you create cognitive dissonance.[1] Users of your taxonomy can never be entirely sure of the behavior they will get from classes without looking inside those classes to see what they really do. This is, of course, an egregious violation of encapsulation.

Class hierarchies can be viewed from an implementation perspective as well as a cognitive perspective. Unfortunately, these two perspectives are not always in concert. When they disagree, it is almost always because the hierarchy is perverted to conform to constraints imposed by a nonobject machine or virtual machine (programming language).

In Chapter 5, "Vocabulary: Words to Think With," it was noted that one aspect of a class was to act as a repository for code and information shared by all instances (objects) of that class. In terms of efficiency, this is a good idea because storage space is minimized and changes can be made in a single place. It becomes very tempting, however, to use this fact to justify creating your class hierarchy based on shared code instead of shared behaviors. A similar error arises from treating object variables (instance variables) as if they were data attributes and then creating your hierarchy based on shared attributes. Always create hierarchies based on shared behaviors, side 1 of the object cube, only.

---

1. Polymorphism—allowing different objects to respond differently to different messages—allows you to create classes that override (replace) a superclass method with one of their own. There are reasons for doing so, but they still create cognitive dissonance and make use of the objects containing overrides more difficult. There are better ways to achieve the same goal—defining template or interface classes, for example.

Collaborates-with Relationship

Collaborations arise if, and only if, object A must use a service from object B during the interval defined by object A receiving a message (request for service) and object A returning the appropriate result object to the sender of the message to object A. All collaborations are synchronous in the sense that object A must invoke and wait for results from object B before it can complete whatever work is required in response to the message it received.

Collaborations are almost always hard coded: they require manifest references in the algorithm of the method where the collaboration occurs. Because of the hard-coded nature of collaborations, we assert that they define part of the intrinsic nature of an object. In every circumstance, in every context, the collaboration will occur if object A receives the indicated message.

Collaborating objects are very tightly coupled. For this reason, collaborations should occur inside the encapsulation barrier, with objects occupying instance variables, objects being received along with messages, and objects occupying temporary variables. Collaborations with objects occupying global variables are good or bad depending on the justification of need for a global variable. Collaborations outside the encapsulation barrier are sometimes necessary but should be avoided (by refactoring the distribution of responsibilities among objects) whenever possible.

Wirfs-Brock introduced a dedicated model—a collaboration graph—that was seldom adopted by actual developers. Figure 9-2 shows an example of such a graph. The graph depended on the use of contracts (side 3 of the object cube) to define potential connection points for potential collaborations. Deciphering the graph was difficult because of line tracing from client to server. Collaboration graphs (probably unintentionally) provide a visual metaphor consistent with the object = software integrated circuit introduced by Brad Cox. Interesting collaboration graphs look like circuit boards when viewed as a gestalt.

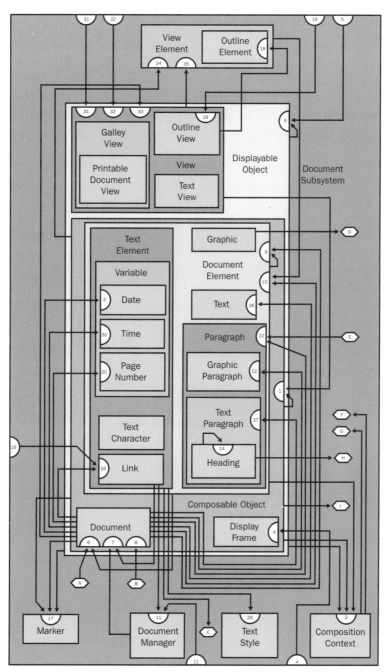

Figure 9-2   A visual model of collaborations, based on a graph in *Designing Object Oriented Software,* by Wirfs-Brock et al., 1991.

Situational Relationship

Collaborations are not the only example of "uses" relationships among objects. It can be said that object A uses object B if object B has asynchronously provided information or services to object A that object A finds useful for its own work. For example, an airplane has a responsibility to identify itself, which requires an *id* object, which leads to the assumption that at some point in the past the airplane asked some national naming authority for an *id* object. That request for an *id* object is an example of a uses relationship between the airplane and *namingAuthority*. (It is not a collaboration because the airplane does not interact with *namingAuthority* each time it receives the *id* request.)

Except for collaborations, the fact that particular objects use the services of others reflects the demands of the application (the situation) and not intrinsic needs of the objects themselves. The same thing can be said of the particular objects that are aggregated into components: the aggregation is a reflection of the demands of a particular circumstance, nothing more. This is not to say that it is unimportant to understand (and probably model) situational relationships, but it is important to recognize, and keep in mind, that you are not modeling the intrinsic nature of any objects.

What then do you need to understand about a situational relationship application?

- The objects that are participating in the work of the application

- The objects that have a need to communicate with others and the general nature of that communication

- The "data"—really, the collective memory of objects involved in the application; any relationships among data items

- An overview, or gestalt, view of the application and its participants

The following sections describe models that might be helpful as a guide to thinking about a situational relationship application.

Static Relationship Model

A static relationship model (the UML equivalent is a class relation diagram or an object relation diagram) can provide all of this information. Static relationship models (SRMs) are models of applications and not domains. They are called *static* because the information portrayed in this type of model is supposedly invariant. It must constantly be remembered that *invariant* applies to the time and space boundary defined by each individual application; the relationships might or might not exist in any other application. This is a major point of difference with data-driven approaches to modeling objects.

A data-driven approach assumes that objects are equivalent to data entities. Data entities *are* expected to be defined at the level of the domain because
it is assumed that they are the basis for creating a database that will be common
to all applications. This is one more example of perpetuating the traditional
view of software as data structures plus algorithms. A data-driven approach to
objects posits a singular database containing all of the data structures and
allows multiple applications—application is equal to algorithms only—to share
a common data structure.

> **Note**   Data modeling and object modeling are so dissimilar that a
> named concept, the *impedance mismatch problem*, was coined to
> reflect the difficulty of integrating object and database applications.
> Some of the problems were simply technical and have been more or
> less resolved. The inability of classical databases to generate
> "changed events" or otherwise notify objects of a need to update
> themselves when a cell in a database table has been altered is one
> example. The basic difference, however, arises from the fact that
> objects are domain-centric models, while schemas are machine/data-
> base models. The effort required to "normalize" a conceptual data
> model into a logical data model (one capable of implementation in a
> database) essentially has to be reproduced in some degree each time
> an object application wants to interact with a database—usually for
> persistence. Immense amounts of effort have gone into the develop-
> ment of middleware that allows objects and databases to interact with
> each other.

An SRM, from an object thinking point of view, is a gestalt view of the
objects participating in an application (cast of characters) and relationships that
exist among those objects when in that application. Relationships most frequently denote *potential* interactions among objects, just as a roadmap shows
potential travel[2] among cities connected by those roads. Relationships might
also denote constraints on object behaviors or associations while the objects in
question are participating in a given application.

Most application SRM diagrams are little more than semantic nets (see
Chapter 6) with more precision, more detail, and an aura of specification

---

2. Roads connecting cities are obviously real. But the existence of a road does not mandate use by
   vehicles; traffic remains a potential, not a certainty.

instead of discovery. A semantic net also identifies the cast of characters—objects—in a domain and reveals relationships among those objects. Semantic nets were used as a heuristic starting point for object discovery. SRMs are intended as a kind of specification: information to guide the developer in the creation of the application.

Most of the information depicted in a semantic net will be used to define and create objects. Some of that information will be used to define applications, especially constraint- or rule-based information on the semantic net. Consider the mortgage trust example discussed in previous chapters. Figure 9-3 shows a fragment of the semantic net dealing with relationships between the price of a home and the median price of homes in a neighborhood. The semantic net fragment shows a specific business rule: the home price must be less than or equal to the median price of homes in the neighborhood. This rule is not a domain rule; it is an application rule. It should not become a basis for defining the home, neighborhood, or price (actually money) objects because it does not reveal the intrinsic nature of any object. Instead, it shows a relationship that exists only in one or more applications (contexts), perhaps the "collect and validate loan application data" application.

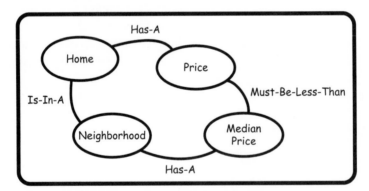

Figure 9-3 A semantic net fragment, showing a constraining relationship among objects in a domain.

Figure 9-4 shows an SRM for the mortgage trust example. Notice that it is very similar to the semantic net: most of the same players are still present, and most of the links among them are still evident as well. It differs from the semantic net in the use of implementation names for many of the objects (classes), it shows some of the interesting details of object construction (instance variables and method names), and it uses terminology more suitable for implementation than discovery. (Technical rather than domain jargon is allowed on an SRM but not on a semantic net.)

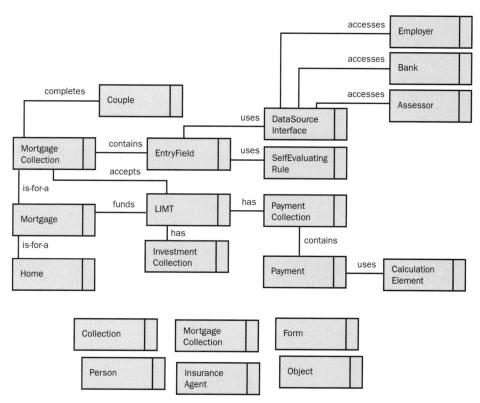

Figure 9-4   SRM depiction of the classes and relationship in the mortgage trust example.

Collective Memory Map

One of the important responsibilities that an object might assume is to portray and maintain some specific bit of information (data). Examples include numbers, integers, floating-point numbers, dates, times, characters, strings, and money. None of these objects limit themselves strictly to the portrayal and maintenance of information; they also have other interesting behaviors appropriate for the kind of information they maintain. Dates, for example, can perform calendar-related calculations and comparisons. Numbers can do arithmetic. Strings have many behaviors similar to those of collections: iteration, insertion, deletion, and arrangement, for example.

Given their specialized nature, *data depiction objects* frequently are found occupying instance variables of other objects. An airplane object, for example, has an instance variable named *id*, which is occupied by a string object.

Given the information-centric nature of the contemporary world, numerous constraints and relationships exist between and among data depiction objects. Although it is possible to capture this type of relationship in a standard SRM, doing so obscures, somewhat, the real nature of the relationship. Suppose, for example:

- An airplane object has instance variables for *id*, containing a serial number such as N543UE; *transponderCode*, a four-digit integer; and *status*, containing a character whose value indicates that the airplane is in normal operation, hijacked, in a declared emergency, or in controlled airspace.

- An airspace object has an instance variable, *assignedAircraft*, that contains a collection of *blips*.

- A blip object has instance variables for *id, transponderCode, altitude, latitude, longitude, vector, priority,* and *status.*

Figure 9-5 shows a fragment of an SRM that relates the three objects under discussion. This fragment obscures a great deal of detail about the actual relationships involved—for example, the following rules:

- Transponder code value must equal 1200 for VFR flight.

- Transponder code value must equal 7500 if plane has been hijacked.

- Transponder code value must equal 7700 if plane is in a state of emergency.

- Transponder code value must equal 7600 if plane has lost communications.

- Transponder code must equal value specified by ATC for its blip representation.

- Transponder code value must be consistent with airplane's status value.

- Blip ID and airplane ID must be consistent.

- Blip priority must be 1A if transponder code is 7500, 7600, or 7700.

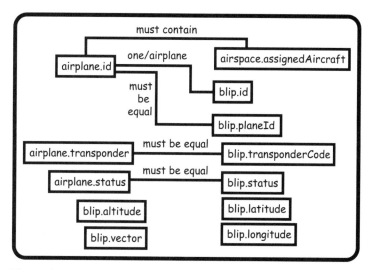

Figure 9-5   Relationships among airplane, blip, and airspace.

It would be possible to model all of these constraints simply by adding relationship symbols between blip and airplane on the SRM—if you are willing to sacrifice a great deal of readability. Alternatively, since all of these relationships are among objects occupying instance variables of other objects, there is value in modeling them directly in a separate model, a collective memory map like that depicted in Figure 9-6.

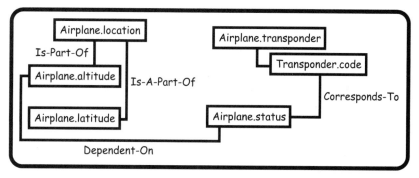

Figure 9-6   Relationships among objects occupying instance variables of other objects in the airplane, blip, and airspace example.

A collective memory map (CMM) is another type of static diagram constructed according to the following rules:

■ Objects appearing on a CMM are occupants of instance variables in other objects.

■ Objects appearing on a CMM must have a primary role of data depiction and maintenance (maintenance implies self-validation, self-persistence, and self-based access control); they can be considered primitives in the same sense that a database defines certain objects as primitives. Most often these include numbers, characters, strings, dates, money, time, and similar objects.

■ A kind of collection that is restricted to containing "primitive" objects, called a *ValueHolder*, can also be depicted in a CMM.

■ Each object depicted is named using dot notation that identifies the container object name and instance variable name—for example, *customer.lastName*.

■ In those cases in which the instance variable contains a *ValueHolder* instead of a primitive, the dot notation is extended to include the label (key) associated with the actual primitive—for example, *customer.description.gender*.

■ Relationships among objects on the CMM are drawn as connecting lines with appropriate labels.

Figure 9-7 depicts a collective memory map for the mortgage trust example. Collective memory maps are situational: they reflect constraints that exist among "data" objects in the context of a particular application. In some cases, it might be useful to create a domain-level version of a collective memory map. A domain-level collective memory map would have some things in common with an enterprise memory model, namely a global depiction of all the "data" in the domain and the objects in which it might be found and any relationships among those objects that were truly invariant across the domain. If your enterprise is interested in constructing such a global model, you need to remember some important caveats:

■ Object thinking presumes that "data" objects represent information or knowledge that objects need to perform their assigned tasks, while enterprise data models presume to depict all the data that the "system" must remember about objects. This is a critical distinction.

- The global model should contain only relationships and constraints that are invariant across the domain.

- A CMM for an application can add, delete, and modify relationships to reflect the situational context. If there is a conflict, the global map must be modified.

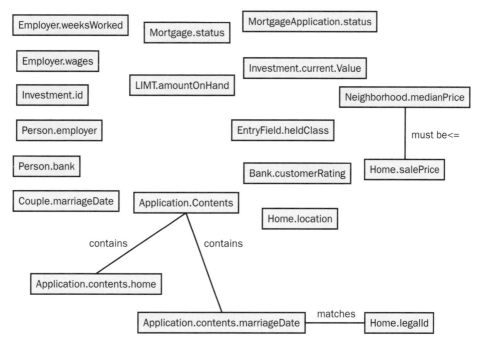

Figure 9-7   A collective memory map for the mortgage trust example.

Architecture

Almost all applications have an overarching structure or means of organization, which might be called *architecture*. Architecture affects the way you think about implementation, especially when the architectural pattern is so common as to be assumed. For example, traditional structured development presumed a hierarchical command-and-control architecture as reflected in a program structure chart (Figure 9-8). This visual pattern is seen in the mainline-plus-subroutines source code organization scheme (Figure 9-9). The hierarchical control architecture is a codification and expression of a lot of ideas about "good" program design, ideas that support most of the rest of structured development approaches.

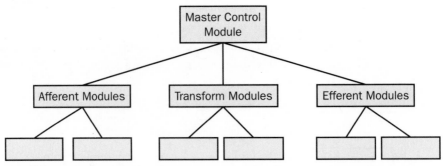

Figure 9-8   The proper organization (architecture) of a program consistent with structured development ideas.

```
Initialize procedure
Main routine
    Input data routines
        conditional flow logic
     end input routines
    Process data routines
        case statement depending on data types
    end process routines
    Output routines
        conditional flow logic
    end output routines
end main routine
Termination routine

subroutine one
    transform code
end subroutine one

subroutine two
    transform code
end subroutine two
```

Figure 9-9   A structure depicting how actual source code might reflect the hierarchical control architecture.

A prototypical architecture that reflects object thinking ideals and principles also exists: model-view-controller (MVC). MVC is not a mandated architecture. You can use almost any of the commonly encountered architectural patterns (see the sidebar "Architectural Patterns and Objects"), but an investigation of MVC is instructive and important for the way it illustrates and reinforces the other aspects of object thinking that have been discussed in previous chapters.

Architectural Patterns and Objects

MVC is but one of a number of architectural patterns or prototypical ways of organizing a group of objects engaged in a collective task. Commonly encountered alternative architectural patterns include hierarchical control, pipes and filters, client/server, and several variations of the blackboard architecture. With the exception of hierarchical control (the antithesis of object ideals), all of these alternative architectures can be consistent with the principles of object thinking.

Regarding *pipes and filters*, readers familiar with UNIX/Linux will immediately recognize this pattern. Two kinds of objects are involved: pipes, which are connectors and possibly temporary storage locations; and filters, which are places where specialized services (transformations) are performed. Figure 9-10 illustrates a small pipes-and-filters architecture.

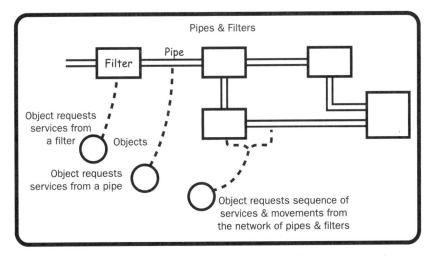

Figure 9-10   Objects move along the route provided by the pipes and obtain services from the objects embodying the filters.

Traditional thought about pipes-and-filters architecture reflects traditional thinking about the separation of data and process. From that non-object point of view, data passes along the pipes (pushed or pulled by the connected filters) and is manipulated by processes at each filter station. Simply reversing the idea about who is in charge and assuming that everything is an object makes this a perfectly acceptable architecture for use by object thinkers. The architecture merely provides transport objects

(continued)

Architectural Patterns and Objects   *(continued)*

(pipes) and service providing objects (filters). A large pool of objects requiring a similar set of services can ask the pipes for transport to the filters whose services they need, take advantage of both, and effect self-processing in a very efficient manner.

Client/server architectures are the mainstay of the networked business world. Two-tier client/server systems are almost identical with MVC, with the model (usually a database) physically located on a server and most of the view and control aspects on clients. Conversely, MVC can be seen as simply an n-tier (or peer-to-peer) client/server architecture. Object thinking will frequently, and naturally, lead to the construction of a client/server architecture, the only difference being the overall distribution of responsibilities and the absence of overt controller, manager, and scheduler objects.

Blackboard architectures actually come in at least three variations, which I'll label bulletin boards, blackboards, and whiteboards. All variants have common elements as illustrated in Figure 9-11: service providers, requesters, a common communication space, requests for service, and results. Each of these elements is, of course, an object.

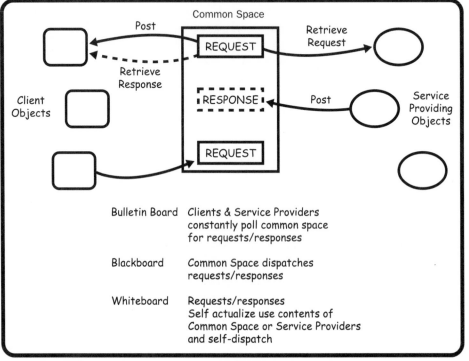

Bulletin Board   Clients & Service Providers
                  constantly poll common space
                  for requests/responses

Blackboard   Common Space dispatches
                  requests/responses

Whiteboard   Requests/responses
                  Self actualize use contents of
                  Common Space or Service Providers
                  and self-dispatch

Figure 9-11   Elements common to all blackboard systems.

Architectural Patterns and Objects   *(continued)*

In the simplest form of blackboard architecture, the *bulletin board*, requesters post requests in the common space, and service providers constantly poll that space looking for requests they might service. Upon finding an appropriate request, the service provider retrieves it and provides appropriate satisfaction, a result, which is then returned to the common space, where the original requester finds it (constantly polling the space—"Are you there yet?") and retrieves it.

Request and result objects are relatively straightforward containers—of the information necessary to specify a result and the result that can be queried by the requester upon retrieval of the information. A ride board, such as that found in most university student unions, is a prototypical example of a bulletin board system.

Give the common space some interesting responsibilities, and you have a blackboard variant. The common space maintains a list of service providers to which it can match a posted request. When a match is found, the request is forwarded appropriately. The common space also retains a list of requesters and their requests so that when a result is posted it can forward the result to the appropriate requester. Care must be taken not to turn these responsibilities into a command-and-control structure.

Whiteboards are similar to the tuple spaces proposed by David Gelernter[3] and implemented in his Linda programming language. In this variant, the shared location—the whiteboard—is called *tuple space* and the request and result objects are called *tuples*. Tuples can actually perform work, transform themselves by combining with and interacting with other tuples, in tuple space. The tuple space itself is also given enhanced responsibilities for filtering and feeding forward (to the next hierarchical level of tuple spaces) its contents (tuples).

All of these architectures are perfectly consistent with the ideals of object thinking as long as the assumptions about control, distribution of responsibility (factoring), and object autonomy illustrated in MVC are respected.

---

3. Gelernter, David. *Mirror Worlds*. Oxford University Press, Reprint edition (January 1993).

Figure 9-12 depicts the model-view-controller architecture. The figure is actually a slight variant of the architecture proposed as the Smalltalk language and development environment was being created at Xerox PARC. MVC is almost always discussed in the context of a graphical user interface environment—invented simultaneously with Smalltalk—but the important principles behind the architecture are not limited to such an environment.

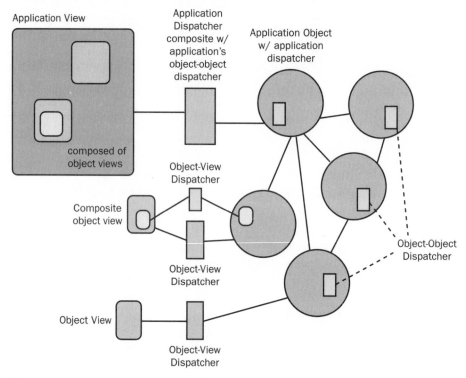

Figure 9-12   Generalized model of the MVC concepts.

MVC is grounded in the idea of specialization and distribution of responsibilities—specifically, the identification of three main categories of responsibility (presentation or visualization, computational work, and coordinating communications) and assigning those to different sets of objects.

The *model* comprises those objects actually engaged in accomplishing the work objectives of the application. Model objects have a need to communicate with one another by sending messages and by notifying other objects of internal state changes. In Figure 9-12, model objects are depicted as round circles.

One of the model objects assumes the role of the *application object*. The application object assumes responsibility for startup and shutdown activities in collaboration with the other model objects and acts as a kind of global (within the application) repository of objects and information that need to be visible to other model objects while the application is running.

The *view* consists of a hierarchically organized collection of objects—for example, widgets, windows, and icons—whose primary task is creating visualizations of objects so as to be comprehensible to human beings. This definition presumes a GUI environment and reflects the history that shaped the original MVC architecture.

A view object does not have to be a GUI element. If an object creates a representation of itself other than its native implementation, that too would be a view object. Examples of nonsensory views would include bit stream serializations that allow objects to exist in a relational database or an XML statement that allows an object to be shared across applications and implementation languages.

In Figure 9-12, view objects are depicted as rounded rectangles. The hierarchical organization of views reflects the fact that simple objects have simple views and more complicated objects have views that are collections of the views of the simpler objects that they comprise. It's also possible for any object to possess multiple views of itself. An integer, for example, might have a simple bitmap view that depicts the value of the integer, and it might have an update view consisting of a widget depiction (rectangular entry field area) plus the bitmap of its value. Figure 9-13a illustrates the hierarchical composition of a complex view, and Figure 9-13b provides an example using the mortgage application.

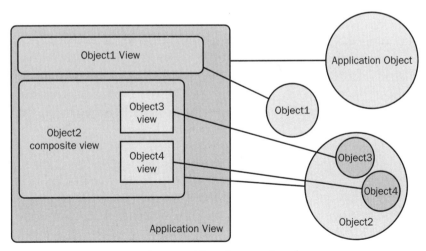

Figure 9-13a   Hierarchical composition of a complex view.

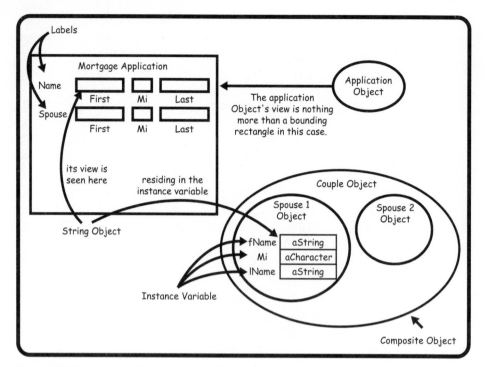

Figure 9-13b   The application completion screen in the mortgage trust example is a hierarchically organized collection of object views.

The *controller* is badly misnamed. Control in the classical programming sense is anathema to object thinkers and right-thinking autonomous objects everywhere. I'll substitute the word *coordinator* for the rest of this discussion. Coordination refers to the tasks involved that allow one object to send a message to another and for an object to notify any interested object of a state change in itself.

Ensuring that it's possible for two objects to exchange messages is a matter of visibility: the objects have to be able to see one another. An example of coordinating visibility is the application object having a variable that contains a collection of all the objects participating in the application. Should one object need to talk to another, it can ask the collection for an object by name or by criterion. Similarly, the application object might have a variable that will contain the currently active or currently selected object, to which other objects might need to send messages. Because the application object is global within the application, all other objects can send messages either to it or to the objects occupying its instance variables.

Event (state change) notification was the main responsibility of historic controller objects, another manifestation of the GUI-centric history of MVC. We will use a special-purpose object, an *eventDispatcher*, to provide all the necessary coordination associated with event notification. Dispatchers were introduced earlier; the following paragraphs will serve as a reminder.

An *eventDispatcher* is a simple two-dimensional table, the first column of which contains a list of events that can be dispatched and the second column of which contains a collection (possibly an ordered collection) of *notification-Request* objects.

A notification request is a dyad consisting of the name/ID of the object requesting notification of an event's occurrence and a message to be sent to that object as means of notification. If the notification collection is ordered (for priority, for instance), the notification request can be a triad of name, message, and priority number.

An *eventDispatcher* can add or delete events, must accept and delete registrations on request, and, when an event is detected, must tell each registration in the associated queue to execute itself (send the contained message to the contained object reference).

If the *registrationQueue* is an ordered collection, it must reorder itself each time a registration is added or deleted.

The *eventDispatcher* objects in Figure 9-12 are depicted as rectangles (long axis is vertical). Each object has a small solid triangle inside itself, indicating that every object has the capability of accepting registrations for changes within itself (as indicated on side 6 of the object cube).

Rectangles appearing between an object (circle) and a view (rounded rectangle) coordinate and ensure consistency between the object and its view. Just as views are composites, so too are these event dispatchers. A composite object (*Customer*, for example) might have a composite view consisting of the views of each of the objects occupying an instance variable of *Customer* (the strings in *fName*, *lName*, and *MI*, for example). Although it's possible for each object participating in this composition to use its own individual dispatcher to coordinate changes, it's also possible to create a single dispatcher and have each object add an event line to that dispatcher as it adds its view to the composite. Figure 9-14 illustrates this composition.

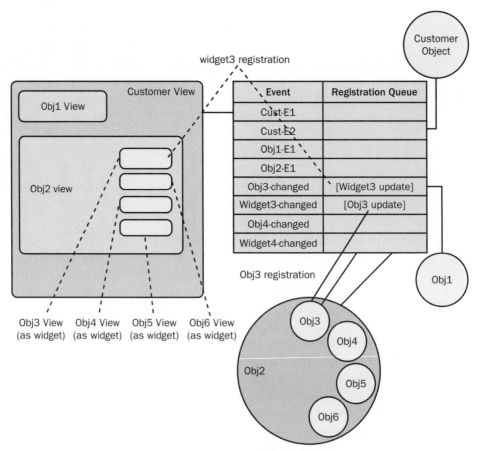

Figure 9-14 The composite object, *Customer*, might use a composite dispatcher instead of each object using its own dispatcher.

In addition to the explicit elements of MVC, we also assume an *outside world* consisting of all the objects outside the application object. This is the realm of human being objects, legacy system objects, and operational platform objects such as hardware, operating systems, mouse managers, and keyboard managers. (Of course, any object whose name includes the term *manager* is immediately suspect and should be examined carefully for violations of object thinking principles.) Although it's true that everything is an object, it's equally true that many of the things in this realm operate in a very nonobject fashion.

From the perspective of the application object and the objects making up its cast of characters, the outside world is a source of information and events. It's the presumed destination of results, but whether someone actually uses the results an object was asked to provide is not of much concern. Objects live to serve. Someone on the outside asked for a service, and it was provided. The object assumes that the client knew what it was asking for and had a use for the result. This is an anthropomorphic way of saying that objects are not and should not be aware of their clients, even when those clients are not other software objects.

The application object, or one of its cast members, might require services from objects in the outside world. In that case, it might need to display itself using an update view, an implicit request to an outside world object to provide information by altering the update view. In other cases, it might need to find and send a message to an object in the outside world, usually by sending a message to the operating system object via the application object.

A composite *eventDispatcher* associated with the application object also handles events generated in the outside world of which objects inside the application (or the application object itself) might need notification. In Figure 9-12, the application dispatcher has three parts (view-object coordination events, outside world events, and global notification events) illustrating its composite nature.

The MVC architecture has been criticized (in some cases by those who created it), but it is an excellent example of how to organize and coordinate a group of objects without imposing any kind of centralized control. The distribution of responsibilities and the creation of special-purpose objects such as the dispatchers allow complete flexibility, even at run time. Dispatcher events, for example, can be added and deleted by sending a run-time message, as can registrations for those events. It's even possible to dynamically configure the event registration dyad at run time. MVC provides an existence proof of how the ideals of object thinking can be realized.

Dynamic Relationships

All of the static relationships (except class hierarchy and collaboration) can be seen as "setting the stage" information. They determine the scenery and props, the marks that actors use to navigate the stage, the cast of characters, and an outline of the plot. A script actually determines what happens on the stage during the performance of the play. A script is simply a collection of messages sent from actor to actor, interpreted by receiving actors, and resulting in subsequent messaging. On occasion, actors respond to cues other than messages—that is, signals, such as the ringing of a phone, which is the phone's way of notifying other objects of a change in its state.

Capturing and modeling the dynamics of an application (following the stage metaphor) consists of detailed modeling of scripts and event notification: the two sources of "cues" for our participating objects.

Scripts

During discovery, we told stories about object interactions. Some of those stories we wrote down on cards; others we modeled with interaction diagrams. Most of those stories exhibited a nested structure, analogous to the way a play is broken up into acts and acts into scenes. Design and implementation activities require that we turn those stories into specifications, program code, or both.

The same tool, an interaction diagram, is used to discover conversational requirements and specify a script. The only difference will be in the labels attached to objects, messages, events, and returned objects. During discovery we want to use, exclusively, domain language in describing our stories. For design purposes, our diagrams should have labels that correspond to actual classes and actual messages as they appear in message protocols recorded on the object cubes. (In the Behavior! tool mentioned earlier, interaction diagrams have color-coded labels: red meaning that the label has not been mapped to an implementation term and reflects user vocabulary, black for user vocabulary that has been mapped to an implementation term, and blue for the implementation term. The diagram itself does not change, only the labels, assuring consistency between our domain and the simulation of that domain we are creating in software.) Figure 9-15 depicts the discovery and script versions of a conversation from the mortgage trust example.

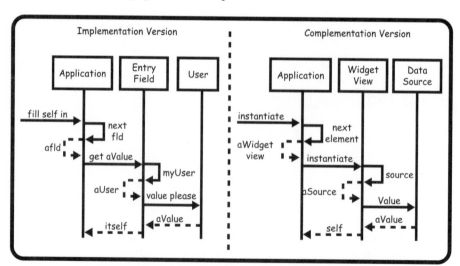

Figure 9-15   The diagram on the left has labels reflecting domain vocabulary. The one on the right is the identical conversation with labels reflecting implementation vocabulary.

Customers, working with developers, spend time factoring their stories into discrete cards with the goal of creating cards that can be estimated (effort required to realize the story in code) and that have a discrete focus. This may require refactoring an ambiguous or overly ambitious story. No intermediary design is required. An XP user story maps to a discrete bit of functionality of a larger program or system and should probably involve fewer than six objects exchanging ten or so messages. Purely as a thought-organizing aid, even XP developers often take the time to sketch a rough interaction diagram as a means of factoring stories and as a prelude to coding. Although not one of the official twelve practices of XP, a quick design session using a whiteboard clearly has a role in clarifying the intent of the story and outlining the participating objects and their interactions.

For example, consider the story card "Application form is completed and validated," a story that almost certainly needs to be factored. Figure 9-16 (a–c) shows rough sketches of interaction diagrams that might have been sketched during a conversation[4] among developers and the on-site customer. Drawing the diagrams reveals ways to factor the original story. (The story might actually stay intact, and only the tests and tasks completed by the programmers are factored to reflect the design implications of the interaction diagram sketches.)

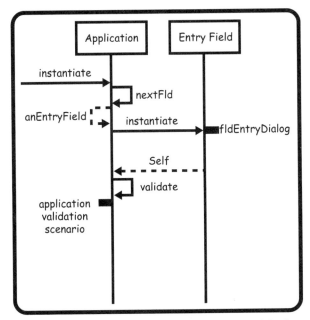

Figure 9-16a   The original story that, whenever it looks as though a lot is going to happen, is factored with a placeholder for a substory inserted.

---

4. An XP story has three parts, *card, conversation*, and *confirmation*. The card is the tangible evidence of the story and a place to record information about the story (estimate and priority, for example). The conversation may be verbal or may involve the use of diagrams such as those depicted here. The conversation is intended to expand understanding and to reveal the design behind the story. Confirmation is the acceptance test, written by the user and implemented by the developers, that proves the code accomplishes the desired task.

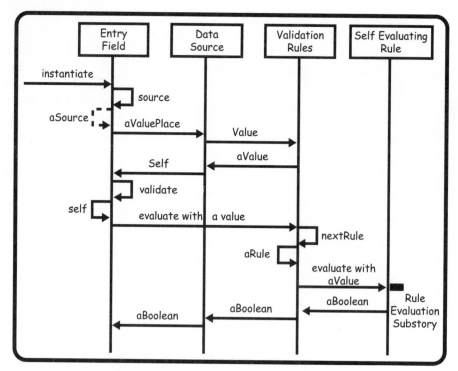

Figure 9-16b   Substory: "Entry field obtains and validates contents."

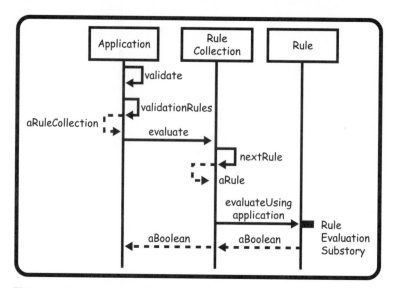

Figure 9-16c   Substory: "Application form validates self."

Note that the interaction diagrams created as part of the conversation about the story expose a need for object interactions that detect and resolve problems—error handling.

A final note on scripts: It's quite possible, and sometimes desirable, to implement scripts as first-class objects, as an ordered collection of messages. When told to execute, the script sends the messages it contains, in order; accumulates the results; and keeps track of its own status in terms of its successful execution. This approach adds discipline to a conversation, ensuring that it occurs as it was supposed to, without adding control. The script object encapsulates a conversational fragment, and it's the script object itself that succeeds or fails in its assigned task. As a first-class object, a script can be modified by adding and deleting message objects without the need to recompile the application containing those script objects.

Event Dispatching

Events are cues that can be used by the developer to script object interactions. Side 6 of the object cube lists the events (cues) available for use. Our stories and the interaction diagrams that might have been created as part of the conversation about those stories provide us the information needed to link an event (cue) with resulting messages sent to the objects being cued. The object cube tells us of the state changes an object deems of potential interest to others, and the interaction diagrams note occasions when state changes affect the flow of a conversation among objects.

The interaction diagrams also confirm an important aspect of object thinking: the only object directly aware of a state change is the object in which the change occurs. The double-headed arrow used in an interaction diagram to denote a state change signal must always be directed to the object in which that state change occurs, never to other objects in the diagram. Figure 9-17 illustrates this important caveat.

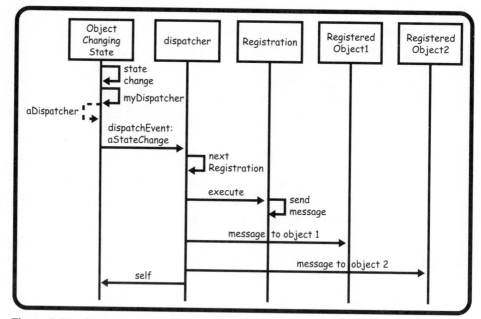

Figure 9-17 State change notification is always a "message" to oneself, never to other objects. A state change can trigger multiple messages to other objects, reflecting the contents of the event dispatcher, as shown in the diagram on the left.

All event notification is performed via an event dispatcher located in each object. Event dispatchers must be *populated* for an application to execute—that is, each must contain a list of events and must have registrations[5] for those events consistent with the needs of the application as expressed stories (interaction diagrams). Because most objects will have little if any interesting state behavior, populating an event dispatcher will be relatively straightforward.

However simple an object's state behavior may be, it would be nice to have some corroboration of the information on side 6 of the object cube and in our stories. Taking the time to sketch a state model can provide this verification. State diagrams are also useful for modeling (revealing) constraints on object behavior (see the following major section, "Constraints") and for modeling event-driven (stimulus-response) scripts. A state chart, as devised by David Harel, has become the modeling tool of choice in the object community.

State Modeling

Figure 9-18 shows a state diagram for a mouse and part of a diagram for a *mouseManager* object. (*mouseManager* is a name reflective of a popular operating system environment—not of object thinking.) The dotted line in the

---

5. Some of these registrations will be made as part of the application initialization process—getting the cast (objects) ready to perform—and others will come and go during the running of the application.

diagram reveals that a mouse really consists of two concurrently operating objects, a movement detector and a button. (Although most mice have more than one button, it isn't necessary for the state chart to model them separately. Scroll wheels and other mouse embellishments are not modeled here but would be additional concurrent state machines within the mouse.) Both objects have very simple state, but the diagram confirms the events that need to be listed on the object cube for each object—*click* and *out of order* for the button; *newXYZ* and *out of order* for the movement detector.

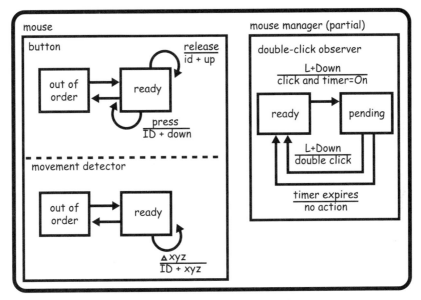

Figure 9-18   This Harel state chart depicts a mouse and its composite parts plus a fragment of a mouse manager.

Inclusion of the *mouseManager* diagram fragment illustrates how object thinking affects distribution of work. Instead of making a complicated mouse capable of generating events for all possible state change combinations, we keep the mouse simple and have other objects assume responsibility for transforming simple events into composite events—in this case, for generating a *double-click* event. This example use of a state chart also reflects the XP commitment to simplicity. By separating the generation and interpretation of mouse events, we create objects that are simpler and more composable.

The partial state chart shown in Figure 9-19 shows partial state charts for a mortgage application and an *entryField*. Assuming that the entry field in question is one of those contained on the form, the diagram represents event registration information that needs to be accounted for and a constraint on the behavior of the application itself:

■   Any change in the contents of an *entryField* object forces the containing application into the nonvalidated state. This means that the *entryField* object cube must contain a *changed* event and that the application must register for notification of that event with all of its contained *entryField* objects.

■   The application cannot be funded if it's in the nonvalidated state, reflected in the fact that the funded trigger operates only while the application is in the validated state.

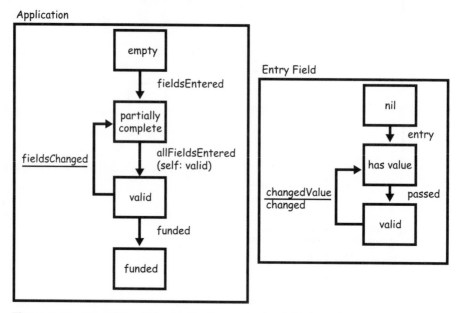

Figure 9-19   Partial charts for application and entry field, from the mortgage trust example.

Unless the developer and customer are discussing an attempt to model a complex event-driven composite object—a graphical user interface perhaps—most state modeling is used only for the purpose of helping us think about possible constraints on an object's behavior, to confirm that we have listed all necessary events on each object's cube, or to confirm/reveal the need for one object to register for events (state changes) with other objects.

Constraints

We have a stage, actors, and a script (application context, objects, and a script object plus populated event dispatchers); and the play (application) is ready to open. Except ... sometimes our actors have to obey rules or are otherwise constrained in their actions. We need to accommodate this need as well.

Objects, like people, can have behaviors that should not be exercised in certain circumstances. All constraints are local and arbitrary (for example, the rules of culture that allow one behavior in one place but not another), and because of this, the modeling and the implementation of constraints are not intrinsic to the definition of objects, only to the context (application) in which those objects perform at any given time.

Classical thinking about object development made this difficult, primarily because rules and constraints were primarily seen, and modeled, in terms of static relationships between or among objects. Because these relationships were supposedly static, they tended to be hard coded in object designs and implementations.

With a few exceptions, object thinking suggests that constraints and rules should be thought of as objects in and of themselves. We have talked in this vein throughout the earlier chapters and will make the idea explicit in the next section, "Self-Evaluating Rules."

Constraints on objects can be direct, inhibiting a behavior (actually allowing or prohibiting the execution of a method) or setting limits on the values of objects contained in instance variables (the knowledge that objects work with when doing their jobs). Constraints can be indirect, reflecting relationships among objects instead of object internals.

Examples of direct constraints include

- Inability to respond to a message because the object is already engaged in performing work in response to a previous message.

- Limiting the set of objects to which an object will respond when sent a particular message. For example, the airplane would allow no one except a manufacturer object to send the message that sets its ID (serial number).

- Restricting the values that can be assumed by an object—telling an integer that it can assume only values between 10 and 100 would be an example.

An indirect constraint is illustrated with the following example: a marriage object must associate two, and only two, person objects. (Of course, this is a local or cultural rule, not universal, and so does not reveal the intrinsic nature of a marriage object.)

Constraints are revealed at different times in the development process. Stories, told to identify objects, are the most common source. Static models (discussed previously) reveal constraints that might have been assumed in the stories without explicit mention. Thinking about implementation reveals many others, especially constraints on values that objects may assume and state-based constraints.

> **Note**   The primary sources of constraints are the definition of stories by the customer, the discussions of stories by the customer and the developers, and the development of tests to demonstrate that the stories are correct. The artifacts discussed in this section (interaction diagrams and state charts) can be used during those three activities.

Implementing constraints must be done with program code. That code is generally located in one of three different places: the affected method, a manager/controller object, or a rule object (by encapsulation). The preferred option is using a rule object. Hard coding makes objects brittle and mandates undue maintenance if changes in constraints occur over time. Manager/controller objects violate object thinking principles (and, from a purely pragmatic point of view, result in unnecessary complexity). Creating a class of objects capable of realizing any kind of rule—production rule, business rule, formula, and so on—is the object thinking solution to the constraint problem.

Self-Evaluating Rules

A dependent is eligible for family coverage if she or he is under 18 years of age, between the ages of 18 and 24 but a full-time student and receiving a majority of her or his support from the insured, or if she or he is dependent due to disability or illness.

Your interest rate is the average prime rate (as published in the *Wall Street Journal*) for the 30 days preceding the issue date of your statement plus 4.5 percent.

An Employee may have 0 or 1 Spouse.

$Py = (1/360 * FA) + (1/12 * (.075 * CB))$

The preceding are examples of business rules. Businesses are rife with these kinds of statements, formulas, conditionals, and mandated relationships. Despite the ubiquity and importance of business rules, they are seldom accorded the status of first-class objects. Instead, rules are documented and presented as static relationships among classes. (Traditional development methods deal with rules in the same way—for example, using entity relationships in a data model.) These static relationships are then supposed to be established and enforced by appropriate code in object methods or by establishing special-purpose objects, such as a database management object, that specialize in the maintenance of relationships.

Object thinking mandates that "everything is an object." A rule[6] should therefore be an object and, like any other object, have the ability to perform a specific set of services: modify itself and evaluate itself. By modify, we mean the rule must be flexible: adding, deleting, or extending clauses. By evaluation, we mean applying computational rules to itself so as to return an object encapsulating a meaningful result—in the simplest case, returning a Boolean object that encapsulates whether the rule was satisfied.

Applying object thinking to the problem of creating a rule object leads to observations about structure and responsibilities.

Structural Abstraction of a Self-Evaluating Rule

A useful object thinking heuristic for decomposition is to take an occurrence of such an object as it appears in the real world and separate its physical parts. We can do this with a simple example of a rule expressed as a formula:

$$X = 4q + (p^*r)$$

Analysis of this equation (rule) yields five distinct types of physical components:

- X, q, p, and r represent things that are currently unknown but knowable. Following convention, we will call these items *variables*.

- *4* represents a *constant* value.

---

6. Many years ago, I formulated the basic ideas of self-evaluating rules and lectured my classes on the concept. I didn't actually have a rule object implemented (leaving that as an exercise for the student). Without implementation, self-evaluating rules were a nice idea, but ... Kevin Johnson, one of my graduate students, who later became a colleague and great friend, would occasionally complain that rules could not be implemented as I was describing them (as described in this chapter). So one day we sat down and implemented them in Smalltalk, with him doing almost all of the programming. The final concept of self-evaluating rules is the result of Kevin and me discussing them over many months and finally implementing them in at least one object language. He and I coauthored an unpublished paper that is the foundation for most of what is said in this section. I want to thank Kevin and acknowledge his invaluable assistance in finalizing the ideas in this section.

- ■   *+*and *** are *behavioral operators.*

- ■   *(* and *)* in combination represent an *aggregation and precedence operator.*

- ■   *=* is an *operator of symmetry*, indicating that the thing on one side of the equation is in some sense symmetrical with, equal to, or to be assigned to the thing on the other side.

The order in which these components appear is important, as is the association of elements with one another (for example, determination of the receiver/operator/argument relationship). Our initial, structural, abstraction of a rule then follows:

A rule is an ordered collection of variables, constants, and operators.

Each of these components can be analyzed to discover its behavioral characteristics. Constants are perhaps the simplest, most often being instances of known classes such as integer, float, real, character, string, and so forth, although nothing prevents them from being any known object with the ability to provide a fixed or constant value.

Variables are more interesting. At first glance, we seem to have two different types: those, like X, that equate (are assigned) to the resolution of the entire rule; and those, like p, q, and r, that represent a discrete value that can be used to resolve the rule.

If we think of variables as a place where a value (an object) could be but currently is not, we can posit a structural abstraction for a variable. In the case of variables like X, that abstraction would consist of a *targetObject* and a *setterMessage*. For the q, p, and r variables, the abstraction is a *sourceObject* and a *getterMessage*. Behaviorally, a variable is responsible for obtaining its value, for instantiating itself. It does so by sending the *getterMessage* to the indicated *sourceObject*.

In the realm of objects, we are accustomed to treating operators as messages. In our simple example, we see three nuances of operator: first, those representing standard messages sent to objects to invoke behavior (+ and * being examples); second, those that instruct the compiler/interpreter/virtual machine to establish precedence; and third, assignment operators. The hardest part of implementing self-evaluating rules was dealing with the relationship between operators and the objects related to each. The solution turned out to be creating a *term* class that had receiver, operator, and (optionally) arguments as instance variables. This turned our rule into an ordered collection of terms, but the conceptual essence of self-evaluating rules was preserved.

Our attention can now turn to behavior and the dynamics of the rule and term structures we have defined.

Behavioral Abstraction

Side 1 (responsibility list) of an object cube for a self-evaluating rule would have the following entries: modify self and evaluate self. The second responsibility requires collaboration with the *ruleElement* objects, namely the constants, variables, and operators.

Side 2 (description and stereotype) might show a stereotype of ordered collection, reflecting the modify self responsibility coupled with the definition of a rule: an ordered collection of variables, constants, and operators.

Side 4 (knowledge required) would indicate a need to know about the *ruleElement* objects that need to be added, deleted, and so forth but, surprisingly, little else.

Side 5 (message protocol) would define messages for the following: add an element at a location, delete a designated element, evaluate, instantiate, and resolve.

Side 3 (contracts) would show that evaluate, add, and delete messages would be public, while instantiate and resolve would be private.

All basic behavior is now defined. A rule is asked to *evaluate* itself. It, in turn, sends itself the instantiate message, causing itself to iterate across its elements and ask each variable object to instantiate itself (turn itself into an actual value by sending its message to its receiver). Once all variables are instantiated, the rule then sends itself the message to resolve—apply the operators appropriately and return the result (with assignment taking place as needed).

Rules are recursive. Any element of a rule can be replaced with a rule. That's more than enough flexibility and power to get yourself into trouble unless you use other object thinking principles, such as simplicity and local action, to eliminate the need for truly complex rules.

Every object can be given the responsibility to validate itself simply by giving it a collection of rules to use as collaborators in that process. Those rules can be modified at run time, just like any other object, merely by sending appropriate modification messages. Variables can be context sensitive in their instantiation.

This type of self-evaluating rule was presumed in examples in previous chapters. The form example assumed that every entry field would have a collection of self-evaluating rules that it would use to validate its contents. Figure 9-20 provides three examples, the first two showing simple *entryField* validation rules and the third showing a more complex rule for form validation.

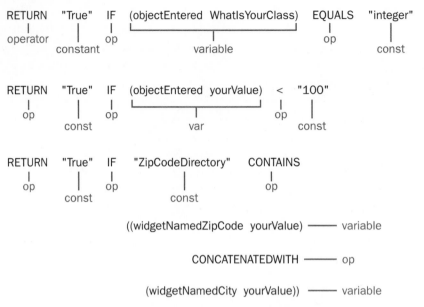

RETURN   "True"   IF   (objectEntered WhatIsYourClass)   EQUALS   "integer"
| | | |_____| | |
operator | op   variable   op   const
      constant

RETURN   "True"   IF   (objectEntered yourValue)   <   "100"
| | | |_____| | |
op | op   var   op const
       const

RETURN   "True"   IF   "ZipCodeDirectory"   CONTAINS
| | | | |
op | op   const   op
       const

((widgetNamedZipCode yourValue) ——— variable

CONCATENATEDWITH ——— op

(widgetNamedCity yourValue)) ——— variable

Figure 9-20   Sample rules with identification of element types.

Creating rules as first-class objects is essential to eliminating the kind of control and management that's endemic to classical software, wherein data is assumed to be passive and special-purpose objects (such as database management systems) assume responsibility for validating all of the elements of data they contain—with inordinate degrees of complexity as a byproduct.

Implementation

Having thought about all aspects of your objects, your stage, and your scripts (the ones necessary to complete the story you are working on), you are ready to write code—almost. If you are an XP developer, you are ready to write tests. No matter what kind of developer you are, you need to think about two more details: what your unit tests and code might look like and some additional information that must be provided to those objects whose primary role is the maintenance of bits of knowledge ("data" objects).

Methods

For every message you listed on side 5 (message protocol) of the object cube, you have to write a method and a test of that method (or tests). The first tests are obvious: When the message is sent to the object, is the expected object returned? Is it an instance of the right class? Is it in the correct state? By state, I mean does it have a reasonable value; or, if it is a composite object, do all of its instance variables have reasonable values?

The next set of tests concerns an object's ability to recover from errors that it might encounter between the time it's asked to do something and the time it returns an object in response to that request. These tests are trickier because they usually involve a group of objects and a script. A very simple case would be an error that occurs when an *entryField* object cannot validate itself with the entered object. It must then invoke a dialog box object, ask the dialog to display an appropriate error message and accept an alternative value, and then reperform the validation tests.

I have talked a lot about scripts and noted the possibility of script objects actualizing the sequence of communications among a group of objects. In practice, a lot of the communications talked about in terms of scripts will be implemented in methods. Thinking about scripts helps you design your next set of tests. Does the precondition (trigger) implied in the script always cause the appropriate message to be sent to the appropriate object? Does that object implement the next bit of the script? Does that implementation satisfy the conditions necessary to continue with the larger script?

The filling in of a form is an example of scripts being implemented in methods rather than in an independent script object.

- The form will receive the instantiate message. The form's instantiate message will be two lines (in some languages) of code: "Self, iterate across all entry fields and tell them to instantiate themselves"; and "Self, send yourself your validate message."

- Each entry field will receive the instantiate message. That method will be about three lines: "Self, ask your source of input (an object in one of your instance variables) to display itself and return a value to you"; "Self, ask your validation rules to evaluate using the entered value"; and "Self, let the form (whoever sent you the instantiate message) know that you have successfully completed your job."

■ Each validation rule will receive the evaluate message. The evaluate method will have two lines: "Self, instantiate" and "Self, resolve."

■ Next the validation rule receives the instantiate message. Instantiate consists of one line: "Self, tell all your elements that are variables to instantiate themselves."

■ Then the validation rule receives the resolve message. Resolve consists of one line: "Send the message value to each of your terms in a recursive fashion."

Writing tests for each of these methods (script fragments) is relatively straightforward—until you start to deal with exception and error handling. But even this complication can be ameliorated by creating a new script that might be implemented in several methods in other objects.

Your tests provide any additional specification you might need regarding the form of your methods. Your selected (or mandated) programming language provides you with the syntactic rules that must be adhered to in order to implement the semantics implied by your tests. Unfortunately, most programming languages were not designed specifically to make it easy to express the semantics that object thinking yields. You almost always will have to perform some translation.

Knowledge Maintenance Objects

A lot (perhaps most) of the objects in your application will have the primary charge of maintaining a bit of information. It's convenient to call these data objects—as long as you remember that they are not passive bits of data; they are real objects!

In addition to the fact that it exists, each data object needs to know a lot of additional information, information that traditionally was specified in a data dictionary or a CRUD matrix.

Note A CRUD matrix gets it name from the actions *create*, *read*, *update*, and *destroy*. It is a simple two-dimensional table that associates users and data items. Each data item in an application appears at the head of a row of the matrix, and each user (user role) appears as a column header in the matrix. Each intersecting cell then contains one or more of the characters *C*, *R*, *U*, or *D*, reflecting that users have privileges (accesses) to the data item.

Items of importance from a data dictionary include

■   The name of each data item.

■   The composition of each data item—for example, Name is-composed-of an optional Honorific, and a First Name, and an optional Middle Initial, and a Last Name, and an optional Generational. (Of course, the structure of a name will vary dramatically across cultures.)

■   The allowed size or upper and lower size limits; for example, a string used for a First Name might have to contain at least 1 character but no more than 35.

■   Any initial or default value.

■   A range of values—what data modelers call a *domain*; for instance, a Zip Code data item would have a domain of all the values listed in the United States Postal Service Zip Code Directory.

It will be essential to obtain this information about all your data objects. But what do you do with it when obtained? Where is it implemented?

Earlier I suggested that certain classes called *primitives* are most likely to be used to maintain knowledge—for example, characters, numbers, strings, dates, times, and money. The obvious place to store CRUD and data dictionary information is in the objects that use that information. However, it is unlikely that you will actually want to modify all of the classes that can be used as primitives. Instead, you might want to create a *DataItem* class.

A *DataItem* class is a way to reify passive data into a first-class object. An instance of *DataItem* would have the following structure (Figure 9-21 shows the object cube representation of this structure):

Label   A string that names the data item.

Class   The name of the class of which this data item is an instance.

Value   The actual value of the data item. This would be an instance of one of the primitive classes.

Composition   An optional collection of *DataItem* objects that actualizes the data dictionary definition.

Validation rules   A collection of self-evaluating rules that would enforce domain constraints.

Access rule   A rule that enforces the line of the CRUD matrix pertinent to this particular data item.

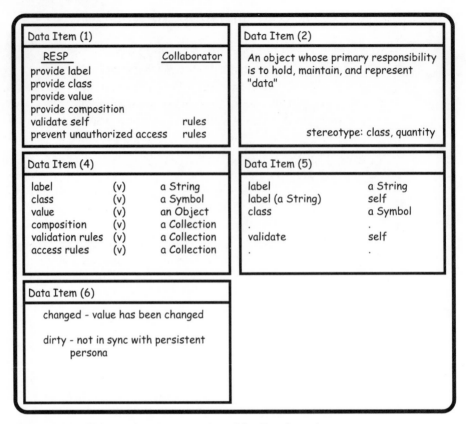

Figure 9-21 Object cube representation of the *DataItem* class.

If you elect the *DataItem* class option, you will then return to your object cube, side 4, and replace a lot of the primitives listed there as *DataItem* objects. Take care to replace only those primitives that are used more or less exclusively as knowledge holders. If you are using a string or number, for instance, for behavioral capabilities and not just to hold a value, you will not want to replace them with *DataItem* objects.

Development at the Speed of Thought

Throughout this chapter (and the preceding two chapters), a lot of information, models, heuristics, and details about objects have been presented. Every discussion of every aspect of objects and object modeling included a caveat: every step and every model is used only as a means of clarifying and communicating understanding and is utilized only as part of the relevant XP activity.

Furthermore, there is an expectation that you will overtly use the material presented in Chapters 7 through 9 only while learning object thinking. Eventually, all of the material in this entire book will be "inside your head," and you will be applying it without conscious awareness and while engaged in other explicit activities—most notably while you are writing and refactoring code.

At first you will be consciously reminding yourself of the concepts and ideas presented here and will make use of the various diagrams as explicit aids to thinking. As you gain proficiency, you will use the aids less and less but still might be seen "talking to yourself" just as a new reader will move his lips while reading silently. Eventually you will just "do it."

XP has three maturity levels—*out of the box*, *adaptation*, and *transcendence*—that apply equally to object thinking. Once you have transcended the material in this book, you will think faster and better about objects, and that thinking will improve and expedite your thinking about design, testing, and coding.

10

Wrapping Up

Despite any appearances to the contrary, objects are not something you do; objects are a way that you think. To illustrate object thinking, it was necessary, in preceding chapters, to distinguish between thoughts you would have at different points in the development process and to differentiate between thoughts reflecting a holistic perspective and those that had a precise focus. It would be easy, but wrong, to see phases, cookbook methods, and even prescriptive modeling requirements in the last three chapters.

The material in Chapters 7 through 9 is an expression of the principles, practices, values, metaphors, and the definitions presented in the first six chapters. Object thinking requires developers to master the ideas so as to understand the sample expressions and, more important, to be able, themselves, to craft appropriate expressions of those ideas in response to the novel problems they encounter in their own work.

An individual's object thinking takes place inside her head—unobserved by others, who can see only the product of that thought. The concerted object thinking of a team is also mostly inside their heads, but it is sometimes manifest in the communication products they produce and utilize as a kind of "external group memory." Ephemera like whiteboard drawings, story cards, poster graphs, and visual metaphors and models are but byproducts of object thinking.

The product of object thinking is software that manifests simplicity and composability, which lead, in turn, to adaptability, flexibility, and evolvability. If object thinking is done in the context of XP (which contributes refactoring and test-driven development techniques that complement object thinking) and agile development, the shared focus on the problem space and the needs of the customer results in software that is usable and demonstrably supportive of business/user requirements.

Unfortunately, there are circumstances in which it is difficult if not impossible to apply object thinking.

Vexations

Sometimes you just can't do the right thing. Or, more accurately, other considerations make doing the right thing very hard. However diligent an object thinker you become, you will encounter situations that tax your skills. The most commonly encountered examples: the necessity of object applications using relational databases for persistence and object-human communications via graphical user interfaces.

The Impedance Mismatch Problem

Traditional computer thinking treats data as passive and helpless, manipulated and moved by active procedures. Procedures, being a bit unruly, have been known to abuse data, to make it something it shouldn't be. Procedures also tend to be egocentric and think that all data, its definitions and its values, are properly determined by the procedure currently using that data. The result is data that is inconsistent in definition, inconsistent in value, inaccessible because some other procedure has possession, or needlessly duplicated.

The solution to these problems was to create a single repository for all data—the database—and create one master procedure—the database management system, or DBMS—to manage the data and protect it from "abuse" by "unruly" application functions. Database philosophy is almost totally inconsistent with the philosophy behind object thinking.

Databases violate the axiom that everything is an object. They violate the principle that no object can do things to another object. Databases celebrate centralized control. And relational databases, especially, are totally enamored of the idea that everything can be formalized. It's not surprising, therefore, to find that objects and databases are frequently in conflict with each other.

Some examples of the kinds of problems encountered when mixing objects and relational databases are as follows. (Extended relational and object databases have been modified and extended in their capability to ameliorate most of the problems noted.)

■   Objects are not defined based on their attributes, but entities and the tables that they inhabit in a database are defined in precisely that manner. Objects can store, in a variable, objects whose primary purpose is to provide a calculation or a service rather than to embody a piece of data. The rules that you follow to make something "persistable" vary radically between the object world and the database world.

■   Objects have variables that can contain arbitrarily complex objects, including collections and multivalued constructs. Databases can store only a defined, and limited, set of primitive types. For an object to be stored in a database, it must be disassembled and translated, making both storage and retrieval complicated and error-prone processes. Several companies have made significant amounts of money providing special-purpose "object-relational mapping" software that "solves" this disassembly-and-translation problem.

■   If a running application uses objects that persist in a database, there is no assurance that an object's value in the application is consistent with its value in the database. Other applications might be updating the database, and there is no way for the database to notify the object that its persistent value has changed through intervention by another program. (Extended relational databases now have the ability to notify objects of this kind of event.)

■   Databases do not preserve the encapsulation of an object. While an object is persistent (in the database), all of its contents, the objects stored in the object's variables and in some cases even the object's methods, are available for direct access by any other program using that database. This leads to all kinds of potential coupling between objects (based on program-specific contexts), which interferes with (destroys) the modularization arising from good object design in the first place.

In an ideal object world, there would be no need for databases. Every object would have its own URL.[1] Persistent storage devices would offer nothing more than space and a path extension for the object's URL so that it could be located when necessary. The object would serialize itself (marshal itself into a

---

1. URL—Uniform Resource Locator—is a technical term for the address of resources on the Web. I am using it more colloquially, still meaning a unique address with the implication that such an address would be as simple as a URL and be independent of physical implementation (i.e., not rely on platform-specific offsets and extents).

bit stream) and de-serialize itself in order to reside on the storage medium.[2] The object would also register its location with a "white pages" object so others could find it when necessary. (The white pages would function much as the domain name servers employed to match text and numeric URLs for the Web—that is, they would be hierarchical and replicated for efficiency of access.)

Why Databases?

Persistence is not the only reason for using a database. Databases also offer computational advantages for certain application needs. For example, they provide functions for efficiently and quickly tabulating and computing across large collections of instances (tuples, or rows, in database vernacular). If I had a large collection of customer objects (a few million, say) and wanted to know which of them lived in a particular postal code, I would have to ask each object in turn where it lived and have it report to an output collection if it lived in the specified postal code. This would take a long time. If that same collection were stored as tuples in a relational database, a simple vector operation would extract the relevant objects in short order. On the other hand, storing a complex object—say the bill of materials for a passenger jet, perhaps—in a set of relations in a database and then asking that database to print a list of all components used to build that airplane would take a long time for the database but would be a relatively trivial operation for the object. In the main text of this section, concern is focused on persistence. But object thinking designers need to give attention to the functional advantages of databases as well as their persistence services.

Services that a database is supposed to provide to data—access control and enforcement of integrity constraints, for instance—would be assumed by each object. An object could queue messages or simply indicate a busy signal if it received multiple messages simultaneously. Each object could carry within itself its own set of rules (self-evaluating rule objects) that would ensure the integrity of its value and allow it to reject messages from sources that have not been given access authorization. (Think in terms of access tables maintained by

---

2. The object-relational mapping software mentioned in this section provides a kind of marshalling where the serialization results in SQL or proprietary data manipulation statements rather than a bit stream suitable for writing to magnetic media.

most operating systems that allow some users access to files while denying it to others. The entries in such tables are merely transferred to the objects instead of being maintained in a central place.)

Until the object vision is realized in full, it will be necessary to compromise and accommodate and make use of existing database systems. Treating the database as a great big object—employing the concept of putting an object wrapper around a nonobject thing—is one way to effect that compromise.

A Problem with GUIs

As noted previously (sidebar, Chapter 8), the advent of graphical user interfaces promoted object thinking while simultaneously distorting what it meant to be an object. The primary problem was trying to design object applications from the interface in. The first step advocated by many object enthusiasts was to sketch or prototype the application interface and then figure out what kind of objects were needed behind the scene. This kind of thinking also reflects pre-GUI computer thinking, wherein it was common to design the (character-based) forms and reports before writing the application code that would use them for input and output.

Object thinking says that a view (sometimes called an interface)[3]—graphical or otherwise—is a means for an object to communicate with another object and nothing more. The need for a view arises when an object needs to present itself in a "non-native" form to some other object (usually a human being) or application (for example, an XML view for data objects being shared across platforms).

Discovery of the need and the parameters that must be satisfied by a view is manifest in the scenarios in which the object participates. Whenever an object is asked to display itself, it must use a view—a representation—appropriate for the sender of that display message. If, for example, an object is trying to instantiate itself (get a value for itself), it must present a view of itself as an implicit request to a human being (or other service-providing object) for a value. If we are building a GUI that will serve as an intermediary between a software object and a human object, we will use glyphs for display purposes and widgets for interaction purposes.

But which glyphs and widgets need to be included in the GUI? Only those necessary to complete the scenario or scenarios[4] of immediate interest as the

---

3. The term *interface* is used, unfortunately, in more than one way. It refers to the object-specific message protocol plus event notification information as recorded on sides 5 and 6 of an object cube. It also means the form assumed by an object in order to present itself to a human user or another application object. We are using the second sense of the word in this section.

4. In most applications, several objects will be simultaneously presenting themselves to or requesting interaction with the human user. The totality of the GUI will therefore be composed of multiple object views. This was noted in the discussion of the MVC architecture in Chapter 9.

application runs. This perspective is counterintuitive for most developers because it suggests that a GUI be defined from the application out.

As an example, consider a brewery. Off to one side are vats filled with beer. At the other side are trucks waiting to take cases of brew to avid customers. In between is a complex production line consisting of bottle washers, filler stations, capping machines, and package assemblers. Above it all is a control station that monitors the brewery and notifies human managers of status and problems. Traditional developers are likely to begin their analysis and design of "a brewery management system" from the point of view of the control panel. This is analogous to designing from the interface in.

Object thinking would suggest, instead, that you consider which object is the prime customer of the brewery and all its myriad machines. On whose behalf does the complex maze of equipment exist? The correct business answer is, of course, "The customer." But an answer more reflective of object thinking is, "The beer." All scenarios are written from the perspective of the beer, trying to get itself into a bottle, with a cap, placed in a package, and resident in a truck. The control panel is a passive observer[5] of the state of the brewery. If the beer encounters a problem at some point, it's the responsibility of the beer to request intervention of the human operators by sending a message to the control panel (or machine-specific control panels) requesting an intervention service.

This perspective will simplify GUI design and, more important, eliminate the host of manager and controller objects that seem to inevitably arise when designing from the control panel's (GUI's) perspective.

Other vexations for object thinkers include programming language implementations that do not allow direct expression of object concepts or that impose safety and control structures that are antithetical to object thinking. Operating systems and hardware also present situations forcing compromise of object principles in order to get anything done. Dealing with these vexations in the most efficacious manner possible requires application of object philosophy, metaphor, and principles.

Dealing with negativity is no way to end a book on object thinking, so we will redirect our attention to some issues that extend the ideas presented in earlier chapters.

---

5. In an experimental microbrewery, the panel (in conjunction with the brewmeister) might be more than a passive observer. It might also be a source of instruction to the beer to modify its behavior. It is still not a controller—merely another interested player that provides services to the beer in its effort to "be the best brew it can be."

Extensions

One of the tenets of extreme programming involves the avoidance of *premature abstraction*. Abstraction, as they are using the term, is a kind of optimization that arises from refactoring code. It's not necessary, however, for every abstraction to be rediscovered every time it's used. Abstractions, once discovered, can be remembered and applied in similar circumstances in the future. This has the effect of accelerating thought and thereby accelerating development—something quite consistent with XP principles and values.

For example, the stereotypes discussed as part of side 2 (the description) of an object cube are abstractions. If you are developing a financial system and encounter an object named *portfolio*, your knowledge of collections—an abstraction—should lead you to discover that a portfolio is just a collection with some added behavior. Patterns and architectures are another form of abstraction that you can learn, as abstractions, and then apply as you think about design and implementation.[6] In Chapter 9, some architectural abstractions were introduced (for example, MVC, blackboards, pipes, and filters). Patterns have also been introduced—for example, the discussion of *blind dispatching*, which is an example of the *observer* or *publish-and-subscribe* pattern—but a full exploration of patterns is best pursued in the patterns literature itself. (See the bibliography for starting points.)

Frameworks

A framework is another kind of abstraction, somewhere between a design pattern and a full architectural pattern. Frameworks are organizational abstractions that provide a set of objects with expected behaviors and the relationships that enable them to interact in order to achieve some collective goal. Good frameworks provide the essential core of a programming solution. Extension of the framework by adding other objects and other relationships is expected. However, a good heuristic is to demand unassailable justification before accepting any addition to the framework. See if the unaltered framework can solve your problem before you embellish it. Following are some examples of frameworks.

---

6. See the work of Alan Shaloway and of Josh Kerievski on refactoring to patterns and Bob Martin's *Agile Software Development* for discussion of how and why patterns serve as guides and targets, not as templates that get dropped into your design. Blind composition of patterns actually leads to very poor code.

Composable Document

A composable document has variable content and constraints on the appearance of the content, which are sometimes determined by the presence or absence of other content. A report is a kind of composable document. A legal form, like a loan disclosure document, is another.

The composable document framework (Figure 10-1) suggests that a *composableDocument* is a collection of elements (which means it has the behavior of adding, deleting, and providing access to the collected elements) that can identify itself, describe itself, and display itself. Display requires collaboration with elements, which can display themselves. Both the document and its elements have extent (the amount of space occupied by the element—for a document, usually the two-dimensional area), which can be reported and, in the case of the document, allocated to an element.

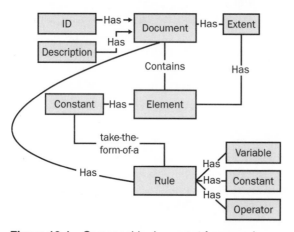

Figure 10-1   Composable document framework.

Both elements and the document must satisfy certain composition rules, which are embodied in self-evaluating rules. (The composition of a rule as a collection of variables, constants, and operators is shown in Figure 10-1.) This framework provides all of the objects necessary to model the construction of any form or report. (Actual display requires a host of additional objects, glyphs, bitmaps, vector graphics, and so on—a vexation in that way too much work is required to paint a screen than would be the case if object thinking had guided the developers of operating systems and graphics libraries.)

Object Routing and Tracking

The object routing and tracking framework (Figure 10-2) is useful as an abstraction for the core description of systems as disparate as a network packet manager and a UPS package delivery system.

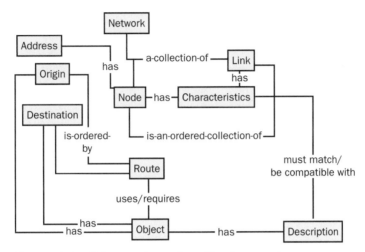

Figure 10-2   Object routing and tracking framework.

This framework suggests that an object has an *originLocation*, a *destinationLocation*, a description, and a unique ID. It obtains a route from a network (an object that specializes in solving np-complete (traveling salesman type) problems. A route is simply an ordered set of nodes and links that connect an *originLocation* to a *destinationLocation*. Nodes and links have addresses and characteristics. An object obtains a route, checks with both nodes and links to track its own progress, and raises an alert if it detects a deviation from its assigned route. This alert enables making a request for an alternate route. Various parameters, which match object description with link or node characteristics, time or priority constraints, and so forth, are encapsulated in rules associated with the appropriate objects.

Resource Allocation and Scheduling

Resource allocation is important in numerous business systems. Scheduling is fundamentally nothing more than a kind of resource allocation, with the resource being time. Three objects form the core of this framework (shown in Figure 10-3):

- *Resource*, which can have other resources (such as a calendar with fine-grained time divisions) as part of its structure and which has a description and an identity

- *Request*, which can recursively be a collection of requests and which also has a description (resource requirements), an identity, and a *Requester*

- *Reservation*, which associates a resource with a request and has an identity along with references to the objects it is associating

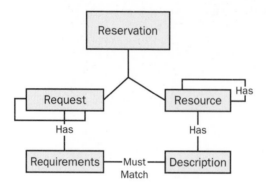

Figure 10-3   Resource allocation and scheduling framework.

Numerous other frameworks can be constructed, each of which captures and embodies the best of object thinking. These abstractions can then be used as shortcuts in future efforts to apply object thinking to solve new problems.

A very different kind of extension to object thinking arises from the principle that objects are simulations. An object does not represent, in some abstract way, a thing in the real world; it simulates that real-world thing. Objects are *evocative* rather than representational. This is why Alan Kay (among others) speaks of the need for objects to preserve the "user illusion" and behave and appear in a manner consistent with the thing being simulated. This evocative property of objects can be utilized in interesting ways—including the depiction of system *architecture*.

Object-Based Evocative Architecture

Figure 10-4 is a photo of a Thangka painting on the wall of my office. This painting is an evocative model of Tibetan Buddhist cosmology and philosophy. Even a cursory glance reveals that it has some kind of structural organization, a significant amount of detail, and lots of interesting and unusual images. Less obvious is that it is a very good object model. The images on the painting are representational in part. Each icon and each organizational segment of the whole can be seen as representing a particular deity or circumstance, but that is almost coincidental—a case of convenient labeling. The real purpose of the painting as a whole, and of each individual element of the painting, is to evoke memories, primarily memories of stories the viewer of the painting was told as he or she grew up in a Tibetan household. As complex as the painting itself appears to be, that complexity pales in contrast with the volume of memories and intertwined stories that the painting recalls in the mind of the viewer.

Figure 10-4   Thangka painting.

Given that XP eschews the development of formal representational architectures as a prelude to development and that some kind of holistic view of the system to be built is desirable, perhaps an evocative model patterned after the Thangka painting and reflecting the simulation aspect of objects will provide a useful informal tool.

Essential elements of the painting that would have equivalents in the XP architectural model include

- A center circle with icons recalling to mind the driving forces behind the system under development. In the painting, these are icons reminding us of attachment, greed, anger, and so on. In a system model, these would remind us of the importance of money (almost inevitable), a particular client (a CEO perhaps) who will pass final judgment on our work, a customer, or a service.

- A large segmented circle, each segment representing some kind of portioning of the system, preferably isomorphic to some degree with the actual portioning of the business for which the system is being built. In the painting, these are the various realms of existence—for example, heaven, hell, material world. In our model, these might represent realms such as order entry, inventory, accounting, and manufacturing; or segments of a smaller-scale system—data entry, back-end processing, backup and recovery, and so forth.

- Icons of various sorts arranged in a tableau evocative of the stories that relate those icons to one another. Each icon evokes a specific story or set of stories about a particular element of the overall system. Icons can appear in more than one segment.

- A narrower outer circle, also segmented, with each segment representing a stage in the "circle of life." This circle, in the painting, is the progress from birth to death that each of us traverses. In a system architecture, each segment would represent a stage in the processing of whatever the system is intended to support or perhaps some kind of business cycle from prospect to customer or raw material to product.

- Finally, outside the circle, icons that recall stories about outside influences, things or forces or people that can affect our system but are outside the scope of what we can actually build.

Dynamism can be added to the model in many different ways. If each icon evokes a particular story and the work required to realize that story, the orientation of the icon (down = not started, right angle left = in progress, vertical = done, right angle right = abandoned dead end) can be used to depict status. A quick glance at the model reveals a rough approximation of total effort and total achievements. This is the same information that appears on many an XP project's walls and whiteboards but in a more compact form.

The dramatic form and the unusual context behind the presentation of this architecture might obscure the fact that it's merely a pictorial representation of the way that object thinkers think of objects and applications: as stories, à la XP.

Provocation—The Future of Objects

Thinking can be focused toward the accomplishment of a task. All of the material in this book so far is intended to aid developers in that kind of thought. To conclude, however, I would like to provoke a different kind of thinking—speculative thinking. Specifically, what might happen if all of the ideas, philosophies, and metaphors presented in this book were taken to the extreme? The following story is one possibility.

Circa 1998 a small group of programmers decided they were "mad as hell and not going to take it anymore." Although the rebellion came in many flavors, the most prominent example of it was extreme programming (XP). Similar, concurrently active groups considered themselves agile and formed, with the XPers, the Agile Alliance. *Xgilista* is an umbrella term covering the spectrum of extreme and agile approaches to software creation.

Among other things, Xgilistas rejected the prevailing idea that software projects, particularly large mission-critical projects, required massive amounts of up-front analysis, design, and specification. They claimed that it was quite possible to realize such systems with an incremental process that was highly disciplined, human-centric, social, and ethical.

Large, successful systems emerged from incremental development—existence proofs of yet another old idea. Grady Booch, in *Object-Oriented Design,* 1991, stated that everyone knew that the only way to build successful large systems was to evolve them from successful small ones.

In rejecting up-front design, Xgilistas essentially rejected the need for large, monolithic programs. They challenged, implicitly and explicitly, the assumption that large systems were actually required.

XP focus on delivering the simplest possible deliverable capable of meeting a real but discrete business need had an unintended side effect. (At least, this result was never explicitly stated as an expected outcome of XP, but one should not underestimate the sly, subtle, and covert intent of a Ward Cunningham or a Kent Beck.) Users started to see their requirements in a very different light. Instead of automatically thinking they needed huge, monolithic software systems, they started to request a set of small, targeted software-based business tools instead. The perceived role of software changed dramatically. Users started to ask for objects capable of providing specific and limited services. The utility of such objects was based on how limited an intrusion they made into the business process and how faithfully they simulated a business role in that process.

Objects (applications are just composite objects with collective responsibilities) came to be seen as analogous to new employees. Just as you would hire a human being with specific skills to perform some well-defined job function, so too businesses started to "hire" individual objects instead of massive systems.

In retrospect, this outcome should also have been obvious. In the late 1800s, Pareto's 80/20 "law" was formulated. Empirical study of the actual use of programs such as Microsoft Windows, Microsoft Word, WordPerfect, and so on revealed a variation of Pareto's Law—80 percent of the users used 20 percent or less of the functionality offered by such programs. No one used all of the features. So why were they built? Why did companies spend millions of dollars on monstrous dinosaurs such as SAP and its kindred "integrated applications"? Market forces and management folly is the short answer.

Until Xgilistas demonstrated differently, advocates of monolithic formal systems claimed that the incremental, bottom-up approach could not yield, at least efficiently, systems that were capable of controlling large businesses or complex systems such as air traffic control. The XP mantra, "Architecture emerges," was dismissed as absurd. But architecture did emerge. Executives and even entire corporations are, after all, just another kind of user with focused business needs. Satisfaction of those needs did require aggregation and distillation of results generated by other objects and job processes. But this was addressed with judicious use of the observer pattern.

Xgilistas finally broke the back of the prevailing software engineering and computer science myth—to wit, software is formally defined and constructed. Users, and even managers, were finally ready to accept what objects had offered 30 years earlier.

Enter the *Objectionary*, a combination of dictionary and object factory. The Objectionary is nothing more than the product of taking object ideas—as originally voiced—seriously. The salient features of the Objectionary include the following:

- The Objectionary itself is a kind of "object vending machine," dispensing objects of various types upon request.

- The total number of Objectionary objects is less than 2000, a number that continues to be sufficient to assemble every software application attempted. (Remember the Lego Brick metaphor and the discussion of how many objects—classes, really—are necessary.)

- Each object is an autonomous executable entity. Smalltalk objects are freed from their dependence on image environments.

- Every object has a unique ID and a unique "address"—a realization of Alan Kay's suggestion that every object have its own URL.

- Objects are nothing more than collections of objects. After all, everything is an object. This means, of course, that messages and methods become first-class objects in their own right.

- Objects are fully executable ("precompiled byte code strings") but do require a hardware-specific Virtual Machine (VM) for access to primitive hardware services.

- There are a few key abstractions, such as the self-evaluating rules conceived of by West and implemented by Johnson. Their work essentially reified source code statements into first-class objects that could be modified at execution time.

Access to the Objectionary almost eliminated one profession—that of programmer—and replaced it with another, *application assembly specialist*. (Again, remember the Lego Brick metaphor and its differentiation between creators and assemblers.) These specialists adopted the rather ugly, but descriptive, appellation of *collagist*, reflective of the kind of artist who creates new works by assembling materials.

End user computing—for real, not the pseudoprogramming that had stifled earlier forays into this area—became all the rage. User-created software was quite analogous to the Lego Brick constructions of children—workable but lacking in certain qualities. Some novice assemblers had a knack for putting together objects in such a way that the resultant assemblies not only were functional but were starting to become beautiful. Others noticed and were more than willing to compensate such "hobbyists" or "tinkers" to assemble on their behalf.

Software assembly became a craft, just as programming once had been. Collagists formed a community of shared expertise. But this time the art went in a much different direction than programming had almost 50 years before. The expertise that set a collagist apart from other software assemblers centered on composition, proportion (e.g., the Golden Mean), aesthetics, efficiency (not the rabid concern with machine efficiency of C and C++ programmers—rather, the efficiency of interaction among humans and objects, and between objects and objects), and simplicity or elegance. Not being amenable to quantification and hence formalist corruption, these skills flourished as they had in other artistic endeavors for centuries.

The basic tools of collagism were all open source, free to anyone to use and modify. Collagists made money doing what "anyone could do for free" simply because they had "artistic skill and style." People were more than willing to pay for style, just as they did with regard to the other arts. It was a matter of prestige to have an original "Jeffries payroll system," and companies were willing to pay for that prestige, just as they did for the Mattisse hanging in the lobby.

Two markets have come to thrive, side by side: Generic "house-brand" assemblies and designer assemblies. Users bought what they could afford and what they most needed. In many cases, generic was more than adequate, but for some highly visible (or core competency) applications, designer quality was required—and paid for.

Aspiring collagists shunned software education offered by traditional departments and universities (even when they stopped calling themselves software engineering programs) in favor of apprenticeship programs located in liberal arts colleges.

Objectionary objects turned out to be self-modifiable. A key idea—self-evaluating rules—was the only prerequisite. Rules can be recursively defined and can be modified simply by adding, deleting, or reordering the member objects. Self-evaluating rules are well suited for use as genetic algorithms. Shortly after the release of the Objectionary, various assembly hackers noticed this fact and took advantage of it to create objects that reconfigured themselves as a function of the environment in which they operated.

The earliest self-modifying software consisted of nothing more than complex rules that evaluated to some result that could be subjected to a fitness test. Later attempts allowed participation of all sorts of objects, applications (as it were) that were free to modify the collection of participating objects, the script object that coordinated the interaction of the objects in that collection, and the rules contained within each object that constrained or enhanced its individual behavior.

An interesting story, or a plan of action for Object Thinkers and Xgilistas?

Bibliography

(Books marked with an * are particularly relevant to the philosophical underpinnings of object thinking as discussed in the first chapters of this book.)

Albin, Stephen T. *The Art of Software Architecture: Design Methods and Techniques.* Indianapolis, IN: Wiley Publishing, Inc., 2003.

*Alexander, Christopher. *Notes on the Synthesis of Form.* Cambridge, MA: Harvard University Press, 1964.

Alexander, Christopher, Sara Ishikawa, and Murray Silverstein. *A Pattern Language: Towns, Buildings, Construction.* New York: Oxford University Press, 1977.

*Alexander, Christopher. *The Timeless Way of Building.* New York: Oxford University Press, 1979.

*Alexander, Christopher. *The Nature of Order: Book One, The Phenomenon of Life.* New York: Oxford University Press, 2001.

Ambler, Scott W. *The Object Primer: The Application Developer's Guide to Object-Orientation.* New York: SIGS Books, 1995.

Anderson, Jim, George Bosworth, Alberto A. Della Ripa, Barbara Noparstak, and Michael Teng. *Methods Owners Manual.* Digitalk,1985.

Arranga, Edmund C., and Frank P. Coyle. *Object Oriented COBOL.* New York: SIGS Books, 1996.

Arthur, Lowell Jay. *Rapid Evolutionary Development: Requirements, Prototyping & Software Creation.* New York: John Wiley & Sons, 1992.

Bahar, Mory. *Object Technology Made Simple.* East Greenwich, RI: Simple Software Publishing, 1996.

Bapat, Subodh. *Object-Oriented Networks: Models for Architecture, Operations, and Management.* Englewood Cliffs, NJ: PTR Prentice Hall, 1994.

Bassett, Paul G. *Framing Software Reuse: Lessons from the Real World.* Upper Saddle River, NJ: Prentice Hall PTR, 1997.

Baudoin, Claude, and Glenn Hollowell. *Realizing the Object-Oriented Lifecycle.* Upper Saddle River, NJ: Prentice Hall PTR, 1996.

Beaudouin-Lafon, Michel. Jack Howlett, translator. *Object Oriented Languages: Basic Principles and Programming Techniques*. London: Chapman and Hall, 1994.

Beck, Kent. *Guide to Better Smalltalk: A Sorted Collection*. SIGS Reference Library. Cambridge: Cambridge University Press, 1999.

*Beck, Kent. *Extreme Programming Explained: Embrace Change*. Boston: Addison-Wesley, 2000.

Beck, Kent, and Martin Fowler. *Planning Extreme Programming*. Boston: Addison-Wesley, 2001.

Bellin, David, and Susan Suchman Simone. *The CRC Card Book*. Reading, MA: Addison-Wesley, 1997.

Berard, Edward V. *Essays on Object-Oriented Software Engineering*. Vol 1. Englewood Cliffs, NJ: Prentice Hall PTR, 1993.

Bergin, Joseph. *Data Abstraction: The Object-Oriented Approach Using C++*. New York: McGraw-Hill, Inc., 1994.

Blaha, Michael, and William Premerlani. *Object-Oriented Modeling and Design for Database Applications*. Upper Saddle River, NJ: Prentice Hall, Inc., 1998.

*Bohm, David. *Wholeness and the Implicate Order*. London: Routledge and Kegan Paul, 1980.

Borland. *The World of C++: The Fastest Way to Become a ++ Programmer*. Borland International, 1991.

Bourne, John R. *Object-Oriented Engineering. Building Engineering Systems Using Smalltalk-80*. Boston: Irwin, 1992.

Bowman, Charles F., ed. *Wisdom of the Gurus: A Vision for Object Technology*. New York: SIGS Books, 1996.

*Brown, John Seely, and Paul Duguid. *The Social Life of Information*. Boston, MA: Harvard Business School Press, 2000.

Brown, William J., Raphael C. Malveau, Hays W. "Skip" McCormick III, and Thomas J. Mowbray. *Anti-Patterns: Refactoring Software, Architectures, and Projects in Crisis*. New York: John Wiley & Sons, Inc., 1998.

Budd, Timothy. *An Introduction to Object-Oriented Programming*. Reading, MA: Addison-Wesley Publishing Co., 1991.

Buhr, R. J. A., and R. S. Casselman. *Use Case Maps for Object-Oriented Systems*. Upper Saddle River, NJ: Prentice Hall PTR, 1996.

*Bulhof, Ilse N. *Wilhelm Dilthey: A Hermeneutic Approach to the Study of History and Culture*. The Hague: Martinus Hijhoff, 1980.

Burleson, Donald K. *Practical Application of Object-Oriented Techniques to Relational Databases*. New York: John Wiley and Sons, Inc., 1994.

Burnett, Margaret M., Adele Goldberg, and Ted G. Lewis, eds. *Visual Object-Oriented Programming: Concepts and Environments*. Greenwich, CT: Manning Publications Co., 1995.

Cattell, R. G. G. *Object Data Management*. Reading, MA: Addison-Wesley Publishing Company, 1991.

Chorafas, Dimitris N., and Heinrich Steinmann. *Object-Oriented Databases*. Englewood Cliffs, NJ: Prentice Hall PTR, 1993.

Coad, Peter, and Ed Yourdon. *Object-Oriented Analysis*. Englewood Cliffs, NJ: Prentice-Hall, 1991.

Coad, Peter, and Ed Yourdon. *Object-Oriented Design*. Englewood Cliffs, NJ: Prentice-Hall, 1991.

Coad, Peter, with David North and Mark Mayfield. *Object Models: Strategies, Patterns and Applications*. Englewood Cliffs, NJ: Prentice Hall, 1995.

Coad, Peter, Eric Lefebvre, and Jeff DeLuca. *Color Java Modeling with UML: Enterprise Components and Process*. Englewood Cliffs, NJ: Prentice-Hall, 1999.

Cockburn, Alistair. *Writing Effective Use Cases*. Boston: Addison-Wesley, 2001.

*Cockburn, Alistair. *Agile Software Development*. Boston: Addison-Wesley, 2002.

Coleman, Derek, Patrick Arnold, Stephanie Bodoff, Chris Dollin, Helena Gilchrist, Fiona Hayes, and Paul Jeremaes. *Object Oriented Development: The Fusion Method*. Englewood Cliff, NJ: Prentice Hall, 1993.

Collins, Dave. *Designing Object-Oriented User Interfaces*. Redwood City, CA: Benjamin Cummings Publishing Co., Inc., 1995.

Cook, Steve, and John Daniels. *Designing Object Systems: Object-Oriented Modeling with Syntropy*. New York: Prentice-Hall, 1994.

Coplein, James O., and Douglas C. Schmidt, eds. *Pattern Languages of Program Design*. Reading, MA: Addison-Wesley Publishing Co., 1995.

Cox, Brad. *Object-Oriented Programming: An Evolutionary Approach*. Reading, MA: Addison-Wesley Publishing Company, 1986.

Cox, Brad. *Superdistribution: Objects as Property on the Electronic Frontier*. Reading, MA: Addison-Wesley Publishing Co., 1996.

*Coyne, Richard. *Designing Information Technology in the Postmodern Age: From Method to Metaphor*. Cambridge, MA: MIT Press, 1995.

*David, Alan M. *201 Principles of Software Development*. New York: McGraw-Hill, Inc., 1995.

*Dahlbom, B., and L. Mathiassen, *Computers in Context: The Philosophy and Practice of Systems Design*. Oxford: Blackwell, 1993.

De Champeaux, Dennis, Douglas Lea, and Penelope Faure. *Object-Oriented System Development*. Reading, MA: Addison-Wesley Publishing Company, 1993.

Deitel, H. M., P. J. Deitel, J. A. Listfield, T. R. Nieto, C. H. Yaeger, and M. Zlatinka. *C#: A Programmer's Introduction*. Upper Saddle River, NJ: Prentice-Hall, 2003.

Digitalk, Inc. *Smalltalk/V*. Los Angeles, CA: Digitalk, Inc., 1986.

*Dittrich, Yvonne, Christiane Floyd, and Ralf Klischewski. *Social Thinking—Software Practice*. Cambridge, MA: MIT Press, 2002.

Dorfman, Len. *Object-Oriented Assembly Language*. Blue Ridge Summit, PA: Windcrest, 1990.

*Dreyfus, Hubert L. *Husserl, Intentionality, and Cognitive Science*. Cambridge, MA: MIT Press, 1982.

*Dreyfus, Hubert L., and Stuart E. Dreyfus with Tom Athanasiou. *Mind over Machine*. New York: The Free Press, a division of Macmillan, Inc., 1985.

Eeles, Peter, and Oliver Sims. *Building Business Objects*. New York: John Wiley and Sons, Inc., 1998.

*Ehn, Pelle. *Work-Oriented Design of Computer Artifacts*. Stockholm: Arbetslivcentrum, 1988.

Ellis, John R. *Objectifying Real-Time Systems*. New York: SIGS Books, 1994.

Embley, David W., Barry D. Kurtz, and Scott N. Woodfield. *Object-Oriented Systems Analysis: A Model Driven Approach*. Englewood Cliffs, NJ: Prentice Hall PTR, 1992.

Evans, Eric. *Domain-Driven Design: Tackling Complexity in the Heart of Software*. Boston: Addison-Wesley, 2004.

*Feyerabend, Paul. *Against Method*. London: Verso, 1975.

Fingar, Peter. *The Blueprint for Business Objects*. New York: SIGS Books, 1996.

Firesmith, Donald G. *Object-Oriented Requirements Analysis and Logical Design: A Software Engineering Approach*. New York: John Wiley and Sons, Inc., 1993.

*Floyd, C., H. Zullighoven, R. Budde, and R. Keil-Slawik. *Software Development and Reality Construction*. Berlin: Springer-Verlag, 1991.

Fowler, Martin. *Analysis Patterns: Reusable Object Models.* Menlo Park, CA: Addison-Wesley Longman, Inc., 1997.

Fowler, Martin. *Refactoring: Improving the Design of Existing Code.* Reading, MA: Addison-Wesley, 1999.

Frolund, Svend. *Coordinating Distributed Objects: An Actor-based Approach to Synchronization.* Cambridge, MA: MIT Press, 1996.

*Gabriel, Richard P. *Patterns of Software: Tales from the Software Community.* Oxford: Oxford University Press, 1996.

*Gadamer, Hans-George. *Philosophical Hermeneutics.* Translated and edited by David E. Linge. Berkeley: University of California Press, 1976.

*Gadamer, Hans-George. *Reason in the Age of Science.* Translated by Frederick G. Lawrence. Cambridge, MA: MIT Press, 1982.

Gale, Thornton, and James Eldred. *Getting Results with the Object-Oriented Enterprise Model.* New York: SIGS Books, 1996.

Gamma, Erich, Richard Helm, Ralph Johnson, and John Vlissides. *Design Patterns: Elements of Reusable Object-Oriented Software.* Reading, MA: Addison-Wesley, 1995.

*Glass, Robert L. *Software Creativity.* Englewood Cliffs, NJ: Prentice-Hall PTR, 1995.

*Glass, Robert L. *Facts and Fallacies of Software Engineering.* Boston: Addison-Wesley, 2003.

Goldberg, Adele, and Ken Rubin. *Succeeding with Objects: Decision Frameworks for Project Management.* Reading, MA: Addison-Wesley Publishing Co., 1995.

Gossain, Sanjiv. *Object Modeling and Design Strategies.* SIGS Books. Cambridge: Cambridge University Press, 1998.

Graham, Ian. *Migrating to Object Technology.* Wokingham, England: Addison-Wesley Publishing Co., 1994.

Grand, Mark. *Patterns in Java*, vol 1. New York: John Wiley and Sons, Inc., 1998.

Greenbaum, Joan, and Morten Kyng. *Design at Work: Cooperative Design of Computer Systems.* Hillsdale, NJ: Lawrence Erlbaum Associates, Publishers, 1991.

Henderson-Sellers, Brian, and Julian Edwards. *The Working Object.* Sydney, Australia: Prentice-Hall, 1994.

Henderson-Sellers, Brian. *Object-Oriented Metrics: Measures of Complexity.* Upper Saddle River, NJ: Prentice Hall PTR, 1996.

Highsmith III, James A. *Adaptive Software Development: A Collaborative Approach to Managing Complex Systems.* New York: Dorsett House Publishing, 2000.

Highsmith, Jim. *Agile Software Development Ecosystems*. Reading, MA: Addison-Wesley, 2002.

Hill, David R. C. *Object-Oriented Analysis and Simulation*. Harlow, England: Addison-Wesley Press, 1996.

Hiltzik, Michael A. *Dealers of Lightning: Xerox Parc and the Dawn of the Computer Age*. New York: Harper Collins, 1999.

Holmes, Jim. *Object-Oriented Compiler Construction*. Englewood Cliffs, NJ: Prentice Hall Inc., 1995.

Hughes, John G. *Object-Oriented Databases*. New York: Prentice-Hall, 1991.

IBM. *Object Oriented Interface Design*. New York: Que Books, 1992.

Islam, Nayeem. *Distributed Objects: Methodologies for Customizing Systems Software*. Los Alamitos, CA: IEEE Computer Society Press, 1996.

Jacobson, Ivar. *The Object Advantage: Business Process Reengineering with Object Technology*. ACM Press. Reading, MA: Addison-Wesley, 1994.

Jeffries, Ron, Ann Anderson, and Chet Hendrickson. *Extreme Programming Installed*. Boston: Addison-Wesley, 2001.

Kemper, Alfons, and Guido Moerkotte. *Object-Oriented Database Management*. Englewood Cliffs, NJ: Prentice Hall, 1994.

*Kiczales, Gregor, Jim des Revieres, and Daniel G. Bobrow. *The Art of the Metaobject Protocol*. Cambridge, MA: MIT Press, 1993.

Kilov, Haim, and James Ross. *Information Modeling: An Object-Oriented Approach*. Englewood Cliffs, NJ: PTR Prentice Hall, 1994.

Kim, Won, and Frederick H. Lochovsky, eds. *Object-Oriented Concepts, Databases, and Applications*. ACM Press. New York: Addison-Wesley Publishing Company, 1989.

*Knorr-Cetina, Karin D. *The Manufacture of Knowledge: An Essay on the Constructivist and Contextual Nature of Science*. Oxford: Pergammon Press, 1981.

Korienek, Gene, and Tom Wrensch. *A Quick Trip to Objectland*. Englewood Cliffs, NJ: Prentice-Hall, 1993.

*Lakoff, George, and Mark Johnson. *Metaphors We Live By*. Chicago: University of Chicago Press, 1980.

*Lakoff, George. *Women, Fire, and Dangerous Things*. Chicago: University of Chicago Press, 1990.

*Lakoff, George, and Mark Johnson. *Philosophy in the Flesh: The Embodied Mind and Its Challenge to Western Thought*. New York: Basic Books, 1999.

LaLonde, Wilf. *Discovering Smalltalk*. Redwood City, CA: Benjamin Cummings Publishing Co., Inc., 1994.

Larman, Craig. *Agile and Iterative Development: A Manager's Guide*. Boston: Addison-Wesley, 2004.

Lau, Chamond. *Smalltalk, Objects, and Design*. Greenwich, CT: Manning Publications Co., 1996.

Lewis, Simon. *The Art and Science of Smalltalk*. London: Prentice Hall PTR, 1995.

Loomis, Mary E. S. *Object Databases: The Essentials*. Reading, MA: Addison-Wesley Publishing Co., 1995.

Lorenz, Mark. *Object-Oriented Software Development: A Practical Guide*. Englewood Cliffs, NJ: Prentice-Hall, 1993.

Lorenz, Mark. *Rapid Software Development with Smalltalk*. New York: SIGS Books, 1995.

Love, Tom. *Object Lessons: Lessons Learned in Object-Oriented Development Projects*. New York: SIGS Books, 1993.

*McBreen, Pete. *Software Craftsmanship: The New Imperative*. Boston: Addison-Wesley, 2002.

McGibbon, Barry. *Managing Your Move to Object Technology: Guidelines and Strategies for a Smooth Transition*. New York: SIGS Books, 1995.

McNally, Clayton L., Jr., and Peter Molchan Jr. *Micro Focus COBOL Workbench*. Boston: QED Publishing Group, 1993.

Martin, James. *Information Engineering: Book 1—Introduction*. Englewood Cliffs, NJ: Prentice-Hall, 1989.

Martin, James, and James J. Odell. *Object-Oriented Analysis and Design*. Englewood Cliffs, NJ: Prentice Hall, 1992.

Martin, Robert, Dirk Riehle, and Frank Buschmann, eds. *Pattern Languages of Program Design 3*. Cambridge, MA: Addison-Wesley Publishing Co., 1998.

Martin, Robert C., with contributions by James W. Newkirk and Robert S. Koss. *Agile Software Development: Principles, Patterns, and Practices*. Upper Saddle River, NJ: Pearson Prentice Hall, 2003.

Masini, Gerald, Amedeo Napoli, Dominique Colnet, Daniel Leonard, and Karl Tombre. *Object Oriented Languages*. Academic Press. London: Harcourt Brace Jovanovich, Publishers, 1991.

*Maturana, Humberto R., and Francisco Varela. *Autopoiesis and Cognition: The Realization of the Living*. Dordrecht: Reidel, 1980.

*Maturana, Humberto R., and Francisco Varela. *The Tree of Knowledge: The Biological Roots of Human Understanding*. Boston: New Science Library, Shambala, 1987.

Meyer, Bertrand. *Object Oriented Software Construction*. New York: Prentice Hall, Inc., 1988.

Meyer, Bertrand. *Object Success: A Manager's Guide to Object-Orientation, Its Impact on the Corporation and Its Use for Reengineering the Software Process*. London: Prentice Hall, 1995.

Miller, Byron. *Object Oriented Design Made Easy*. Minneapolis, MN: Impatiens Publications, 1993.

*Minsky, Marvin. *Society of Mind*. New York: Simon and Schuster, 1987.

Montgomery, Stephen L. *Object-Oriented Information Engineering: Analysis, Design, and Implementation*. Boston: Academic Press Professional, 1994.

Morris, Derrick, Gareth Evans, Peter Green, and Colin Theaker. *Object-Oriented Computer Systems Engineering*. London: Springer-Verlag, 1996.

Mowbray, Thomas J., and Raphael C. Malveau. *CORBA Design Patterns*. New York: John Wiley & Sons, Inc., 1997.

Muller, Robert J. *Productive Objects: An Applied Project Management Framework*. San Francisco: Morgan Kaufmann Publishers, Inc., 1998.

*Nardi, Bonnie A., and Vicki L. O'Day. *Information Ecologies: Using Technology with Heart*. Cambridge, MA: MIT Press, 1999.

Newkirk, James, and Robert C. Martin. *Extreme Programming in Practice*. Boston: Addison-Wesley, 2001.

Oliver, David W., Timothy P. Kelliher, and James G. Keegan Jr. *Engineering Complex Systems with Models and Objects*. New York: McGraw-Hill, 1997.

Orfali, Robert, Dan Harkey, and Jeri Edwards. *The Essential Distributed Objects Survival Guide*. New York: John Wiley and Sons, Inc., 1996.

Page-Jones, Meilir. *The Practical Guide to Structured Systems Design*, second edition, Englewood Cliffs, NJ: Prentice-Hall, Inc., 1988.

Palsberg, Jens, and Michael I. Schwartzback. *Object-Oriented Type Systems*. Chichester, England: John Wiley and Sons, 1994.

Papurt, David M. *Inside the Object Model: The Sensible Use of C++*. New York: SIGS Books, 1995.

Parsaye, Kamran, Mark Chignell, Setraqg Khoshafian, and Harry Wong. *Intelligent Databases: Object-Oriented Deductive Hypermedia Technologies.* New York: John Wiley and Sons, Inc., 1989.

Partridge, Chris. *Business Objects: Re-engineering for Re-use.* Oxford: Butterworth-Heinemann, 1996.

Pawson, Richard, and Robert Matthews. *Naked Objects.* Hoboken, NJ: John Wiley & Sons Ltd., 2002.

Poppendieck, Mary and Tom. *Lean Software Development: An Agile Toolkit.* Boston: Addison-Wesley, 2003.

Pree, Wolfgang. *Design Patterns for Object-Oriented Software Development.* Wokingham, England: Addison-Wesley Publishing Company, 1995.

Rasmus, Daniel W. *Rethinking Smart Objects: Building Artificial Intelligence with Objects.* SIGS Books. Cambridge: Cambridge University Press, 1999.

Riel, Arthur J. *Object-Oriented Design Heuristics.* Reading, MA: Addison-Wesley Publishing Co., Inc., 1996.

Rumbaugh, James, Michael Blaha, William Premerlaini, Frederick Eddy, and William Lorensen. *Object-Oriented Modeling and Design.* Englewood Cliffs, NJ: Prentice Hall PTR, 1991.

Rumbaugh, Dr. James. *OMT Insights.* New York: SIGS Books, 1996.

Schach, Stephen R. *Classical and Object Oriented Software Engineering.* Chicago: Irwin, 1996.

Schwaber, Ken, and Mike Beedle. *Agile Software Development with Scrum.* Upper Saddle River, NJ: Prentice-Hall, 2002.

Shlaer, Sally, and Stephen J. Mellor. *Object-Oriented Systems Analysis: Modeling the World in Data.* Yourdon Press. Englewood Cliffs, NJ: Prentice Hall, 1988.

Shlaer, Sally, and Stephen J. Mellor. *Object Lifecycles: Modeling the World in States.* Englewood Cliffs, NJ: Prentice Hall, Inc., 1992.

Selic, Brian, Garth Gullekson, and Paul T. Ward. *Real-Time Object-Oriented Modeling.* New York: John Wiley and Sons, 1994.

Sessions, Roger. *Object Persistence: Beyond Object-Oriented Databases.* Upper Saddle River, NJ: Prentice Hall PTR, 1996.

Stapleton, Jennifer. *DSDM: Dynamic Systems Development Method.* Harlow, England: Addison-Wesley, 1997.

*Suchman, L. *Plans and Situated Actions*. Cambridge, England: Cambridge University Press, 1987.

Succi, Giancarlo, and Michele Marchesi. *Extreme Programming Examined*. Boston: Addison-Wesley, 2001.

Sullo, Gary C. *Object Engineering: Designing Large-Scale Object-Oriented Systems*. New York: John Wiley and Sons, Inc., 1994.

Sully, Phil. *Modeling the World with Objects*. New York: Prentice Hall, 1993.

Szyperski, Clemens. *Component Software: Beyond Object-Oriented Programming*. Harlow, England: Addison-Wesley, 1999.

Taylor, David A. *Object-Oriented Technology: A Manager's Guide*. Reading, MA: Addison-Wesley, 1990.

Taylor, David A., PhD. *Object-Oriented Information Systems: Planning and Implementation*. New York: John Wiley and Sons, 1992.

*Taylor, David A., PhD. *Business Engineering with Object Technology*. New York: John Wiley and Sons, 1995.

Tkach, Daniel, and Richard Puttick. *Object Technology in Application Development*. Redwood City, CA: The Benjamin Cummings Publishing Co., 1994.

Vlissides, John M., James O. Coplien, and Norman L. Kerth. *Pattern Languages of Program Design 2*. Cambridge, MA: Addison-Wesley Publishing Co., 1996.

Wake, William C. *Extreme Programming Explored*. Boston: Addison-Wesley, 2002.

Walden, Kim, and Jean-Marc Nerson. *Seamless Object-Oriented Software Architecture: Analysis and Design of Reliable Systems*. New York: Prentice Hall PTR, 1995.

Webster, Bruce F. *Pitfalls of Object-Oriented Development*. New York: M&T Books, 1995.

White, Iseult. *Using the Booch Method: A Rational Approach*. Redwood City, CA: The Benjamin Cummings Publishing Company, 1994.

Wilkie, George. *Object-Oriented Software Engineering: the Professional Developer's Guide*. Wokingham, England: Addison-Wesley, 1993.

Wilkinson, Nancy M. *Using CRC Cards: An Informal Approach to Object-Oriented Development*. New York: SIGS Books, 1995.

Williams, John. *What Every Software Manager Must Know to Succeed with Object Technology*. New York: SIGS Books, 1995.

*Winograd, Terry. *Bringing Design to Software*. New York: ACM Press, 1996.

Winston, Patrick Henry. *On to Smalltalk*. Reading, MA: Addison-Wesley, 1998.

Wirfs-Brock, Rebecca, Brian Wilkerson, and Lauren Wiener. *Designing Object-Oriented Software.* Englewood Cliffs, NJ: Prentice Hall PTR, 1990.

Wirfs-Brock, Rebecca, and Alan McKean. *Object Design: Roles, Responsibilities, and Collaborations.* Boston: Addison-Wesley, 2003.

Witt, Bernard I., F. Terry Baker, and Everett W. Merritt. *Software Architecture and Design: Principles, Models, and Methods.* New York: Van Nostrand Reinhold, 1994.

Yourdon, Edward. *Object-Oriented Systems Design: An Integrated Approach.* Englewood Cliffs, NJ: Prentice-Hall PTR, 1994.

Zeigler, Bernard P. *Object-Oriented Simulation with Hierarchical Modular Models: Intelligent Systems and Endomorphic Systems.* Academic Press, Inc. Boston: Harcourt Brace Jovanovich, Publishers, 1990.

Index

About the Author

Currently Dr. David West is a professor in the School of Business at New Mexico Highlands University, where he is developing an object-based curriculum in software architectures, business engineering, and management information systems. He also teaches at the University of New Mexico, where he is engaged in developing a software development track for students in graduate and undergraduate computer science.

Prior to joining the faculty at NMHU, he was an associate professor in the Graduate Programs in Software at the University of St. Thomas and a consultant/trainer to several Fortune 500 companies. He has taught courses in object-oriented development ranging from three-hour introductory sessions for managers to multiday technical seminars for professional developers, as well as semester-long courses at both the graduate and the undergraduate level.

He founded and served as the director of the Object Lab at the University of St. Thomas. The Object Lab was a cooperative effort with local corporations dedicated to researching and promoting object technology.

He was a cofounder of the Object Technology User Group (the original, not the Rational-sponsored group), the first editor of its monthly newsletter, and the principal organizer and chair of two regional conferences sponsored by OTUG.

Digitalk's Methods (the first incarnation of Smalltalk for the personal computer, later named Smalltalk/V) was his first object development environment, used to construct an "automated cultural informant," a teaching tool for cultural anthropologists learning ethnographic fieldwork techniques. His object experience is complemented by more than 20 years of software development work, ranging from assembly-language programmer to executive management.

His undergraduate education at Macalester College (oriental philosophy and East Asian history) was capped with an MS in computer science (artificial intelligence) and an MA in cultural anthropology followed by a PhD in cognitive anthropology. All the graduate degrees were earned at the University of Wisconsin at Madison.

-depth learning solutions for every software user

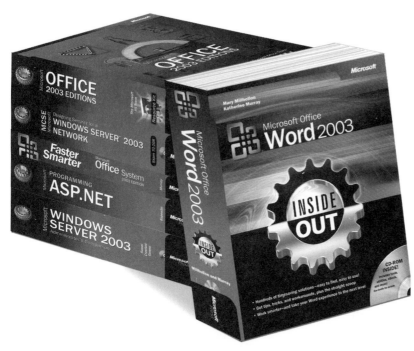

**The tools you need
to put technology to
work.**

rosoft Press produces in-depth learning solutions that empower home and corporate users, IT professionals, and software elopers to do more exciting things with Microsoft technology. From beginning PC how-to's to developer reference titles to aining and technical resources, we offer hundreds of computer books, interactive training software, and online resources, esigned to help build your skills and knowledge—how, when, and where you learn best.

To learn more about the full line of Microsoft Press® products, please visit us at:

microsoft.com/mspress

Create awesome multimedia solutions *with* code, tools, and tips from *Microsoft Digital Media developers!*

Fundamentals of Programming the Microsoft® Windows Media® Platform
ISBN 0-7356-1911-5

Learn how to develop and deliver exceptional digital media solutions using the powerfully enhanced Windows Media 9 Series platform. Created by a technical expert on the Microsoft Windows Media team, this guide walks you through platform architecture and components—providing inside insights, real-world programming scenarios, automation techniques, and reusable code samples to help power your own streaming media solutions. You get step-by-step instructions on how to create applications to encode Windows Media files and streams, serve and receive audio and video streams, create customized players, and even build a complete broadcasting system—your own Internet radio station.

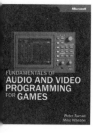

Fundamentals of Audio and Video Programming for Games
ISBN 0-7356-1945-X

Deliver console-rocking sound, music, and video effects to your games with this all-in-one toolkit for C++ game programmers. Load the CD—and experience Microsoft's Digital Media developers at play, learning how to use Microsoft DirectX® 9 technologies to produce amazing, professional-quality effects. From mixing and moving sounds around a 3-D space to taking video to the third dimension, you get expert insights and performance tips direct from the developers, along with a game-ready arsenal of code, copyright-free audio and video, and ready-to-use effects on CD. It's everything you need to fuel your creativity—and take your game players to spectacular new 3-D worlds!

crosoft Press has many other titles to help you put development tools and technologies to work. To learn more about the full line of Microsoft Press® products for developers, please visit:

microsoft.com/mspress/developer

Get a **Free**
 e-mail newsletter, updates,
special offers, links to related books,
 and more when you
register online!

Register your Microsoft Press® title on our Web site and you'll get a FREE subscription to our e-mail newsletter, *Microsoft Press Book Connections.* You'll find out about newly released and upcoming books and learning tools, online events, software downloads, special offers and coupons for Microsoft Press customers, and information about major Microsoft® product releases. You can also read useful additional information about all the titles we publish, such as detailed book descriptions, tables of contents and indexes, sample chapters, links to related books and book series, author biographies, and reviews by other customers.

Registration is easy. Just visit this Web page and fill in your information:

http://www.microsoft.com/mspress/register

Microsoft

- -

Proof of Purchase

Use this page as proof of purchase if participating in a promotion or rebate offer on this title. Proof of purchase must be used in conjunction with other proof(s) of payment such as your dated sales receipt—see offer details.

Object Thinking
0-7356-1965-4

CUSTOMER NAME

Microsoft Press, PO Box 97017, Redmond, WA 98073-9830